Here is your personal password to become a member of The Mind Gym Online. To join, simply visit www.themindgym.com and enter this code.

4652 5536

Press

'What's next? The Mind Gym' *Newsweek*
'Re-invent yourself in 90 minutes' *Financial Times*
'Think short, punchy and fun' *Guardian*
'Send your mind for a workout' *The Daily Telegraph*

People

'Revelation, revelation, revelation – I love The Mind Gym for all its helpful tips that I use every day and make my life so much easier and more enjoyable; a really super invention' Kirstie Allsopp, Presenter, *Location, Location, Location*

'Whatever jungle you are doing battle with, The Mind Gym's tips and techniques are highly likely to give you the confidence and skills to come out victorious' Dr Sandra Scott, Psychological Consultant on *I'm a Celebrity, Get Me Out of Here!*

'To stimulate, order, de-stress and ultimately secure peace of mind, whether for personal or professional use, this book is a bedside necessity which you can rely on for the best advice' Emilia Fox, Actress

'This is the perfect intelligent and intuitive guide for everyone who wants power, wealth and influence – without bloodshed' Simon Sebag-Montefiore, author of *Stalin: The Court of the Red Tsar*

'This is my kind of gym: you can do it wherever you like, you see the benefits immediately, you're never bored and no communal showers' Richard Reed, Co-founder, innocent

'Finally a way to unlock the vast amount of our brain capacity that we all have but few of us ever use, my mind feels more toned already – I love it!' Sahar Hashemi, Founder, Coffee Republic

'When it comes to improving our minds, The Mind Gym is the number one brand – you can trust it completely and may even fall in love' Rita Clifton, Chairman, Interbrand

Professors

'The best psychology turned into neat ideas for living smarter. Credible, imaginative and practical: you can't ask for more' Professor Guy Claxton

'I am very impressed by the intellectual rigour and academic integrity of this immensely enjoyable and practical book' Emeritus Professor Peter Robinson

'Filled with everyday uses for some of the best psychological research of the last fifty years, this is a must for anyone who is serious about making better use of their mind' Professor Ingrid Lunt

'Packed with helpful directions for people struggling with the challenges of daily living, The Mind Gym puts the new positive psychology into practice and offers a multitude of ways to live a strong and healthy life' Professor Michael West

The Mind Gym ran the first 90-minute workout, a fast-paced, face-to-face workshop filled with practical ways to use our mind better, at Deutsche Bank on 1 September 2000.

Since then:

- 66 different workout subjects have been developed including 'Sorted for stress', 'Your impact on others', 'Remembering whatsisname' and 'Wood for trees'
- 100,000 people have taken part, 93% of whom say they will apply what they learnt
- 270 organisations have run workouts, ranging from the BBC and London Business School to Prêt A Manger and Guinness
- The workouts have been run in 5 languages in over 20 countries by qualified Coaches based in the UK, US, Australia, Ireland, France, Spain, Italy and Austria

But that's just figures.

More importantly, a month or so later participants can usually cite examples of what they have done differently at work and in the rest of their lives – 'so far I have given up smoking (after 16 years) and embarked on a healthy eating programme (so far lost 1 stone). Perhaps not all due to The Mind Gym, but it certainly played a part', enthused one participant. 'The team used to get into arguments all the time but I've used The Mind Gym techniques and things are a lot more positive and constructive now', explained another; 'I have learnt to believe in myself and do the things I can control', remarked a third.

'I'm a convert . . . the stickiness of The Mind Gym learning is extremely impressive', declared Steve Crabb, industry expert and editor of *People Management*. 'What Fosbury did for the high jump, The Mind Gym has done for learning', exclaimed Dr Bill Lucas when Chief Executive of the Campaign for Learning.

The Mind Gym's Academic Board of four psychology professors (all Fellows of the BPS and one past President) ensure that The Mind Gym's content has integrity and is up to date. One way that they do this is judging The Mind Gym prize for new research-based insights on how we can use our mind more effectively – the latest thinking on thinking, if you like.

The Mind Gym: wake your mind up is packed with many of the most popular hints, tips and techniques from the workouts and is The Mind Gym's first book (the first of a series from Time Warner Books). The Mind Gym Online is also a new adventure, launched with this book.

For more information on all of this, and plenty more, visit www.themindgym.com.

the mindgym

wake your
mind up

timewarner
books

A *Time Warner* Book

First published in Great Britain in 2005
by Time Warner Books

Copyright © 2005 by The Mind Gym

The moral right of the author has been asserted.

All rights reserved. No part of this publication may be reproduced,
stored in a retrieval system, or transmitted, in any form or by any
means, without the prior permission in writing of the publisher, nor
be otherwise circulated in any form of binding or cover other than
that in which it is published and without a similar condition including
this condition being imposed on the subsequent purchaser.

Every effort has been made to trace copyright owners. Please notify
Time Warner Books of any omissions and they will be rectified.

A CIP catalogue record for this book
is available from the British Library.

ISBN 0 316 72992 2

Typeset in Avenir by M Rules
Printed and bound in Great Britain
by Clays Ltd, St Ives plc

Time Warner Books
An imprint of
Time Warner Book Group UK
Brettenham House
Lancaster Place
London WC2E 7EN

www.twbg.co.uk
www.themindgym.com

Contents

For a little more about what is in each chapter go to pages 20–21.

Wake your mind up

When there is something wrong with your body you go and see a doctor. When you are perfectly well but want to be fitter, nimbler, healthier, thinner or more flexible, you might well head to the gym.

As with the body, so with the mind.

In summary, The Mind Gym is for all of us who want to discover how we can use our minds more effectively so that we can get more out of life and give more to others.

So, what can I do?

There is a wealth of psychology that, were we to know it, would improve our lives. But the vast majority of this enlightening science is hidden in complex academic papers and specialist tomes. There is, of course, a lot that is easy to read about how to improve our minds but much of this is based more on whim or wishful thinking than rigorous research.

There was a van doing the rounds a while ago which had written on its side: 'Patel & Patel plumbers – you've tried the cowboys now try the Indians'. Most of us smile both at the cheeky humour and also at the familiar truth that lies behind it. When we want to improve our lives we face much the same challenge as when we want to fix the pipes. There is a seemingly endless supply of books promising to reveal the secrets of how to understand men (or women), ways to guarantee success at work, the key to a fulfilled life and much, much more. However, it is all but impossible to tell the good from the bad.

The Mind Gym aims to provide a map through this maze of psychology and personal development by making the former accessible and the latter rigorous.

What is The Mind Gym?

The original idea for The Mind Gym came out of a conversation over supper. Someone asked: if the 1980s saw the emergence of people caring about their bodies (gyms, vegetarianism, etc) and the 1990s saw a sudden growth in matters spiritual (yoga, feng shui, and so forth) then what will the 2000s be about? The trinity of mind, body, soul was mentioned and, with a fervour largely found in the truly naïve, the group decided that the next decade would, without doubt, be about improving our minds.

This could have been the end of it but, despite a heavy head the morning after, the idea of a gym for the mind lingered on. Cabals would gather after work and at weekends to sketch out what this mind gym might actually do.

The original intention was to run workouts for the mind in regular health and fitness centres. These would be like mini-workshops that would last no longer than 90 minutes. Each would focus on a different subject, such as conflict or procrastination, and would be packed with practical tips that people could use immediately they walked out of the door, at work, at home and pretty much anywhere in between. The design of the workouts would follow Albert Einstein's maxim 'Everything should be made as simple as possible but no simpler'; the content would be based on applied psychology or related science; the experience would be as much fun as going out for dinner with your friends (more naïve, wishful thinking).

It soon became clear, after talking with various gym owners, that this vision of The Mind Gym wasn't going to work. Nevertheless, the idea of 90-minute workouts packed with practical ways to think and communicate more effectively had an enduring appeal. The original plan had always included an element of running these workouts in organisations for their staff. Would employers give sufficient value to bite-size workshops that helped their people use their minds better?

The answer is 'yes'.

Over 100,000 people have now taken part in one of The Mind Gym's 90-minute workouts, run in their office, factory or wherever they work. And the vast majority seem to love it: 93% say they will apply what they learned and 88% say they would recommend it.

So where does the gym thing fit in?

We often talk about the connections between our physical well-being and our mental strength: 'Looking good, feeling good', 'A healthy body means a healthy mind'. But how does a gym for the mind compare with the more familiar one for the body?

Here are six similarities.

1 **We all go for our own, different reasons**
   Turn up at a gym and you are likely to be asked by an eager fitness coach what you want to improve. Do you want to lose weight, have more stamina, be able to sprint faster? He or she will then design a programme of exercises that will do most to help you towards your objective.

   It's similar at The Mind Gym. Your 'fitness coach' is in the next chapter, helping you to decide where to focus your effort. Of course, you may want to do everything, but even then there are likely to be some areas to work on as a priority.

2 **Working on one area may help another**
   I want a firmer stomach. I therefore take up a programme with various kinds of sit-ups. One of the side benefits is that my backache all but disappears.

   I want to be better at influencing. As a result, I discover how other people look at the world and adapt my style to suit them. Therefore, I also become more popular.

3 **It makes us better equipped for whatever life may bring**
   If we train to run a marathon we become fitter. This is likely to mean that we can recover faster after an unexpectedly sleepless night.

   When we find it easy to manage the stresses at work we'll be better able to deal with the strains at home too.

4 **No pain, no gain (what a shame)**
   Afraid so. Some of the tools and techniques are easier than others but all of them will require effort and application to get the maximum benefit.

5 **It's for everyone**
   We can all improve our minds. Everyone is welcome at The Mind Gym regardless of age, gender, intelligence, fitness, religious beliefs, occupation or anything else. We can come whenever we like: there are no peak time/off-peak restrictions here.

6 You get to watch all the latest pop videos and TV programmes as you train

OK, we made this one up.

The Mind Gym's beliefs

The following are some assumptions that lie behind everything The Mind Gym does. They may need to be changed as new discoveries are made but, for now, they seem to work well.

- We can choose how we think. We are not pre-programmed to see the world in a certain way but are largely free to decide how we think and how we communicate.

- We can all improve. Rather like going to a physical gym where we can make ourselves physically fitter, we can all become more mentally capable. This does not mean that we can turn ourselves into Albert Einstein or Leonardo da Vinci, any more than enough trips to the physical gym will turn us into Maria Sharapova or Ronaldo, alas.

- Intelligence, in its broadest sense, involves much more than abstract problem-solving (or IQ). In addition to systematic thinking, intelligence includes physical skills and social skills, as well as perception, imagination, emotions and many aspects of personality. All of these can be enhanced.

- We tend to underestimate the extent to which what we do is habitual rather than set in stone, reflecting mental 'default settings' that we have forgotten we can change. By uncovering more of the options that are available it is easier to escape our current habits or 'settings'.

- There is sometimes one new 'default option' that is better than the old one. Swapping a faulty way of remembering people's names for a reliable one is useful. But it is more useful to keep at the back of our minds a range of possibilities, because different circumstances require different approaches. So The Mind Gym does not tend to propose a set of prescriptions but, instead, suggests a range of options.

Will Super Mario make me super smart?

There is a movement that offers a seductive promise: by repeatedly doing exercises that require thought, our brain will grow.

Called, amongst other things, neurobics or mental callisthenics, it suggests, for example, that if we complete online mental puzzles against the clock, this will improve our reaction times in the car or when we need to make decisions; and that if we learn to eat Maltesers with chopsticks using our left hand (or right, if left-handed) this will somehow make us more mentally agile.

Alas, there is precious little independent scientific evidence to suggest that it will make any difference at all (save making us better at eating Maltesers with chopsticks). The response from serious academics to this new fad ranges from sceptical to downright scornful.

When independent research demonstrates that playing lots of video games does anything more than make us better at video games, The Mind Gym will take another look. Until then, let's just enjoy them without kidding ourselves that they are good for us too.

What's new?

Is The Mind Gym content original or just borrowing lots of other people's ideas? The answer is a bit of both.

To develop The Mind Gym content, a century of psychological research has been explored. Different theories have been adapted and combined to make them relevant to today's needs. Hundreds of tips and techniques have been tried, initially on the home team and, when they were found to be effective, on the tens of thousands of people who have taken part in one of The Mind Gym's workouts. The result is a wealth of practical tips and techniques about how to think and communicate more effectively. These are based on what others have discovered and are, in large part, refreshed, updated and revised to meet our needs today. Yet, where the old methods are still the best they are repeated just as they were found.

Take, for example, stress. There is more written on this than any one person could read in a lifetime. Much of it repeats what has gone before. The Mind Gym approach draws on the thinking of the now largely forgotten psychologists Yerkes and Dodson, who were writing at the beginning of the last century, and combines it with the thinking of the Austrian-born Canadian Hans Selye (published in the 1960s) and the more recent work of Americans Richard Lazarus and Sue Folkman.

Each of these has very valuable ideas to contribute. The Mind Gym builds on their ideas and adds a new twist. The result is a series of practical ways to deal with 21st-century stress (see the stress chapters for more details).

Do I want a bigger brain?

Research conducted in 2000 showed that the part of the brain devoted to long-term memory (called the posterior of the hippocampus) is larger for drivers of London's black taxis than for the population as a whole. As these drivers have to pass a complicated test that requires an extensive memory of London's streets, this is not surprising, and the research also showed that the longer someone had been a taxi driver, the larger the posterior of their hippocampus was. Many commentators deduced, however, that this made them cleverer.

This was a mistake for two reasons. First, the study also found that another part of their brain was correspondingly smaller and so the total size of their brain remained similar to the national average.

Second, the physical size of the brain does not correlate with intelligence. Men's brains weigh, taking into consideration average body height or body surface areas, 16% more than women's brains but it would be a foolhardy man (or woman) who concluded, therefore, that men are 16% cleverer.

Where now?

You are now a member of The Mind Gym and you are free to come and go as you wish. The next chapter suggests different ways you can use this book and introduces The Mind Gym Online, but if you'd rather just get stuck in, go right ahead.

Only one piece of advice before you start: as Thomas Dewar said, 'Minds are like parachutes, they operate only when open.'

Don't read this book

You walk into a gym for the first time. There are rows of peculiar-looking machines that could as easily be designed for torture as for exercise. You sit on the padded seat of one but aren't sure what to pull or push or how it works. You try a more obvious-looking machine but when you pull on the bar nothing happens. Something familiar catches your eye. You sit on a stationary bicycle and start pedalling. Seems fine, but why are all these lights flashing on the panel in front of me?

The Mind Gym isn't like this. It is designed so that we can all use it straight away and very much as we like. Each tool (and chapter) can be explored in isolation. The directions are clear and the exercises in each chapter can be done where and when you choose.

You don't have to read this book from cover to cover. You can, for example:

Read a chapter that appeals to you and leave it at that
If you simply want some practical guidance on how you can let a friend down and yet keep them as a friend, then there is no need to mess around, just go straight to the relevant place (Bad news, p. 182).

Like a book of short stories, you can pop in and out as you like.

Read a section
As you may have noticed on the contents page at the start, there are five sections which combine all the chapters on a specific subject

- Taking control

- The right impression

- Tough conversations

- Stress and relaxation

- Creative juices

Each section starts with a brief summary about what you will find inside. If your priority is to manage stress or be more creative, then it may be best to go straight to the relevant section and get stuck in.

Follow one of the programmes outlined on pages 11–14
Rather like a fitness regime designed for strength or stamina, each of these programmes has been developed to help address a specific desire.

Design your own programme
There is a questionnaire on pages 17–19 that can help you decide which chapters are most likely to help you address your current priorities. Fill it in and use the results to create a tailor-made programme.

Or, if you prefer, you can always start at the beginning and read through to the end, as with a normal book.

This is your gym for you to use as and when you want.

The Mind Gym Online

The Mind Gym Online is always open and there to help you practise, prepare, share and, if you want, compete. Here you can:

- complete questionnaires with a more in-depth explanation about what the results mean. You can also send the questionnaire to a selection of friends and colleagues and discover how their views fit with your self-perception

Available online

- get support for some of the exercises in the book that are easier to do online. For example, there are recordings of the visualisation instructions in Tranquillity – much easier than trying to read with our eyes closed

- use specific tools, like the influencing strategy builder, to prepare and revise your own powerful plans

- share ideas and seek advice from other, like-minded members of The Mind Gym

- keep a record of how you are doing, the progress that you have made and details of your personal goals or anything else you'd rather no one else knew about

And there will be new goodies being introduced all the time based on what members want and use.

To start your membership of The Mind Gym Online, simply visit www.the mindgym.com and enter your password which is on the inside front cover of this book.

Wherever you see ✎ in the book, there is something at The Mind Gym Online that is directly relevant. But if you don't have access to a computer, don't worry, everything you discover in these pages makes complete sense without any further support.

You now know all you need to get going. If, however, you would like to follow a particular programme, or design your own, read on.

The Mind Gym programmes

There are four programmes that have been developed to help you get what you want from The Mind Gym as quickly and efficiently as possible.

1 Get what you want
For people who know what they want but don't know how to get it, especially when new obstacles keep getting in the way.

2 Be liked
A programme for people who would like more friends, allies and acquaintances who think they're great.

3 Be respected
A programme for those of us who want to be admired or at least treated as an equal by everyone we meet.

4 Ride the storm

For people who are feeling the turbulence in life and who want to be ready to deal with the unexpected challenges whatever they may be.

See pages 11–14 for these routes.

Get what you want

For people who know what they want but don't know how to get it, especially when new obstacles keep getting in the way.

Be liked

For people who would like more friends, allies and acquaintances who think they're great.

Be respected

For people who want to be admired or at least treated as an equal by everyone they meet.

Ride the storm

For people who are feeling the turbulence in life and who want to be ready to deal with unexpected challenges, whatever they may be.

5 steps to design your own programme

Step 1
Fold the section of page 17 to the right of the dotted line back on itself so you can see the circles on page 19 (but nothing else on that page).

Step 2
Complete the questionnaire about what you would most like to become true on page 17. Look through each of the statements that start 'I wish that' and pick the option that is closest to your view. There are five options:

1   This is already largely true or not that important to me

2   Nice to have but there are other things I'd prefer to have first

3   Yes please. This would be great

4   Wow. That would be absolutely fantastic. How soon can I have it?

5   I'd give my right arm (metaphorically) for this

In order to get a good idea of where to start, try to give a range of scores to the different statements. If everything gets a 5 then you will be none the wiser.

Step 3
Turn the whole page back so you can see pages 18 and 19. Transfer the score for each question to each of the chapters that are suggested to the left of the dotted line.

Step 4
Add up the scores for each chapter and write them in the Total score circles.

The chapters with the highest score are the ones that you should probably focus on. You are now equipped to design your own programme.

Step 5
You could, for example, start with the chapter with the highest score and then go to the one with the second highest score and work down your list (where two chapters have the same score, start with the one that comes earlier in the book).

Alternatively, you could calculate your average score (say 7) and develop a programme with all the chapters that scored over 7, starting at the beginning of the book and working through. Over to you.

Design your own programme

Fold this portion of the page back on itself and write your score directly into the relevant circle on page 19

I wish that ...

	already largely true	nice to have	yes please – great	absolutely fantastic	give my right arm
When I want someone to do something differently they willingly agree	1	2	3	4	5
I could turn the most heated argument into a constructive conversation	1	2	3	4	5
I could find answers to issues other people found insoluble	1	2	3	4	5
I didn't suffer from nerves	1	2	3	4	5
I didn't get bothered so easily	1	2	3	4	5
I could do the things I'm no good at	1	2	3	4	5
I could make a fresh start	1	2	3	4	5
When I give tough messages the person on the receiving end is grateful	1	2	3	4	5
I could look at familiar problems with fresh eyes	1	2	3	4	5
I had more energy	1	2	3	4	5
I could sleep better	1	2	3	4	5
People gave me their full attention when I had something to say	1	2	3	4	5
I didn't put off telling people what they don't want to hear	1	2	3	4	5
I could put my worries away	1	2	3	4	5
I knew where my life was going	1	2	3	4	5
I could get analytical people to think creatively	1	2	3	4	5
I had more time	1	2	3	4	5
I always got on with new people/complete strangers	1	2	3	4	5
I felt that I was controlling circumstances more than they were controlling me	1	2	3	4	5
I didn't let arguments get out of hand	1	2	3	4	5
Important people treated me as their equal	1	2	3	4	5
People usually agreed with me	1	2	3	4	5
I got on with people better	1	2	3	4	5
I could achieve more without any extra effort	1	2	3	4	5
I could think creatively just as well as I can think logically	1	2	3	4	5
I was an original thinker	1	2	3	4	5
I could relax when I want to	1	2	3	4	5
The people around me behaved as I'd like them to	1	2	3	4	5
I had more flashes of inspiration	1	2	3	4	5
People naturally looked to me for advice in difficult situations	1	2	3	4	5

Taking control

- Ⓐ Lucky you
- Ⓑ The hardest argument
- Ⓒ New chapter
- Ⓓ In charge
- Ⓔ Jump start

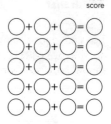

The right impression

- Ⓕ Impact
- Ⓖ Influence
- Ⓗ Connect
- Ⓘ Presence

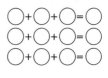

Tough conversations

- Ⓙ Conflict detox
- Ⓚ My honest opinion
- Ⓛ Bad news

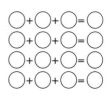

Stress and relaxation

- Ⓜ The joy of stress
- Ⓝ Stressbusters
- Ⓞ Deep breath
- Ⓟ Tranquillity

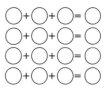

Creative juices

- Ⓠ Let the juices flow
- Ⓡ Creativity for logical thinkers
- Ⓢ Creativity for free thinkers
- Ⓣ Creativity for wannabe daydreamers

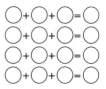

Transfer your score for each question into all the relevant circles on the opposite page (18). When you have finished there should be a number in every circle.

G K ◯

F J ◯
Q S T ◯
N O P ◯
D M N ◯
B ◯
C ◯

L ◯
Q ◯
A B E ◯
P ◯

I ◯
K L ◯
M N ◯
C ◯
R ◯
D E ◯
H ◯

A C D ◯
J O ◯
F G I ◯
G H ◯
H J ◯
A B E M ◯
R ◯
Q R S T ◯
O P ◯
F K ◯
S T ◯
I L ◯

A summary of each chapter

(A) Lucky you

Attentive optimism – a mindset that helps you achieve more and live longer. Have you got it? What can you do to get it?

(B) The hardest argument

The vast majority of the conversations we have are with ourselves, in our head. But do yours help or hinder? Find out how to win the arguments in your mind.

(C) New chapter

I'd like to start a new chapter in my life but something is stopping me. Find out what and how to make the big decisions that will shape your destiny.

(D) In charge

Feel helpless, or that the situation is out of your control? Discover how to take charge, get back in the driving seat and make the right things happen.

(E) Jump start

Everything you wanted to know about procrastination but hadn't quite got round to asking. One chapter you shouldn't put off reading.

(F) Impact

Want to have the right impact? Find out how to spot the way the other person is looking at you and so get it right on the night (and the morning after).

(G) Influence

Discover the nine primary influencing tactics and how to combine them to maximise your chances of winning people round to your point of view.

(H) Connect

Want to get on better with more people? Explore techniques to help build a connection with everyone from long lost friends to complete strangers.

(I) Presence

How to gain gravitas so people listen to what you have to say no matter how important they think they are.

(J) Conflict detox

Find out how to stop disagreements from going toxic and keep arguments constructive so you create strong relationships, not bitter enemies.

Ⓚ **My honest opinion**
Discover how to change the way people around you behave without embarrassing, offending, upsetting or looking stupid.

Ⓛ **Bad news**
Not all bad news can be turned into good news but it can always be shared in a way that softens the blow. The techniques in this chapter show you how.

Ⓜ **The joy of stress**
Some stress is good for us; some is deeply damaging. Discover how to spot the difference and so end up with more of the former and none of the latter.

Ⓝ **Stressbusters**
Nine practical techniques to turn bad stress into the good kind and how to combine them for maximum effect in any distressful situation.

Ⓞ **Deep breath**
How to achieve instant calm by changing the way you breathe.

Ⓟ **Tranquillity**
Quicker than a massage, cheaper than shopping, visualisation is a practical tool for complete and immediate relaxation.

Ⓠ **Let the juices flow**
The magic ingredients for creative thinking – what they are and how to use them to get your creative juices flowing.

Ⓡ **Creativity for logical thinkers**
Simple techniques that use logical thinking to come up with off-the-wall ideas – ideal for those who don't think they are creative but want to be.

Ⓢ **Creativity for free thinkers**
Techniques to take us off our familiar mental routes so we come up with innovative solutions to age-old problems.

Ⓣ **Creativity for wannabe daydreamers**
How to encourage your mind to boldly go where no mind has gone before.

The beginning
How to make best use of what you've discovered so that it improves your life immediately, and for ever. A new beginning?

Taking control

The computer crashing before we saved that all-important document. The vital ingredient forgotten for the meal we're cooking for our hot date. The old lady inching across the zebra crossing as we're late to catch a plane. Sometimes it feels that the world is out to get us. This is not a good place to be. Fortunately, it is not a place where we have to be for very long either.

One of the most significant discoveries in contemporary psychology is that we choose how we think. Sounds obvious? Well, for years the experts thought we were either pre-programmed in our early years or only changed our behaviour as a result of being rewarded or punished. Not so. The good news is that just as we 'choose' to think that the world is out to get us, we can also choose to think that we are in charge of our destiny. The chapters in Taking control are filled with techniques that we can use to help us think differently and get back in charge of our lives.

Some of these approaches are for the everyday challenges such as being more proactive so that things get done, rather than letting them hang over us like a cartoon rain cloud. Check out Jump start and In charge to feel in control of life, day-to-day, today.

For the bigger issues – where is my life going? Am I doing the right things to get what I want? What can I do to reinvigorate or change direction? – then head to New chapter for a new you.

And this whole section starts off with a way of thinking that will help us whatever situation we are in: attentive optimism. Lucky you outlines what it is and The hardest argument how to get it when gloom is all around.

For the 'brightness' control on your future, read on.

(A) Lucky you

Some people have all the luck. So what's their secret?

The answer is perfectly simple: it's a sort of magic. And like any magic trick or illusion, we think it's incredible until we discover how it's done. Once the mystery has gone, we can't believe how obvious it is.

When we understand what makes some people apparently luckier than others, we can learn how to become 'lucky' ourselves. It won't happen instantly. Rather like a budding magician learning his magic tricks, it will take determination and practice to master these new capabilities so that they are effortless and effective. But it's worth it: as we become more accomplished, things will have a knack of increasingly working out as we'd like them to. You may also be closer to it than you imagine.

All the techniques in this book are designed to help us achieve what we want and so, in some way, appear luckier. This chapter, however, takes a more general approach; it shows that the way we look at things can have a huge effect on how fortunate we are.

Even if you don't use any of the tools in the subsequent chapters, simply adopting this way of thinking will mean that you can

- achieve more (optimistic salesmen sell better than pessimistic ones)

- live longer (research shows optimists live longer than pessimists)

- be liked by more people (in a survey on American elections, optimistic candidates consistently picked up the most votes)

- have better relationships (those who believe they are lucky at cards are also lucky in love)

This chapter begins by looking at the difference between optimists and pessimists, and why it is generally better to be the former than the latter. It then goes on to look at different types of optimism and which sorts are the best in a variety of situations. Finally, for all optimism's strength, we explore when we may be better off thinking pessimistically.

How do you think?

The following questionnaire is designed to help understand how we look at the world. For each of the following questions, try to imagine the situation that is described and allocate 10 points across all the options depending on how much they best represent your reaction.

So if answer A fits your response the best by far, B and C fit in certain situations and D not all, then you might answer

A ⑥
B ②
C ②
D ⓪

The only rule is that the total score for each question must add up to 10.

---

1 Someone is rude to me for no obvious reason

A They are having a bad day ○
B They are a rude person ○
C I barely noticed ○
D I must have done something wrong ○

---

2 My proposal for a new project is rejected

A I can learn from this for next time ○
B I messed up ○
C They wouldn't know a great idea if it was in front of their nose ○
D That destroys my chances of promotion ○

---

3 I ring to book a table at my favourite local restaurant but it is already full

A I may well find somewhere better ○
B It's my fault for not ringing earlier ○
C Why is it me who always has to book the restaurant? ○
D I've ruined the whole evening ○

---

4 I cooked supper for friends and though they said it was delicious most of them barely touched the food on their plates

A In future, I'll practise a new dish before trying it out on guests ○
B How embarrassing; I am a terrible host ○

C They said it was delicious and I've no reason to doubt they were
   telling the truth
D My friends will never want to visit me again

5 I get lost on the route to visit a friend

A I can see where I went wrong; it'll be easier next time
B I am a lousy navigator
C Their directions are useless
D They'll be very upset that I'm late

6 I read an article in the newspaper which gives me the information I need to impress a client or important acquaintance

A It's a good thing I keep up to date with current affairs
B What a fluke
C Good things happen to me
D That's the least they'd expect of me

7 I win a tennis doubles tournament

A We're a great double act
B The opposition wasn't up to much
C I am a fantastic tennis player
D It was all thanks to my partner

8 My partner/close friend really likes the birthday present I bought them

A I am good at buying presents
B Thank goodness they gave me a hint
C I bet there aren't many partners/friends who would have chosen so well
D I'll never be able to get them something as good for Christmas

9 I cooked supper for friends and they praised my food

A I'm a good cook
B My friends are easily pleased
C When I turn my hand to something I can make a success of it
D There was nothing special about that meal – they must have low
   expectations after last time

10 Someone compliments me on my clothes

A I look good in this outfit
B They clearly don't have much of an idea about style themselves
C They fancy me
D What a nice thing to say

We'll come back to what the answers suggest later on in this chapter.

Optimists and pessimists: who gets the better deal?

Optimists live longer
In the Mayo Clinic in the US, researchers selected almost 900 people who referred themselves for medical care. When they were originally admitted to the clinic, they took a series of examinations and as part of the series were tested for their level of optimism. Thirty years later, 200 of the original 900 had died, with the optimists living 19% longer than the pessimists.

But the sceptic would respond, there may have been lots of other variables that had come into play: diet, work pressure, a sexually transmitted disease and so on. So where could you do a study where all these remain the same for the whole population? Answer: a convent.

A group of psychologists analysed an autobiographical story which nuns wrote as they were completing their final vows before entering a convent in 1900. The scientists discovered that 90% of the most positive quarter were still alive at 84. In contrast only 34% of the least positive quarter were still alive.

Furthermore 54% of the most positive quarter were still alive at 94. And after studying many other factors, level of optimism was the only one that had a significant correlation with lifespan.

Optimists achieve more
And not just because they live for longer. Optimists tend to be more persistent and resilient and so get more (or better) results.

In a large-scale experiment conducted by the pioneering psychologist Martin Seligman, a group of optimists and pessimists were recruited to become insurance sales agents with the intention of comparing their performance. By the second year of the experiment the optimists were outselling the pessimists by 57%.

Identifying the comparative levels of optimism between competing candidates in the 1988 Senate elections in the US, and backing the greater optimist, produced a more accurate prediction of the final outcome than any of the opinion polls.

Pessimists are more likely to be right
It's not that everything in life goes an optimist's way. Far from it. For all their good fortune, you might be surprised how much optimists tend to get things wrong.

In the study with the insurance sales people, the pessimists were far more accurate about the conversion rate, ie, the number of calls required to make a sale. The optimists generally got it wrong, usually thinking it was many times better than it actually was. The result? The pessimists gave up making calls earlier than the optimists, who ploughed on and got the extra sales. But the pessimists were right.

And realists?

In the same way that a tourist might call himself a 'traveller', some pessimists prefer to go under the label 'realists'. And that is a fair assessment: they are more realistic than the optimist in their analysis of the situation.

Not only can the realist school of pessimism bask in the fact that it is more 'right' than the optimist, it can go further by offering a justification for this mode of thinking. By being realistic about the world, the realists argue, they are never going to find themselves disappointed or let down by events.

However, the irony is that even with this play-safe behaviour, the realist is still more likely to be disappointed than the optimist. This is because when something apparently bad does happen, the optimist will tend to focus on the upside. Say, for example, an optimist and a realist get turned down for a bank loan. The realist/pessimist says, 'I suspected as much' and congratulates himself on not having built up false hopes. The optimist, however, thinks, 'I now know what I need to do to increase my chances of being approved next time' and goes back for a second attempt. No prizes for guessing who has the greater chance of actually getting the loan.

The difference between optimists and pessimists

In what ways, then, do an optimist and a pessimist look at the same events and draw such different conclusions?

Last night, Mark and Janet held a highly successful party for a group of friends. The following morning, Mark wakes up with a slight hangover and remembers the night before. He smiles and thinks to himself, 'We always do give good parties.' On the other side of the bed, Janet rouses from her slumber and slowly recalls the same events. 'We were lucky,' she thinks. 'Last night there was just the right collection of people for a good party.'

Mark's analysis of events shows all the characteristics of an optimist. He considers the success to apply to a wide range of situations (all parties, as opposed to, say, dinner parties or, more specific still, weekend dinner parties with 6–10 people) over a long period of time (if not for ever).

Janet's reaction, by contrast, shows the traits of a pessimistic explanatory style. She associates her success with a very specific type of event (intimate dinner parties) and associates it with one moment in time (last night).

Luck and superstition

Professor Richard Wiseman, while conducting research into what made people lucky and unlucky, wanted to find out whether superstition affected lucky people more than unlucky people. He asked volunteers to rate whether they agreed or disagreed with well-known superstitions like black cats bringing bad luck, or the number 13 being unlucky.

Unlucky

He found that people who considered themselves unlucky are also more likely to be superstitious. He believes that this provides evidence that unlucky people tend to rely on ineffective ways of trying to alter the difficult situations they may encounter.

In summary, there are two dimensions that help to illustrate the difference between how an optimist and a pessimist explain events.

A Scope
This ranges from the highly specific (dinner parties for 6 people on a Friday in September) to the universal (being good at entertaining).

B Time-span
This ranges from the one-off or temporary (last night) to the permanent (always).

When considering positive past events, an optimist will explain them as universal and permanent (as Mark did). Pessimists like Janet, however, will see them as specific and temporary.

By contrast, when it comes to analysing negative past events, the opposite occurs: the optimist will see them as temporary and specific; the pessimist will see them as universal and permanent.

Suppose that, after a summer of struggling, Mark and Janet's garden is still a mess. Mark looks out of the window and thinks, 'The weather this year hasn't been good for my garden.' Janet gazes into her cup of tea and tells herself, 'I'm destined to be a useless gardener.'

Mark, the optimist, explains the situation by making it temporary (this year) and specific (my garden). Janet, the pessimist, does the opposite, making it permanent and applying it to all gardening situations (fairly universal).

The best kind of optimism

In the early academic thinking on optimism, it was believed that optimists took responsibility for positive events and put the responsibility on external factors for negative events (pessimists, of course, did the opposite). In the example of Mark above, he allocates responsibility based on this view, taking credit for the party and blaming the weather for the garden.

There is, however, a danger that if someone gets carried away with their optimism, they end up ducking responsibility: they ignore a problem until it grows out of proportion or rely too much on wishful thinking as the route to achieve their aims.

The attentive optimist is the sort who treads a careful path between taking too much responsibility and too little. For example, after a positive event they will take some credit but only what they consider is their due. Like the goal-scoring footballer in the post-match interview, they may not even share this openly, instead choosing to be gracious and give praise to others. But you can be sure they will recognise and be pleased with what they have accomplished.

In contrast, the undiluted optimist will be inclined to see this one example as definitive proof of their brilliance, charm or never-ending good fortune. And the pessimist will, as suggested above, give the credit to external factors (which may be other people) and so reap very little or no satisfaction from their contribution.

With negative past events the attentive optimist will accept appropriate responsibility and then see what good can be taken from the situation. This might include the lessons they can learn for the future (I won't start a speech with that joke again) or the relative impact on this occasion compared to what it could have been (at least there weren't any journalists there). This is in sharp contrast to the out-and-out optimists who will tend to place the responsibility elsewhere (they were a difficult audience who were in a bad mood because they had already sat through three boring lectures in a row).

The attentive optimist, then, is the sort we should all strive to be. But how much of one are you? To find out, let's go back to the questionnaire at the start of the chapter.

How do you think? – the results

Total up your score for each option in the questionnaire at the beginning of the chapter and capture the raw data here:

A ◯   B ◯   C ◯   D ◯

To see how much of an optimist or pessimist you tend to be, add the scores

$(A + C) - (B + D) =$ ◯

If your score is positive then you tend to think optimistically and if it is negative then you tend to look at things pessimistically. The higher the figure the more you tend to think in this way (the maximum is 100 on either side).

How much of an attentive optimist are you?
'A' represents the attentive optimist's typical response and 'C' those of an undiluted optimist. If your total for C is higher than your total for A then your optimism probably needs reining in or it will be counter-productive. You are likely to be missing out on the 'attentive' part of attentive optimism.

If you gave 2 or more points to the answer 'C' for the following questions, it suggests certain kinds of unrealistic optimism.

Question	Type of unrealistic optimism
1, 2, 4	Ignoring the problem – suggests a tendency to dismiss problems that may need to be addressed. The danger is that the problem grows when you could have taken action earlier to keep it in proportion.
3, 5	Ducking responsibility – suggests that you may not accept your share of the blame when things go wrong. This will not only annoy others but means that you will be less likely to get on and make important changes yourself and so the same problem is more likely to recur.
6, 7, 9	Wishful thinking – this implies that you are looking through rose-tinted spectacles and extrapolating more than appears reasonable about your abilities or prospects. The danger here is that you may assume things will just happen and so not make enough effort to make sure they do.
8, 10	Over-interpretation – similar to wishful thinking, this happens when you decide what other people are thinking or capable of without much evidence. You may well misinterpret their motives or underestimate their capabilities as a result.

And what kind of pessimist?

In a similar way, the two scores for pessimism (B and D) have different meanings. The B score is straightforward pessimism based on the explanatory style described above. D represents more accentuated pessimism where additional elements are at work.

If your pessimism is mainly B-type, then the best way to go about becoming more of an optimist is to explain situations differently. With negative events, try describing them as specific and temporary (the shower curtain didn't stay up this time) and with positive ones try making them more universal, permanent and personal (I'm great at DIY).

If you gave 2 or more to 'D' for the following questions, it suggests there are some things other than your explanatory style that are worth looking at if you want to get the benefits of attentive optimism.

Question	Type of unrealistic pessimism
1, 3	Over-identification – you are in danger of taking more responsibility for a negative outcome than is reasonable.
2, 6, 8, 9	Maximising/minimising – you run the risk of exaggerating the negative impact or dismissing the positive aspect.
4, 5	Over-interpreting – as with undiluted optimists, you are assuming what other people think or are capable of without much or any evidence.

| 7, 10 | Misallocation of responsibility – you are generous in your praise but may not value your own contribution enough. This modesty could be attractive to others but may also leave you with less appreciation of your strengths. |

When pessimism pays

So far we have suggested that optimism is preferable to pessimism, and broadly speaking this is true. However, there are a handful of circumstances in which it is better to switch to a more pessimistic outlook.

Mark is an undiluted optimist. He always sees the best in every situation. He also thinks that giving up his career as a successful banker and opening up a bar in Mustique will be a breeze and he will be a great success. He is wrong and will end up losing all his money and returning home with his tail between his legs.

Janet is a pessimist. She sees what could go wrong in any situation. She decides not to take on a project that Mark left half finished as she can't see how it is going to be completed in time and fears that she will be made responsible for the mess that Mark has left, which happened to her once before. She will stay at the bank but progress only slowly to a mid-ranking level.

Rachel is an attentive optimist. She was offered Mark's project after Janet had turned it down. She assessed the pros and cons and what the worst outcome for her might be, as well as calculating the chances that this 'worst outcome' would happen. She also reminded herself that she had successfully completed difficult projects before. After quite a lot of consideration, she decided to take on the project. From this moment she switched from pessimist/realist and became entirely optimistic in her outlook. The project will be completed on time and Rachel will be promoted which marks the beginning of a meteoric career.

One of the tricks to being an attentive optimist lies in knowing when to be optimistic and when to be pessimistic. In summary, there are three situations when it is best to be pessimistic in outlook.

1 When making big decisions
This is where Mark goes wrong with his move to Mustique. The unbridled optimism that helped him succeed in his day-to-day work in banking is a disadvantage when considering big decisions such as changing his lifestyle completely. This is the risk of wishful thinking.

2 When the implications of being wrong would be extremely serious
How comfortable would you be if you knew that the pilot of your plane is being optimistic about having enough fuel to get to your destination?

3 When you start trying to comfort someone who is very unhappy
Try telling someone whose mother has just died that they are really lucky as they will get to inherit and will no longer have to spend Christmas being reminded of all their faults.

In almost all other situations we are better off being broadly optimistic.

Conclusion: watch out for the rut

Most of us have decided how we look at life and the events in it and we tend to use the same approach for everything. If we found that a sense of realism is helpful in one part of our life, say, buying a house or submitting budgets at work, then we are likely to use it in every other part of our life even if it is having the opposite effect from the one that we want.

Our upbringing also has a strong influence. If you wanted to fit in with the cool crowd at school it almost certainly required a level of cynicism and criticism that you may have taken with you into adult life. Equally, if your parents were always telling you how everything is possible, you may have adopted their positive perspective or rebelled against it.

Once you are aware of how you look at things, whatever the reason, you can then decide whether to change it. The results from the questionnaire will help you realise how you could change the way you look at things to be more attentively optimistic (or, for that matter, pessimistic).

Knowing is one thing, doing is quite another.

The next chapter suggests a technique to help turn pessimistic beliefs into optimistic ones (a challenge that most of us have from time to time). For the time being, appreciate what you have achieved – knowing and recognising the difference between optimism and pessimism is half the journey.

Give your mind a workout

I SPY Listen out for someone, it could be a friend, a colleague or a celebrity being interviewed on the radio or TV, who is entirely pessimistic in the way that they describe their situation.

Listen out for someone being entirely optimistic in the way that they describe their situation.

I TRY A one-week programme for pessimists who want to be attentive optimists.

Day 1   Think about a positive event in your recent past both optimistically and pessimistically, using the explanatory styles outlined above, and then do the same for a negative event.

Day 2   Repeat this with two different events but this time add two more optimistic interpretations for each of the events.

Day 3   When you hear yourself explain something negatively, reword it to explain the same thing optimistically, maybe even joking with the other person, 'or you could put it like this . . .'

Day 4   Every hour of the day make sure you think about something using an optimistic explanatory style.

Day 5   Consciously explain something using an optimistic explanatory style to two different people during the course of the day.

Day 6   Listen out for when someone you know well uses a pessimistic explanatory style. Suggest an alternative, optimistic explanation.

Day 7   Spend the whole day thinking and speaking like an attentive optimist.

By now you should have got the hang of how to think like an optimist. Keep trying it out. The more you practise the more natural it will become.

(B) The hardest argument

'Tidy your room.'
'Why should I?'
'Because if you don't you won't be allowed to watch any TV.'
'That is so not fair. You didn't make Sarah tidy her room before she was allowed to watch TV.'
'Sarah's room is not as messy as yours.'
'Yes it is, I'll show you . . .'

We learn to argue from an early age and most of us never give up. With practice we might become subtler and, we hope, more effective. Some of us even get beyond the stage of stamping our feet, slamming the door behind us and locking ourselves in the bathroom for three hours.

Whether it's about politics, money, who is going to win the Oscar for Best Actress, the shortest route to the station or what colour to paint the bathroom, most of us have some subjects we feel strongly about and some people we are happy to argue with about them.

There is, however, one person who none of us tends to argue with and, when we occasionally try, tend to do so pretty badly.

That person is ourselves.

This is a shame because we are the person we need to convince when it comes to changing the big things in life: whether it's branching out in a career, giving up smoking or debating the future of a relationship.

We've all seen or read those books that tell you how to get in touch with a veritable safari park of animals inside your body: find the wolf within, you can be a tiger, think like a dolphin and so forth. In this chapter we explore how you argue with yourself, and, by doing so, unleash the most vicious internal creature of them all: your inner Paxman.

Why arguing with ourselves is good for us

Meet Kevin. Kevin likes playing chess. The person Kevin most often plays chess with is himself. When his friend Alan saw him playing white, and then swapping seats and playing black, he was confused. 'Don't you find you always lose?' he asked.

'No,' replied Kevin, 'I always win.'

Quite apart from the difference between the optimistic Kevin and the pessimistic Alan, the story of Kevin playing chess against himself seems a little odd to most of us. How can you develop your own strategy when the other side is going to know what it is and therefore will be more than capable of defeating it?

Kevin's response to this is that he deliberately blocks his previous thoughts and, by physically moving to the other side of the board, looks at the problem completely afresh. He admits that it isn't quite the same as playing against another person but is confident that it improves his game.

Win or lose? You decide

When it comes to the idea of arguing with ourselves, our reaction is a little like Alan's: we find it odd because we assume that we are right in the first place. After all, if we didn't think we were right we would have changed our view already. So why bother? Not so much checkmate as stalemate.

The weak point in the argument above (there we are, at it already, arguing with a previous paragraph this time) is this 'assumption' that we are right. Once we have made the assumption, we don't seriously consider that it may be false. Through a combination of mental idleness and the desire to reinforce our view of ourselves, we rarely open our assumptions up to scrutiny.

The strongest reason for any of us to argue with ourselves is that we may have beliefs that are limiting us from achieving what we are capable of.

If I believe I'm no good at languages, then I won't try to improve my French. If I believe you'll never come round to my point of view, I am very unlikely to persuade you.

Six steps to arguing with yourself

Sean was a participant at one of The Mind Gym workouts, Create Your Own Luck. During the course of the workout, the following discussion happened between Sean and The Mind Gym Coach, though it could quite as easily have happened inside his head. The important point is the thought process that was followed – a process that we can all learn from and apply to our own internal arguments.

Step One: The belief
Sean believed he was bad at giving presentations. As a result he tried to avoid taking on roles that required standing up and talking to groups of people (even though he had to make a presentation roughly every eight weeks in his current job). This limited his exposure in his company and in his industry, which meant that he had not been promoted into the position that someone with his track record could have expected.

'Whenever I make a presentation,' Sean explained, 'there is always someone who disagrees with me. They ask me questions that I can't answer on the spot and it looks like everything I am saying is rubbish. In addition, my boss always interrupts when he is there, making points that I hadn't considered; everyone looks at me with totally blank faces; I always have to use notes; and in all my career not one person has ever said they thought I made a good presentation. I'm not making it up. I really am a bad presenter.'

At first glance, Sean's argument that he is a bad presenter seems strong. But there is always a danger with a pessimistic opinion that it is a self-fulfilling prophecy: we are so determined to maintain our self-belief that we will go out of our way to prove it is correct, even if we suffer as a result. Is this what Sean was subconsciously up to?

Step Two: The evidence
On closer questioning, Sean admitted that people didn't always stare with blank faces, they sometimes nodded and took notes, even though he gave out copies of the slides that he used. This could be a sign that they were interested and keen to remember what he had said rather than, as Sean saw it, proof that his visual materials weren't any good.

Sean also agreed that, over the years, some people had said things like, 'that was interesting' or 'that could be useful on project Alpha'. So, whilst they didn't directly compliment his presentation style, they clearly valued what he had to say.

Sean also accepted that in his company compliments were rare and that when you did something well most people assumed that you were just doing your job. They were, however, quick to point out when things went wrong. Had anyone ever told Sean he was a bad presenter? The answer was no, even though, when we counted, Sean had done eighteen different presentations.

The difficult questions, it emerged, invariably came from the same department. The reason Sean often couldn't answer the questions was because they weren't relevant at this stage or because it wasn't his area of responsibility.

The evidence

But because Sean believed that, as the presenter, he should be able to answer whatever questions come his way (another false belief) he floundered and apologised which made him appear less convincing.

When tested, Sean's argument that he is a poor presenter didn't look quite so strong. In fact, we could argue that on cross-examination it has been shown to be largely false. But the evidence still hadn't convinced Sean and it is his view, not ours, that matters.

Step Three: Alternative explanations
If the evidence itself is not enough to disprove the argument, then the next step is to look for alternative explanations.

First, let's look at the specific points in Sean's argument. It transpired that Sean's presentations were to people in other parts of the organisation and were often about quite technical and complex subjects. As a result, the blank faces he saw were likely to be signs of deep concentration rather than disbelief or boredom.

As for Sean's boss interrupting him, maybe it wasn't because Sean was bad but because his boss wanted some of the credit for himself. When this was suggested, Sean immediately thought of other times when the boss had taken some of the glory for Sean's work.

And as far as using notes is concerned, the fact is that many good presenters use them, especially when they are talking about complex subjects.

Second, let's consider the general assumption behind Sean's argument: quite often, when we see ourselves as 'failing' it may well be that we just have a misguided definition of success. In this instance, the question is this: what does a good presentation consist of? Some people (Sean included) think that it is about making people laugh, speaking fluently and not using notes. Certainly, if you are a stand-up comedian this is true. But not, necessarily, if you are a presenter in business.

Step Four: So what?

By this stage, Sean was beginning to see that there might be another side to his argument. But what if he hadn't considered changing his view? The question to ask when both the evidence and the alternatives aren't very convincing is, so what? In Sean's case, what would the consequences be if his initial assumption that he is not a good presenter was true?

Sean's view was clear. As a bad presenter he damaged his reputation each time he stood up to speak. As a result, he was usually in the background and so did not tend to be considered for new roles and promotions. Also, the more senior roles tended to require more presentations and as he hated doing these he wouldn't want to take the roles in any case. He had therefore hit a ceiling in his career and he was only 32.

But when pressed further about the consequences of being a bad speaker, it seemed that Sean had exaggerated its effect. There were people more senior than Sean, he agreed, who weren't great presenters. They'd succeeded either by joining up with someone who was a more proficient communicator and doing double acts, or by writing clear papers that were widely shared and published.

The consequences of being a poor presenter were less serious than Sean initially assumed.

Step Five: A waste of thought

When all the arguments above have been tried and found wanting, the last resort is to ask ourselves, is there any use in holding this view?

For Sean, the value in seeing himself as a bad presenter was, well, nil. And so, for that reason if no other, it is worth Sean's while to change his view. The only way Sean's self-belief about being a bad presenter could be helpful is if he uses it as a prompt to take action and so become a better presenter.

Step Six: Call to action

Challenging the way we look at a situation is probably the single most powerful thing we can do when it comes to altering our beliefs. It is certainly possible that simply by thinking differently about his presenting

The second hardest argument you'll ever have

There are some people we know we're not going to be able to convince even before we start trying. Sometimes we wonder why we bother. Just as we expected, we don't get a pay rise, an extra person to help out on the project, or an exemption from lunch with Aunt Anne.

One of the reasons why we have next to no chance of succeeding is the conversation that we have in our head before we have even started. In The Mind Gym's Influence and persuade workout, participants consider what goes through their mind before they try to win over a particularly tricky adversary. They then look at how they could rewrite the conversation.

Here are some examples of the most frequently cited blocks and the most helpful alternatives.

Unhelpful self-talk	Rewriting the conversation
I don't know as much as they do	I know more about some things than they do; we'll learn from each other
They are more senior than me	They are just another person with hopes and fears and insecurities, just like me
I always lose arguments with them	What I am proposing is in *their* interests; we are both on the same side
They never agree with me	I know lots about what doesn't persuade them so I am well equipped to try a better approach
I'll fail	The worst that can happen is that I learn from the experience
There's no point – they've made up their mind	I wonder why they think like this? I'll use this opportunity to find out more about how they make their mind up

capability, Sean could become a more confident and effective presenter. Perhaps as he becomes less bothered by his lack of polish, Sean could gain gravitas as an authority in his subjects.

But thinking differently is not the only thing Sean could do. The next step he could take is to tackle his perceived weaknesses head on.

Sean could be trained or coached to answer difficult questions more effectively; he could spend more time anticipating the questions that might be asked and so prepare some answers; he could develop some standard techniques for questions that he doesn't know the answers to; and, no doubt, there is plenty more that Sean could do to become a better presenter.

Having changed our self-belief by arguing with ourselves, we are now ready to get out of the pessimistic torpor we started in (I am not good enough and there's nothing I can do about it) and do something positive (I am capable, now let me get on and do something useful). Deciding what to do and when is the final, seventh, stage in the self-argument (also called a 'disputation').

The seven steps: a summary of the disputation process

In the steps above, we have charted the 'argument' Sean had in our work-out. As a result of which he

- considered himself a perfectly adequate presenter

- appreciated that the level of his presenting skills isn't as critical to his future success as he had previously thought

- knew what he could do to become a better presenter.

This argument or 'disputation' happened between two people, but it could just as easily have happened in Sean's head. It is a process any of us could use when we have a pessimistic or negative assumption we want to challenge or change.

Win yourself over

The 'person' you have the argument with is up to you, though the tougher and firmer they are, the more likely you are to have your opinions over-turned. You could imagine, for example, that your inner voice takes the persona of a top TV interviewer: you know they're not going to let you get away with anything, they'll always be sharp but fair and won't let you

The seven steps of arguing with ourselves

1 **What is the belief that I have?**	This will be a pessimistic view. If I am already thinking optimistically about the situation then I don't need to argue with myself about it.
2 **What evidence is there to challenge this view? (The case for the prosecution.)**	Work hard to unearth all the evidence against this view. Imagine you are Columbo, V I Warshawski, Poirot and Sherlock Holmes rolled into one.
3 **If the evidence isn't enough: What alternative explanations are there to explain the situation?**	There are almost certainly other reasons. Come up with as many alternative explanations as you can before picking out the ones that are most likely to be valid.
4 **If the alternative explanations and the evidence aren't enough: What are the real consequences if my belief is correct? (So what?)**	I might well have built this up into an enormous thing in my mind. A reality check will help put it back into perspective. Indeed, so much so that it may become largely irrelevant.
5 **If you still hold on to your original belief: How useful is it to have this view?**	Even when all other arguments haven't worked, holding this negative belief is unlikely to help. Better to see it differently, say as a good base from which to build.
6 **Given this argument with myself, what do I need to do to improve the situation?**	There are usually lots of things that I can do to improve the situation. It can be good to write them ALL down (and then some more) before deciding what to do – otherwise we do roughly the same things we did last time, and as they didn't work then they probably won't this time either.
7 **What will I do? When?**	Of all the options, which ones will I actually do and when?

Mirror, mirror

One overly common and very unhelpful self-belief that people have is 'I am not attractive'. It comes in many forms, from 'I'll never find someone who wants to marry me', through 'No one ever looks at me in that way any more' to 'My looks aren't even good enough for radio'. The feeling is often particularly acute at the end of a relationship but it can happen at many different times to pretty much any of us. Essentially, it means that the people we want to find us attractive, don't.

Working through the seven steps outlined above, how could we argue ourselves out of this viewpoint?

Evidence
- Has anyone I care about ever found me attractive?

- Have any of my friends told me that I am attractive, or acted as if they thought so?

- What character and physical traits do I have that people might find attractive?

Alternative explanations
- Everyone has this feeling from time to time – it has nothing to do with me and how I look

- Just because one person doesn't find me attractive, albeit someone I care about, doesn't mean that no one will find me attractive

- Am I comparing myself with the people photographed in magazines and who appear in TV advertisements? Is this a reasonable comparison? Maybe I am much more attractive than them but in different ways

- Am I considering the right people to be good judges of how attractive I am? Am I deliberately focusing on those who don't obviously find me attractive?

Consequences
- Different people find different looks beautiful

- The worst consequence is that I will find it difficult to find the perfect partner. I can still achieve much else in my life, arguably more

- The sort of people who judge someone on attraction alone are the superficial sort of people I want to avoid

- I won't start a shallow relationship that will end quickly

Usefulness
- The more I think like this the more unattractive I will become. The first stage to being more attractive is to think you are. True or not, I am better off changing my self-perception

Plan of action
- Be happy as I am

- Diet, gym and other forms of physical improvement

- New wardrobe

- New passion or interest

- Go to a new hairdresser

- Change the type of person I want to find me attractive

dodge the question. If you're going to have the hardest argument you'll ever have, you might as well do it properly and have the hardest person to argue with.

Imagine the following argument in the head of Ashley, who is constantly toying with giving up smoking, but never quite gets round to it. As Ashley discovers, not only is your Inner Interviewer brilliant at arguing, he is also perfectly briefed: as your inner voice, he knows everything there is to know about you . . .

INTERVIEWER: So Ashley. You want to give up smoking then, do you?

ASHLEY: Well. You know, at some stage, probably.

INTERVIEWER: I'm sorry, I don't quite understand your answer. Do you want to give up smoking, yes or no?

ASHLEY: Yes, but does it have to be now?

INTERVIEWER: (Snorts) You tell me, I'm not the one thinking about giving up. Are you normally the sort of person who puts things off?

ASHLEY:	(Bristling) No, not really.
INTERVIEWER:	So you're going to get on with it then? You're going to give up smoking now?
ASHLEY:	OK. Here's the thing. I actually really enjoy smoking.
INTERVIEWER:	You do? What, always? (Raises eyebrow.) Even the first one in bed in the morning?
ASHLEY:	Well, OK, maybe not that one . . .
INTERVIEWER:	So you don't enjoy smoking?
ASHLEY:	You're putting words into my mouth here. Yes, so the first one in the morning isn't great. But there are plenty of cigarettes that are fantastic. I love that cigarette after dinner, especially if I'm sitting on a moonlit terrace in a Mediterranean villa.
INTERVIEWER:	Right, and that happens how often? Weekly? Monthly? (Raises eyebrow again.) Yearly?
ASHLEY:	Once a year.
INTERVIEWER:	And the cigarette you don't enjoy in the morning? That out-weighs the Mediterranean fag by what? 365 to 1?
ASHLEY:	I think you're twisting things a little here . . .
INTERVIEWER:	They're your statistics, Ashley, not mine. (Sits back in chair, looks bored.) But come on, apart from 'enjoying' smoking, what else has it got going for it?
ASHLEY:	Er, I know lots of cool people who smoke.
INTERVIEWER:	Oh *come on*. (Pulls face.) You're not *seriously* using that as an argument are you? (Stares at Ashley in unbelieving manner.) Cool? I don't remember ever seeing a Premiership footballer bending a free kick with a Benson in his hand.
ASHLEY:	Maybe, but I'm not sure that proves anything.
INTERVIEWER:	With the greatest respect, Ashley, it's your argument, not mine. I mean, look at the people who do smoke. They are giving no thought to the fact that they are seriously damaging their health. You're not like that. You wouldn't drive a beat-up old car with no brakes, so why smoke?
ASHLEY:	Are you suggesting I'm superficial?
INTERVIEWER:	I'm just trying to understand why you smoke, and, so far, I don't think you've come up with anything *approaching* a decent

reason. It's been suggested that you light up at a party as a sub-stitute for thinking of something to say. It's also been claimed that you light up by yourself when you're bored. These are fairly damning accusations, Ashley. What have you got to say about them?

ASHLEY: (Thinks) Well, OK, so sometimes I do smoke when I'm bored or can't think of what to say . . .

INTERVIEWER: (Adjusts tie) So you're not denying the claims then?

ASHLEY: If you'll let me finish my sentence. Yes, so sometimes I do, but what's the alternative? Do I really want to go through the night-mare of giving up? I'm not even sure I definitely want to give up for ever.

INTERVIEWER: I don't think anyone's suggesting you should say never for ever. Why not just take a break for a while? See how it goes?

ASHLEY: And what if I have a cigarette during my 'break'?

INTERVIEWER: It's hardly a big deal, is it? Just see it as the exception and return to the smoking break. One chocolate does not end a diet. The research shows that the physical addiction lasts only three days; after that it's strictly mental. You are strong-willed?

ASHLEY: Yes, if I want to be.

INTERVIEWER: Well, do you want to be? Yes or no?

ASHLEY: Yeah, maybe.

INTERVIEWER: No one's suggesting it's going to be easy. Each time you are in a situation where you used to smoke, you're automatically going to want to light up, it's a sort of click-whirr, as guaranteed as a grandfather clock chiming on the hour.

ASHLEY: So what am I supposed to do?

INTERVIEWER: Recognise that this is the reason why you want a cigarette. You don't actually want it, only you react automatically in this situation. What you need to do is to re-programme yourself so that you see it as a smoke-free situation and find something else to do with your mind.

ASHLEY: And what about when I really *do* want a cigarette?

INTERVIEWER: Think about the benefits of not smoking, even for just a few weeks or months. The money saved, walking up the stairs with-out feeling out of breath, no nicotine hangovers, enjoying good food and wine more, less stuff to have to remember and carry around. Also, if you can give up smoking, what can't you do?

ASHLEY:	OK, so maybe I'll take a break for a couple of weeks and decide at the end whether to carry on.
INTERVIEWER:	I'd say a month – it sounds better and gives you something more specific to aim for.
ASHLEY:	Well, I guess that's . . .
INTERVIEWER:	Ashley, I'm going to have to stop you there. Thanks for talking, and, er, good luck.

The arguments above may not convince you. It doesn't matter. You will need to have your own debate with your own arguments.

Ashley's argument would be much less likely to work if it was between two people as each would want to defend their position. As these two voices are in the same person's head, and as that person can guide the debate as they wish, there is more chance of the side you want to win actually winning.

Note too that the interviewer's tone changes from assertive to ally; this is intentional. He is trying to persuade, not win an intellectual argument. Ultimately, he has much more chance of this as the forceful friend.

These kinds of arguments may happen once but they are just as likely to be stopped and returned to on future occasions. You can keep returning to your inner arguments – until the side you want to win has its final, convincing victory.

To be optimistic or not to be: this is the conclusion

By learning how to argue with ourselves, we give ourselves a great chance of overturning any unhelpful, pessimistic thought. And it may be comforting to learn that, by doing so, we are not alone: literature is full of such questioning characters.

In the children's story of *Doctor Dolittle*, there is the mysterious double-headed creature, the pushmi-pullyu, who goes to show that two heads can sometimes be more argumentative than one. Then there is Gollum/Smeagol in *The Lord of the Rings*, continually torn between good and evil.

But where the one-man argument finds its greatest exponent is in Shakespeare and his soliloquies. Think of *Hamlet*, and perhaps the most

The inner Paxman: a user's guide

Jeremy Paxman is one of the most feared and respected interviewers in the media today. For your 'inner Paxman' to rise to similar perceptive heights, you might want to adopt one or more of the following techniques.

1 Be sceptical
A sceptical starting point means that your answers have got to be robust to convince.

2 The snap
If Jeremy has a catchphrase, it is 'Oh, come on!', spat out to catch the interviewee off guard. Try the same response with your arguments. If you can handle your inner Paxman snapping at you like that then you're probably on the right lines.

3 The raised eyebrow
A similar tactic to The snap, but ten times as powerful, and capable of reducing a Cabinet minister to tears at ten paces. Can your assumptions survive the same deadly treatment?

Oh, come on!

4 The repeated question
In one of Jeremy Paxman's most famous interviews he asked the same question fourteen times in a row. Let your inner Paxman try the same tactic: if he keeps asking the same question, it's because you're avoiding answering it.

famous passage in English literature: 'To be or not to be'. Here the young prince persuades himself away from the most pessimistic outlook of all: whether or not to end his life. And if Hamlet can argue himself back from the brink, there should be no pessimistic viewpoint which the rest of us can't overcome.

Nine top tips on how to argue with yourself effectively

1   Choose a view that you would, ideally, like to change, for example a negative view about yourself and what you are capable of.

2   Don't become too entrenched in your position to start with. If you do, be willing to agree in principle that you will compromise or change your view if the arguments are compelling.

3   Imagine you are the prosecutor challenging your original hypothesis; give it everything you can. As the prosecutor, you don't need to be fair. You need to make the best case possible. Don't put up a defence as you go along but assemble all the arguments against your original view.

4   Is there a case for the prosecution? If so, accept this without necessarily launching a counter-attack.

5   Search for alternative explanations. There is almost always more than one reason. We tend to over-emphasise the examples that support our belief and underplay any counter-examples that suggest an alternative cause.

6   Try to find the right path between firm and supportive. Too lenient and your views won't change; too aggressive and you won't want to change.

7   Challenge your assumptions about the importance of your view. So what if you can't play a musical instrument or master all the functions on your mobile phone?

8   The ultimate fall-back is to decide if your view is helping or hindering. Even if it is, in your opinion, true, that isn't enough of a reason to hold on to a view. If the belief is getting in the way, then best to put it to one side.

9   The hardest part of arguing with ourselves is being willing to be swayed. Ask yourself if you are being obstinate.

(C) New chapter

You are sitting in your rocking chair on the terrace of your Spanish villa, watching the sun set with a glass of sangria by your side. With your 100th birthday only a few weeks away, you're thinking back on your life, and you recall how the major decisions you made at different stages affected the course it would follow.

You remember the decision to quit studying law and take up Spanish. You remember moving out to Madrid and, after a few lonely nights, venturing into a bar and talking with a stranger who would later become the love of your life. You remember both of you deciding, after barely seeing each other for weeks, that your well-paid jobs weren't worth the ridiculous hours you had to work – and so you quit. Less romantically, but infinitely more profitably, you remember buying the licence to import computers and writing your own Spanish manuals to go with them.

If you'd listened to other people, you'd never have done any of these things. Your father said you couldn't give up law (because of the sacrifices he and your mother had made to get you there). Your closest friend said you couldn't move to Spain because of the political regime there at the time. Your Spanish neighbour told you that you couldn't go into a bar in that district alone, especially as a foreigner. Your colleagues said that if you stopped working in a 'proper' job you'd end up starving on the streets. You look out across the sky at the sun going down, and smile.

A few weeks later, at your birthday party, one of your daughters asks you to give advice to all your grandchildren and great-grandchildren now that they are all together. You decide to share the reflections that you had the other evening.

'I guess my advice is that, whatever everyone says, there is very little that we can't do. The choice we have is between "will" and "won't". In my experience, people tend to say that they can't do something, or that you can't do something, as a way to disguise the fact that there is a choice. But there is always a choice. What they actually mean is that they won't do it, or they don't want you to do it. Sometimes it may be better not to do it, but you always have the option.'

'Does that mean you can become a gorilla?' asked Fred, the smart(ish) eight-year-old son of one of your granddaughters.

'There are some things that are impossible,' you smile. 'But for most things there's a choice. You can become an astronaut, a professor or a beach bum [his mother gives you a sharp stare] or the boy with the tidiest bedroom in the world [her frown turns into a forgiving smile]. Then again, you may choose not to [Fred smiles again, and you avoid looking at his mother]. That's how life works. It's your choice.'

Can't is a four-letter word

'Free Will (he's innocent)' is a good line of graffiti but a bad line of argument. For free will, like it or not, is responsible for the actions that we take.

The existentialist philosophers, led by Jean-Paul Sartre and Martin Heidegger, were the first significant body of thinkers to claim that man(kind) is totally free and totally responsible for his (their) acts. This may sound less radical now than it did in the middle of the 20th century. But it is plenty more radical than many of us allow when we consider what to do to make our lives better.

Fifty years on, our lives are full of rules, guidelines and principles that we invent, or are invented for us, to help us make choices (and provide excuses for poor decisions). But though they masquerade as immutable laws (as in the laws of physics), they are more like local by-laws, often out of date, irrelevant and better breached than obeyed.

Here are a few so-called laws or principles that you may have come across, or live your life by.

- Job security is greater in large, well-known companies

- If you want a successful career you need to go to university

- Marriages with a large age difference don't work

- People who finish at the top of their class get the best jobs

Yet many of those who we now consider as remarkable people became successful by doing what 'couldn't' be done. Only it could and they did . . .

- Andy Warhol (They said: you can't reproduce the image from cans of soup and call it art.)

- Michael O'Leary, CEO of Ryanair (They said: you can't fly people between countries for less than ten pounds.)

- Dick Fosbury (They said: the only way to do the high jump is the scissors technique. Fosbury was the first person to do a back flip and so greatly increased the potential maximum height for high jumpers.)

What they all knew, and what we should always remember, is that when it comes to making choices in life, 'can't' is the wrong word.

Will. Or won't?

The lunch has been cleared away and you are settled in a favourite, slightly worn armchair. Your newly teenage great-granddaughter, Jasmin, comes to sit by you.

'I loved your advice that everything is possible; that's what I believe. But it does make everything much harder. With so many options, how do you decide when you will do something and when you won't? Do you think the way we are taught at school and what Mum and Dad say at home encourage us to go more in one direction than another?'

You're really in the wise old guru seat now. You feel like a bit of an impostor; after all, do you really have any wisdom that is worth sharing? Would they be better off discovering their own insights for themselves rather than listening to your out-of-date, simplistic mantras? Nonetheless, it is rather flattering and Jasmin's questions are on the nail. You've enjoyed the wine at lunch and you succumb.

'I'll let you into a secret.' You beckon Jasmin to come closer. 'When I was eight years old we moved house and ended up living next to a family who had a son who was a year older than me. We had been there only a couple of months when they asked me to his birthday party. I was scared of going to a new house with lots of strangers and imagined them ignoring me or, even worse, teasing me. And so I said "no".

'On the day of the party I looked out of the window and saw all the kids at the local school, some of whom had become friends in the intervening weeks, going into our neighbours' house and heard them playing and laughing all afternoon and late into the evening. I sat next door wishing I was there too and I cried.

'I realised that it was in me to turn down what could be great opportunities because of made-up fears. I didn't like this about myself and so I decided to change it. That day I made a decision never again to turn down an opportunity because I was unreasonably scared about what could happen.

'So, in answer to your question, I guess I was programmed by fear towards "can't" but I rewrote the programme so that I would make better choices between "will" and "won't".'

How are you irrational?

For all that man is the 'rational animal', there are two irrational attitudes that many of us allow too much sway over our lives.

Much of our upbringing is filled with threats about horrible things that will happen if we don't stick to the rules. Santa Claus won't visit us. Our father/mother will be told when he/she comes home. The bogey man will get us. And this carries on in later life where we are fearful that our friends or family won't approve, or our motives will be misunderstood. Reputation, Theodore Zeldin once observed, is the modern form of purgatory.

For those of us who tend to be swayed by **irrational fear**, our regrets tend to be based on the things we didn't do and the opportunities that we didn't take: Why didn't I leave accountancy once I had qualified? Why didn't I take the chance to go to Memphis when I had it? How different would life have been if I'd proposed to her that night on the boat?

Equally, there are others amongst us who suffer from **irrational exuberance**. These people might be described, especially by those with irrational fears, as not having their feet firmly on the ground. The regrets they are most likely to have are along the lines of 'Why did I rush into that?' Some of the small businesses that collapse every year are started by people with irrational exuberance, who didn't think through the decision they were making.

There is a danger that each 'side' encourages the other. A failure for an irrational exuberant convinces someone with irrational fears that their fears are actually well justified – see what happens if you give up a good job. To the irrational exuberant, the sight of someone unhappily stuck in a rut is evidence that we have nothing to fear but fear itself – they may be rich in financial terms but look how unhappy they are.

People with irrational exuberance are, however, the exceptions. Because of our upbringing and the society in which we live, we are much more likely to be worried about failing in some way or letting someone down than keen to give something a go and not worry about the consequences.

The rest of this chapter is similarly weighted. There are a few tips for those who are more used to saying 'I wish I hadn't', but the majority of advice is for those of us who want to avoid looking back and saying 'If only' or 'I wish I had'.

Get ready for the ride of your life

A helpful way of illustrating the main steps that we go through as we re-order our lives is the grandly named 'existential cycle'. The cycle has four spokes: doing, contemplating, preparing and experimenting.

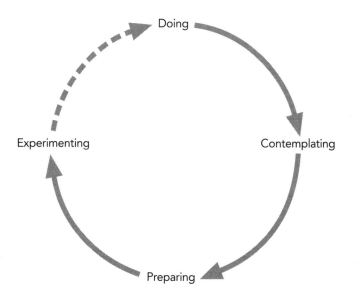

Doing is where we spend most of our lives: it is our settled, equilibrium position. The 'doing' may be all sorts of things – writing emails, riding horses, reading books, washing up, going to meetings, changing nappies, sitting in lectures, cooking, dancing, running, sharing tales about friends, telling jokes and making love. Though not all at the same time, not unless we're really clever. Whatever it may be, and however enjoyable or dull it is, we are doing it and it tends to keep us occupied.

Sometimes, however, we get around to **contemplating** about whether or how things could be different. 'I wonder what life would be like if we moved to Bali', 'Do I really want to be a pig farmer for the rest of my life?', 'Am I leading a "good" life?'

Occasionally, we move on from reflecting to actually **preparing**. We search for estate agents in Bali on the web, find out what property prices are, check the weather patterns, possibly even go to Bali for a holiday. We have moved beyond imagining how things could be different to investigating the practical options for how to make them different.

What goes around . . .

Here's an old joke that illustrates how, just sometimes, the cycle isn't worth starting.

A businessman is on holiday by the sea, sitting on the beach and watching the locals fishing and lazing in the sunshine. In the bar that evening, he decides to give one of the fishermen some advice.

'You're wasting yourself here,' he tells the fisherman. 'You should use your brain, make some money. Have you ever thought about opening a restaurant? Fresh fish dishes, you could make a fortune. And once the first restaurant works, you could set up another, and then another. Before you know it, you've got a whole chain on your hands. And if it works in this country, why not abroad? Then all you have to do is float your company on the stock exchange, retire to the coast, and spend the rest of your days fishing and lazing in the sunshine.'

'Another beer?' smiles the fisherman.

The next stage is actually making the change. We leave our jobs, get a residential visa, buy the house and move all our possessions. This stage is called **experimenting**. After a while when we have settled in and started the beachside bar that we'd dreamed about, this becomes our normal way of living and we are, once again, in a state of 'doing'.

The cycle in itself is not complicated. The challenge, however, is moving round it at the right pace and in the right way.

The 'doing' magnet
As we are travelling round our cycle we all have conversations with ourselves that stop us moving on to the next stage and instead take us back to 'doing'.

'Cyc'ology: two tour de forces

The Tour de France is one of sport's most prestigious and gruelling events. Cycling thousands of miles over three weeks, including stages in both the Alps and the Pyrenees, simply reaching the finishing line in Paris is a challenge for most cyclists. But for two of its recent champions, the race itself was only half the battle.

In 1987, American cyclist Greg LeMond was involved in a horrific shooting accident: over forty shotgun pellets ripped through his body, including two that lodged in his heart lining. While waiting for rescue, Greg's right lung collapsed and he lost three-quarters of his blood supply. When he finally got to hospital, Greg was lucky to be alive, and certainly would never race again.

In 1996, Lance Armstrong was a promising young cyclist who was about to receive the shock of his life: he had advanced testicular cancer that had spread to his lung and brain. He had the malignant testicle removed and underwent both brain surgery and chemotherapy. Even so, his chances of survival were put at no more than 50/50. As for returning to cycling, that was just a pipe dream.

But here's the astonishing thing. For both Greg and Lance there was no such word as 'can't'. Couldn't race again? Just watch them. Both set their sights on proving the doctors wrong and returning to cycling. And both went on to win the Tour de France, in Lance's case six times.

Sometimes these thoughts can be very sensible and prevent us from wasting time or following the wrong path. But sometimes, unfortunately, these internal conversations prevent us both spotting and taking opportunities that could dramatically improve our lives. The trick lies in recognising the conversations that we are having and so being able to make an informed decision about whether to listen to them, or to ignore them and move on.

Conversation One: Dreamers are losers

- I must get on with things

- No point in dreaming, I'll only be disappointed

- I should be grateful for what I've got

- I've got my feet on the ground

- Let's deal with today

These are some of the conversations that we have that stop us contemplating and bring us straight back to 'doing'. They struck a particular chord with a participant on The Mind Gym's Me, me, me workout, who, on seeing the cycle, realised that she had never really left 'doing': or at least had reflected only ever on the mundane issues of daily living rather than the big questions about her life.

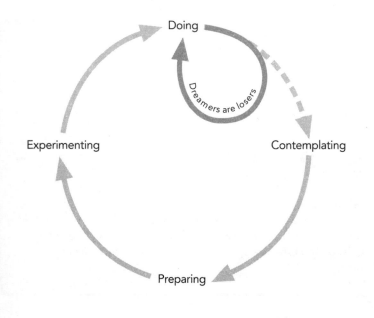

'I am always worrying about the next project,' she explained, 'about what I should be doing to get ahead at work, about the state of the house, about what my mother will complain about when she next visits and how to pre-empt her. I don't think I have ever asked myself how my life could be different or better, only how to make sure it keeps going as it is. That's not to say that I'm unhappy, only that I've never really thought about what I could do that would make me happier.'

This woman, in her early forties, married, financially secure and in a successful career, has a strong internal conversation that dismisses reflecting about how her life could be very different and keeps her in a constant state of 'doing'. When significant changes do occur, they are likely to be led by outside events to which she responds. And even then, her efforts will be geared towards getting back to 'normal life' as quickly as possible.

A couple of years earlier, for example, she had been made redundant. Instead of wondering what opportunities this opened up or how to use the extra money from the redundancy to pursue a new career or learn new skills, she immediately rushed into looking for jobs which were almost identical to the one she had just left. It wasn't that she loved the job and didn't want to do anything else, she explained, only that it seemed the most obvious route to follow.

Conversation Two: Get real

- It would never work in practice

- Nice idea but better get on with the day job

- Someone else will have got there already

- There's no way that I could do that

- It's too much of a risk

Even once we get past the 'Dreamers are losers' conversation, and reach the contemplation stage, the 'doing' magnet is still very much there and just as powerful. At this stage, however, it works in a different way. Here we put up a string of practical objections to explain to ourselves why the dream, whilst very nice as a dream, wouldn't work in reality. 'A shame, but it's just not practical,' we decide, and then get back to doing.

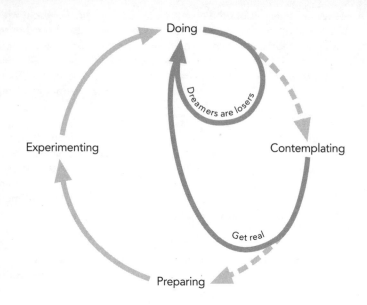

Doing

Dreamers are losers

Experimenting

Contemplating

Get real

Preparing

The Rubicon

In the film *Ghostbusters*, the biggest weapon in the ghost-busting armoury (Bill Murray's wisecracks aside) is the proton gun. But these poltergeist pistols come with a warning: you must never 'cross the streams'. Once that happens, there is no telling what might result. In the end, though, crossing the streams is the only way that the Ghostbusters can save New York.

Just over two thousand years ago, another stream was crossed with similarly dramatic results. The Rubicon is a stream that marked the boundary of Ancient Rome. Any army that crossed it was declaring war against the state. So when Julius Caesar, who was at that stage still a General, crossed the Rubicon in 49BC, he automatically declared war on the Roman Senate after which there could be only one of two outcomes: he would conquer or he and his armies would be destroyed. This is the origin of the phrase 'to cross the Rubicon', meaning to take an irrevocable step.

In the existential cycle, the irrevocable step occurs when we move from preparing to experimenting. This is the stage when we turn ideas into action, when we hand in our letter of resignation, tell our husband that we want a divorce, throw out all our old clothes, sign up for the Foreign Legion, stop using contraceptives. It is the most difficult stage in the cycle and the one where the 'magnet' back to 'doing' is the strongest. This is why it is often referred to as 'crossing the Rubicon'.

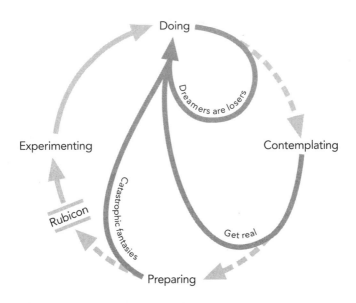

Conversation Three: Catastrophic fantasies

The most common reason why we don't cross the Rubicon is that we create what are called catastrophic fantasies. A catastrophic fantasy is a bleak prediction of what would happen if we did experiment with something new, ie, if we did cross our own Rubicon.

An advertising campaign for the American soft drink Dr Pepper was built on just this point. Although popular in the US, the drink is less well known in the UK – it's not a cola, it's not a fizzy fruit drink, what is it? – and so the advertisers played on tempting consumers to cross the 'soft drink rubicon' and try something new. The strapline for the advert was: What's the worst that could happen?

In the advert, the worst thing that could happen – the catastrophic fantasy – does happen. Arriving at his girlfriend's house to take her to the prom, the boyfriend is offered a Dr Pepper by her father. The boyfriend (like the consumer) is unsure about drinking Dr Pepper but agrees to try it, whereupon the father challenges him to wrestle for it. The resulting play-fight ends up with the sitting room being trashed and the father lying unconscious on the floor, just as the girlfriend walks down the stairs . . .

This catastrophic fantasy is, technically, possible. But is it a realistic worst-case scenario? In the real world, of course not. The realistic worst-case scenario is the boyfriend tries the Dr Pepper and doesn't like it. At least then he'll know he doesn't like it, and won't spend his life wondering what he'd missed. The much more likely scenario is that the boyfriend tries Dr Pepper, finds it a bit different, and isn't sure about it. He may not like it instantly, but after a few more bottles might come round to it, and possibly end up discovering a new favourite drink.

We all create catastrophic fantasies, particularly when contemplating big decisions, and quite often they scare us into sticking with the status quo. Most men who have proposed marriage have, before they did so, created catastrophic fantasies about married life. These may include a nagging wife, gorgeous women desperate for their attention whom they will have to resist (so what if this has never happened so far?), never being able to go out with their mates, the end of bachelor freedom, and so on.

The men who do propose recognise the catastrophic fantasy as nonsense and appreciate that the likely outcome is very different. The men who didn't spot that they were creating a catastrophic fantasy may have missed out on the opportunity of a lifetime.

There is, of course, a third category: those who made a realistic assessment and decided that they did not want to commit to one person for the rest of their life, or that the particular person they would be committing to was the wrong person. And there is nothing wrong with that.

Putting the brakes on: Rational fears
Crossing the Rubicon is not always a good thing. In reality, some of our fears and worries may be accurate.

I dream about being able to swim across the English Channel. However, I also believe that I am not nearly fit enough: I might set out from Dover and end up too tired to make it to France. Rather than risk drowning, I therefore decide not to swim the Channel.

The challenge we all have when venturing round the existential cycle is knowing whether our decision not to experiment with the new but to go back to 'doing' is realistic and sensible or ill-founded, damaging and based largely on irrational fears. While there is no definitive way of knowing for sure, there are some tell-tale signs to help gauge whether the decision not to cross this particular Rubicon is based on rational concerns or irrational fears.

Five signs that you are probably right not to cross the Rubicon
- You can see the arguments for both sides and have decided that, on balance, your decision makes most sense. If pressed, however, you could make the case for the opposite view.

- You are confident that you won't regret it later. You have thought about what the realistic best outcome is and either it isn't good enough or it isn't likely enough.

- You have thought through what the worst-case scenario is (as opposed to the catastrophic fantasy) and it is something you want to avoid at all costs (to cross the Rubicon you really need to have decided that the worst-case scenario is worth the risk).

- You can imagine advising someone else in your situation to do the same (ie, not to cross).

- You are relieved to have reached a conclusion and also pleased about the journey that you have taken to get there.

Five signs that say don't leave the banks of your Rubicon yet
- The worst outcome that you are imagining is extreme, verging on the absurd (not just failing to cross the Channel but being eaten by sharks).

- You feel nervous and unsure about your decision; you keep putting it off but aren't doing anything constructive to help make the best choice.

- You can imagine circumstances where, looking back, you would regret your decision.

- The decision to keep things roughly as they are doesn't fit with how you see yourself. Maybe it seems cautious whereas you see yourself as courageous, or it feels contradictory to some of the values that you hold most dear.

- Everyone else may disagree but you are still excited by the prospect of the change.

Putting the brakes on: Irrational exuberance
Irrational exuberants are those people who are forever saying things like, 'I wish I hadn't rushed into that' or, 'If only I'd thought about it first'. Rather than never crossing the Rubicon, they're happy to head over far too easily – without considering the size of the army on the other side first. In terms of the existential cycle, their 'doing' magnet is relatively weak – the centrifugal momentum of the 'next new thing' is stronger than the gravitational force of the status quo.

If you find that you can't keep down a job or a relationship, you never make any savings or haven't got round to turning your home into a place you like living in, AND you regret it, then you may well be suffering from a form of irrational exuberance. The best advice in this situation is this: spend longer at the preparing stage before wading across your Rubicon. For example, you may choose to

- think through all the possible disadvantages of taking this course of action as well as the advantages – really make an effort to present the case for caution on this occasion

- contrast the elixir of the new with how your existing life might improve even if you don't make this big change. People who are always moving on to new jobs often fail to consider how their current job could get better. The new job may well be attractive, but it is wrong to assume the old one will stay the same: new possibilities may open up (what might happen when your boss retires?) and these need to be considered too

- contemplate the bigger and better gains and pleasures that you could have if you didn't always go for some instant gratification

- consider how the decisions that you made in the past have led to situations that you later regretted; what can you learn from these that would help you make a wiser decision this time?

Heart or head?

One acquaintance of The Mind Gym's recalled trying to decide whether to continue a relationship with her boyfriend.

She divided a page into two columns and listed on the left reasons to leave him and on the right reasons for staying with him. She filled the left column with a long list of reasons ('he won't commit', 'he's always late', 'he never tells me he loves me', 'he forgot our anniversary') and had to go on to another page. On the right column she wrote only one thing: 'I love him'. She is still happily with him several years later.

In this case the heart prevented her from crossing a Rubicon and a good thing too. Just as often, it is our emotions that persuade us to make the leap. When it comes to life-altering decisions, a balance of both heart and head is usually the winning combination.

The road to Rome

We all have a choice in how we run our lives. There is no 'can't', only 'will' and 'won't'. The trick for all of us is knowing why we are or aren't moving round the cycle and, in particular, crossing the Rubicon. There may be very good reasons for not experimenting in which case it is excellent that we had the idea and even better that we decided not to go ahead with it. Often, however, our reasons are not so strong. We are worried about outcomes that have virtually no chance of becoming reality or are frightened because we can't see a guaranteed course to a future paradise. Better the devil you know.

These are poor reasons. The decision not to cross the Rubicon for the wrong reasons is why people look back on their lives and think, 'if only . . .' All of us who look back and are proud of what we have done have crossed the Rubicon at least once and maybe many times.

There's a famous Latin motto, carpe diem, which translated means 'seize the day'. The question you have to ask yourself is, when it comes to crossing Rubicons, just how much of a 'Caesar' are you prepared to be?

Give your mind a workout

I SPY If you enjoy reading profiles or biographies of famous people or, for example, listening to 'Desert Island Discs', look/listen out for the Rubicon(s) that these people have crossed.

Next time you read a novel, pause at certain stages and imagine where the main characters are in the existential cycle. Often the protagonist (the central character) will go the whole way round the cycle during the course of the story, often agonising about whether to cross a Rubicon before finally doing so and becoming a different person as a result. Lady Chatterley (arguably twice), Oliver Twist (many times) and Gatsby (just once, but it was a big one) are a few examples from the classics.

I TRY Think about one of the main areas of your life, say your career or your home. Which stage of the existential cycle are you at most of the time? Is this a good place to be or are you preventing yourself from moving round the cycle? Is there a danger that you may be saying 'if only . . .' in a few years' time? If so, how can you change your internal conversations to help unblock?

Next time a friend tells you about a particular crossroads in their life and asks for your advice on whether to make a big change (or you have a dilemma of your own), see if you can help them solve the challenge simply by asking questions.

First, ask what the options are and why it is such a difficult decision.

Next, try to find out whether they have a catastrophic fantasy by asking, for example:

- What is the worst outcome you can imagine?

- What would be the consequences if this outcome actually happened?

- What is the likelihood of this happening?

- What do you think is the more likely outcome?

- (If they are very unclear) What information do you need to have a better idea of the likely outcome?

- How could you get that information?

Also, ask about what would happen if they decided not to make a significant change but follow the route that is closer to the status quo.

- How are things likely to change in any case?

- What do you think the likely outcome would be if you took the option closer to the status quo?

If your friend is still undecided then try some of the following questions.

- What does your gut instinct tell you?

- What puts you off following your instinct? How valid are these reasons?

- For each option, how might you feel if you followed it a year from now?

- What decision do you think you will feel most proud of a year from now?

You don't have to stick rigidly to these questions and it is probably wise to probe further in some areas depending on the answers. Discovering where someone is in the existential cycle can be challenging, but it is also the basis from which to decide whether to start a new chapter.

D In charge

I am going to give a party for my birthday. I plan to invite a hundred or so friends to my house for a night of celebration, dancing and Twister. Actually, the Twister's optional (and my version is slightly different from the one you probably know), but the celebration isn't.

I am worried, however, whether it will be a success. Will this be remembered as the party of the year or will my friends leave after an hour wishing they had stayed in and washed their hair?

After all, there are a lot of things that could go wrong and it seems that I can't do anything about them. It could pour with rain in which case some people won't want to make the journey. The fancy dress shop might have a run on wigs. Chris might be rude to Nick, after all he is still upset about Susan: maybe they'll end up having a fight. Or maybe it won't even be memorable for all the wrong reasons: maybe it'll just fall flat and no one will talk to anyone they don't already know.

St Francis of Assisi's guide to party planning

The thoughts and preaching of St Francis of Assisi may not be the most obvious place to start when organising a birthday spectacular, but a truism he described in a prayer eight hundred years ago still has much resonance today:

> God grant me the Serenity to accept the things I cannot
>   change;
> Courage to change the things I can;
>   and Wisdom to know the difference.

The best part of a millennium further on, absolute insight may still be beyond the reach of humankind but the ability to differentiate between what is in our control and what is not is very firmly within our grasp.

Let's return, then, to my concerns over why my party might be a disaster, and see what possible solutions we can think up to overcome them – the 'courage', as St Francis put it, to change the things we can.

My challenge: a birthday party

Worry	What I can do
Bad weather so fewer people come	Negotiate a bulk discount from a mini-cab firm and enclose the details with the invitation to make the journey easier
	Organise great music/a DJ so that the party is more appealing
	Call my friends who are most likely to drop out to say how excited I am that they are coming – it will be harder not to show up once they have told me they are definitely going to be there
Fancy dress shop running out of wigs	Give the shop plenty of advance warning so they have time to order some more in
	Widen the party theme from Motown to music giants or cultural icons
Chris and Nick end up arguing	Talk with Chris and Nick in advance and ask if they can keep calm given that the other one will be there, maybe emphasising how much it will mean to me to have them both at the party to celebrate my birthday
	Talk to a friend of Chris's to get advice on what to do
People don't mix	Plan who to introduce to whom because I think they will get on and also, perhaps, what to say to help them make the link
	Ask my best-networked friends to help by introducing people
	Bring in help to serve food and drink so I can give all my attention to mixing people, not cocktails

Are you a spanner or a planner?

Some of the ideas for what can be done to tackle the party problems may be impractical or inappropriate. Then again, there may be many more things that one could do to reduce the chances of these problems actually happening than are on this list. Even so, a sceptic might say that there is no guarantee that these solutions, or any others, will solve the problems. They are absolutely right. There is no guarantee.

What is 100% certain is that I have a choice whether to focus on the list on the left or the list on the right.

The person who focuses on the list on the left we'll call the 'spanner', because they are continually throwing one into the works. They worry about all the things that might go wrong which they feel they can't do anything about, and are likely to

- be reactive, responding to what happens, often feeling like a victim, buffeted by events rather than leading them

- spend a lot of time worrying in ways that will drain their energy but won't improve the situation

- blame and accuse other people for the problems and challenges in their life

- put off doing things for as long as possible, in the end often doing much more to achieve the same or a poorer result

- fail to take action that would be likely to improve their circumstances

The person who creates and then focuses on the right-hand list we'll call the 'planner', because they are coming up with a plan of action to tackle these problems. Their focus is on all the things that they can do that might have a positive influence on the situation, and they are likely to have the opposite experience to the spanner. For example they are more likely to

- take action proactively, doing things that will help

- feel more in control of the situation (and their life)

- find they have more free time to do what they want

- be seen as leaders and/or people who are strong

Planners work out what they can do about the situation and concentrate on doing it. As a result they are more in control of their lives and get more done. They also give better parties.

To know the difference

If you wanted a friend to read this book you could recommend it. You could offer them a reward if they read it, you could tell them why you think it is worth their while, you could even buy them a copy – all these things are in your control. But whether they read it or not and whether they like it or not is out of your control.

Sometimes the difference between what is in our control and what is not is obvious. But often it's not so clear, and it is this ability to distinguish between the two that makes the difference between those of us who can banish the worry demons and those who can't.

Danny is concerned about selling his house. The market is soft, the agent doesn't seem very efficient, the last people who made an offer pulled out and he won't be able to afford the mortgage when the discount stops at the end of next month. He is losing sleep and it is affecting his work. 'Please will someone fall in love with my house and make an offer today,' he says to himself as he waits for the bus.

The chances are they won't. Danny is focusing on what is out of his control: the market, the agent's efficiency, the reaction of the last people who made an offer, the end of the discount on his mortgage. As a result, he is likely to feel powerless and is using up lots of

Is this you?

energy without achieving very much. Danny is in 'victim' mode, at best reacting to events and at worst waiting passively for them to show him his destiny, which is unlikely to be a particularly rosy one. This is not a good place to be.

The solution for Danny, or at least the beginning of the solution, is to switch from 'spanner' to 'planner' and think about what he could do.

The science behind being in charge

The idea of having a 'locus' of control was put forward by Julian Rotter in 1966. He suggested that externally orientated individuals (the spanners) typically believe that rewards in life are controlled by forces such as fate, luck or other people. People with an internal locus of control (the planners) tend to see events being triggered by their own behaviour or capability.

Crandall and Crandall's research in 1983 suggested many benefits for people with an internal locus of control (planners), including

- Better thinking skills

- Better memory to pick up new insights

- More likely to choose challenging tasks

- More willing to delay gratification and keep going when things get tough

- More likely to deal with and recover from illness

- Better personal relationships and more emotionally well adjusted (greater self-esteem and less anxiety)

- Greater satisfaction with life and overall contentment

So what causes us to have an internal or an external locus of control?

The general view from the scientists is that people with parents who were controlling or authoritarian are more likely to develop an externalised locus of control. Similarly, stressful life events, eg, the death of a parent or sibling, particularly when young, tend to have the same effect.

By contrast, those of us whose parents encouraged us to do things where we could see the direct result of our efforts (eg, learning to play a musical instrument) are more likely to have an internalised locus (planner). Kindness also made a difference: children with an internal locus also seemed to have parents who showed affection and love.

My challenge: selling my house

Worry	What I can do
The market is softening	Find out if similar properties really are being sold for less and what the market rate is for a house like mine
	Reduce the asking price
The agent's efficiency	Give the agent a time limit before giving it to another agent
	Talk with the agent about why he is finding it difficult to sell and what I can do to make it easier
The reaction of the last people	Ask the agent why the last people decided not to buy the house; maybe get my own survey done to show to potential buyers up front
	Make some cosmetic improvements such as repainting the hall
The mortgage discount is running out	Talk to the bank and explain the situation. They may well be able to organise a loan at a discounted rate
	See if there is another bank that will take on the loan at the same terms (and if there is a penalty clause for leaving my existing bank)

If Danny focuses his attention on the right-hand list two things will start to happen:

- Danny will feel better about the situation as, rather than feeling impotent, he will feel that he can make a difference.

- Danny's energy will be used thinking about and doing things that could help.

This positive and constructive mindset is a good thing in itself. It is, however, likely to lead to a third benefit. As Danny starts to take action, new opportunities will emerge that he hasn't even thought of. Perhaps by talking with the estate agent he discovers that he could make better use of the internet or clear out the spare room so that it looks larger.

Proactive people will always focus on the right-hand column. As a direct result, they will achieve more and feel more in control.

Spot the difference

One way to spot how reactive/proactive you are about a situation is to notice the way you are thinking about it.

Imagine if you are frustrated because your boss keeps changing her mind and makes unreasonable demands on you. Here are some different ways of looking at this problem split between what you might be thinking if you were focusing on being in control and what you would be thinking if you were, in effect, out of control.

Out of control (spanner)	In control (planner)
She's an unreasonable person who doesn't appreciate the pressure I'm under	I can set up an early morning meeting to agree priorities for the day
She's got problems in her personal life and is taking them out on me	I can take her out for coffee and ask if there's anything I can do to help
Her boss is being unreasonable (too)	I can ask colleagues if they have the same problem and how they deal with it
I am finding it really difficult to work in this environment	I can pick some situations where I say that I cannot do the extra work and so set a precedent

Of course, it's easier to be in the 'out of control' column. In the short term, it may even be necessary, for example, grieving after the death of someone close. However, if you stay there the situation is probably going to get worse. Choose the 'in control' column and you are much more likely to improve the situation.

Going for a run three times a week may be hard work to start with but it will make us fitter than slouching in front of the TV. In the same way, focusing our energy on what is in our control will make us more proactive, less stressed and far more likely to achieve our goals.

Make me a planner, now

Take a blank sheet of paper. Put at the top the issue that is on your mind that you want to address. You would be wise to choose something that matters to you and that you can do something about. Winning the World

A partial cure

A lady at a workout had a son-in-law who was very ill with a fatal lung disease. She was very upset and spent most of her time feeling helpless, worrying about what would happen and how her daughter would cope.

She had a go at this exercise, noting down what was out of her control and what was in her control. She realised that there were in fact lots of things she could do to make the situation better. She could regularly visit her daughter and look after their children so her daughter could spend more time at the hospital; she could cook her daughter's family meals to help free up her daughter's time; she could help with legal issues and interpret many of the complex forms as she was a compensation and benefits expert.

Helping out in these ways made this lady feel much better and helped her daughter too, not just in a host of practical ways but also by having a mum who was focused rather than fretting.

Cup may be on your mind but isn't a great example for this exercise as there probably isn't that much you can do about it. Equally, whether you'll get round to reading the newspaper tomorrow may be a little trivial (unless you are its editor).

Once you have written the issue at the top draw a vertical line down the middle of the page. On the left side, write down all the aspects of this issue that are bothering you that you cannot control, and on the right all the things that you could do that might have an impact.

Often when people complete this exercise they are surprised by how much they can put in the right-hand column. A long list here gives us the confidence to take control of the situation and make useful things happen.

There's nothing I can do

Are there times when there is nothing I can do? Not many. There are times, it's true, when there is very little that we can do. If the problem that is concerning us is the damage being done to the environment, we can

- vote for the the political groups that promise to do most to support your cause

- buy products that are more environmentally friendly

- recycle our waste

- write to newspapers and companies presenting the arguments

- invest exclusively in environmentally friendly funds

- take part in peaceful protests

These actions aren't going to lead to an immediate or enormous difference to the hole in the ozone layer or instantly replant the Amazonian rain forests, but they are more likely to help than doing nothing at all.

Party time

In the end, it is my party. I could cry if I wanted to. But instead, there's lots I'm going to do to make it rock.

Give your mind a workout

I SPY Next time you sit down for a chat with a friend, listen out for where their locus of control tends to be (internal/external). As you start to talk about what is going on in your life, see if you can spot where your locus is.

I TRY Take a new challenge and work through what you can do (and what is beyond your control). Look at p. 69 or 73 for some ideas on what sort of things to put in each column.

(E) Jump start

Lord, make me good; but not yet

Putting things off is one of life's guilty secrets: everyone says that they don't do it, but everybody knows they do. Whether in work or in relationships, achieving good health or breaking bad habits, we all have the capacity to turn into an ostrich, put our head in the sand and hope it will all go away (whatever it is).

Sometimes it is the small things, such as leaving that pile of washing up until later on. And at other times it is bigger issues, maybe ending a relationship or asking for a promotion. When we want to put off doing something, we are usually pretty good at coming up with a fine list of excuses: the student who wants to give up drinking coffee but 'can't' until his exams are over; the single man who won't ask someone out because he doesn't feel strong enough to cope with the possible rejection; the office worker who knows they should write that report but is too stressed to even start; the Scorpio who won't send off that form because their horoscope warned about an unpredictable reception.

But while we all procrastinate from time to time, it's all too easy for an occasional lapse to turn into a pernicious vice. It's as if life is a credit card: just as we can treat ourselves to some new clothes and decide 'I'll worry about the cost next month', so we can go to the cinema thinking 'I've lots of time, the closing date isn't until Friday'. The problem is that at some stage we still have to 'pay' for 'spending' the evening in the cinema – and with the added 'interest' of the stress of doing the application at the last minute.

Just like credit card bills, it's all too easy to build up debts in the 'life bank', putting off one little thing after another. And paying back these time debts can be long and painful.

The good news is that procrastination, rather than being a characteristic that some of us are born with, is actually more of a bad habit that we pick up over the years. And just as we learn how to put things off so we can 'unlearn'. As a result, we will not only feel less stressed and more in control but also we have a lot more time to spare.

Everything you wanted to know about procrastination but never quite got round to finding out about

The secret to overcoming procrastination is to find out how, in any given situation, we are procrastinating. It is then a short step to working out what we can do to put it right.

Scientific and psychological research have shown that there are five main reasons why people put off doing things. Read on to discover what they are, how to spot them and ways to brush them aside.

Can procrastination be good for you?

'Rational procrastination' is good for us. It occurs when there is no time pressure, you are likely to discover more information, the situation itself may improve, or you feel that mulling over a challenge might help you solve it. Calvin Coolidge (a former president of the US) called it 'calculated inactivity'.

What's your excuse?

Think about something you're putting off. What is it? Look at the fifteen statements which follow, and circle the relevant number depending on how true you think each statement is for the situation you've chosen.

1	This doesn't concern me much	1 2 3 4 5
2	I'm not going to enjoy doing this	1 2 3 4 5
3	I really won't be able to do this properly	1 2 3 4 5
4	I'm too stressed/tired/excited to do this now	1 2 3 4 5
5	I'm very busy, so I must be making some progress	1 2 3 4 5
6	It's not very difficult, I can do it any time	1 2 3 4 5
7	I'm not in the right frame of mind	1 2 3 4 5
8	I'm very busy, so the results should follow soon	1 2 3 4 5
9	It won't take very long, I'll start another time	1 2 3 4 5
10	I've failed at this before, I'm bound to fail again	1 2 3 4 5
11	This is going to take a really long time	1 2 3 4 5
12	I'm not in the mood to do this now	1 2 3 4 5
13	It's a big step, I'm scared I may not be able to cope	1 2 3 4 5
14	It's really unpleasant, I'll start another time	1 2 3 4 5
15	I know what I have to do, so I'm halfway there already	1 2 3 4 5

We'll come back to what the answers suggest later in this chapter.

The five habits of procrastination

1 Complacency
It's not very difficult, I can do it any time
It won't take very long, I'll start another time
I know what I have to do, so I'm halfway there already

The first form of procrastination comes from an over-strong sense of self-confidence, that one is on top of the situation and needn't bother dealing with it now. It can also come across as laziness or a general lack of concern – that so certain is the outcome, there is no reason to try or make a special effort.

But rather than coasting to success, quite often this form of procrastination leads to the opposite result. In the fable of the tortoise and the hare, the hare is so sure of victory over the tortoise that he settles down for a quick sleep, only for the tortoise to overtake and defeat him. Similarly, in almost every James Bond film, there is a scene where the arch-villain has the spy in his grasp, only to let him escape and thwart his plans for world domination. In these situations, evil cunning and over-confidence always seem to go hand in hand.

Dealing with complacency

One way of dealing with this form of putting things off is to imagine a great opportunity later on, but one that we can only take advantage of if we've completed the task at hand. So, for example, if our passport needs renewing but we leave it until the day before we go on holiday because it's so easy, we need to imagine a friend ringing up with a spare free ticket for a weekend abroad: if we haven't got an up-to-date passport, we can't go.

Bob had decided to fix the tap tomorrow

Alternatively, we can set ourselves more challenging goals. If a situation isn't motivating us to finish it, let's change the situation. With the story of the hare and the tortoise, it clearly isn't enough incentive for the hare to just beat the tortoise: he feels (wrongly as it turns out) that he can do that in his sleep. But if the hare had set himself the challenge of not just beating the tortoise but also breaking the course record, he would have carried on sprinting until the finish line and would never have lost the race.

Finally, if the task is relatively easy, just get it done. If you're an arch-villain in a James Bond film, just pull the trigger and carry on with taking over the world: don't pause to gloat and show 007 the evil genius of your plans; before you know it, he'll be raising an eyebrow, delivering a sharp one-liner and you'll be plunging to earth without a parachute. If you're not an arch-villain in a James Bond film you won't be rewarded with a new world order but your own world will be a little more ordered, and that's a start.

2 Avoiding discomfort

I'm not going to enjoy doing this
This is going to take a really long time
It's really unpleasant, I'll start another time

This sort of procrastination is all to do with the unpleasantness of the activity, particularly compared with a far more enjoyable alternative. When there are dishes to be washed, that television programme about gardening can suddenly become *really* interesting. Perhaps the visit to the dentist can wait until next month, that telephone bill can be left until after payday, the tax return can be done tomorrow.

There are more serious examples, too. We might be unhappy in a long-term relationship but can't face the unpleasantness of ending it.

In each case, our worries about the 'pain' of taking action are enough to make us delay.

Dealing with avoiding discomfort
When the discomfort comes from the size of the task (the tax return?), we can break it down into bite-size tasks instead (get the bank statements, read the form, fill in Section A and so on). Doing one of these smaller activities feels easier, and once we get on a roll the whole project may be completed before we know it.

A second idea comes from the Mary Poppins school of philosophy: the spoonful of sugar to help the medicine go down. Many of us don't enjoy doing the washing up but that doesn't mean we can't make it less of a chore: we could allow ourselves a cup of coffee or a glass of wine while we scrub away (but only if we do it now); we could burn ourselves a compilation CD of our favourite tunes — Music to Wash Dishes By, Volume One.

Finally, here's a challenge: every day do one frustrating activity that you would normally put off until tomorrow. Not only will you be amazed by how much more you get done, but soon you'll run out of really frustrating things to do.

3 Fear of failure
I really won't be able to do this properly
I've failed at this before, I'm bound to fail again
It's a big step, I'm scared I may not be able to cope

Sometimes the prospect of not succeeding is enough to put us off starting. Imagine there's someone you find attractive and want to ask out, but don't because you're afraid they'll say 'No'. Or perhaps there's the possibility of a promotion at work but you don't put yourself forward because you're worried you might not get the job.

Trying to get into a fashionable club, making sales calls, taking up salsa classes — there are hundreds of things we may give all sorts of reasons for putting off but the real reason is fear of failure.

Some of us even use this form of procrastination as a sort of get-out or escape clause. By not doing the work, not trying, not making an effort, we have an excuse for when things go wrong: *It's not that I'm not good at French, it's just I didn't bother with the revision.* As a result, we may dull the pain of failure but we will never taste the satisfaction of succeeding against the odds.

Dealing with fear of failure
The problem here is nothing to do with failure: it's all to do with fear. Mistakes are often the primary source of learning. As Simon Woodroffe, founder of Yo Sushi!, explains, 'I looked at what every entrepreneur has in common and I found one thing: they all make mistakes, lots of them.' Successful people fail a lot, they just aren't afraid of it.

Think, for example, about relationships. Which is worse: never going out with anyone, or being rejected sometimes? You only need one person to say 'yes'. Put the 'no's down to experience and learn from them: *Is it my deodorant? Or am I playing it too keen from the start?* Likewise with jobs: it doesn't matter if we get turned down so long as we learn from the experience; we'll keep improving and sooner or later someone's going to say 'yes'. But no one's going to say 'yes' if we never apply in the first place.

Self-fulfilling beliefs

The psychologist Albert Bandura argued that one of the reasons why effective and decisive people are effective and decisive is because they *believe* they are effective and decisive. Similarly, if people think they are ineffective and indecisive, then pretty soon that's what turns out to be the case. Think proactive, and you're halfway to making it happen.

---

4 Emotional barriers
I'm too stressed/tired/excited to do this now
I'm not in the right frame of mind
I'm not in the mood to do this at the moment

Sometimes we use emotion as a reason to stop ourselves from taking action. We convince ourselves that, for whatever reason, the time isn't right to do something now and we are better off waiting for that 'perfect moment'.

Imagine suffering a nightmare journey into the office: the bus doesn't arrive, there's no seat on the train and you arrive late and flustered. Rather than answering the urgent email in your inbox, you decide you need a coffee, two biscuits and a chat to your friend before you can get in the right mood to start work. Or maybe you've already had two bits of bad luck so you'd rather not make any big decisions until the third one is out of the way. Or maybe you want to save some money by cutting down on going out for a few weeks, but there are so many birthdays coming up you decide to leave it for another month.

Dealing with emotional barriers

The problem with waiting for this perfect moment is that it never arrives: there'll always be another good reason to put things off and you'll still be waiting as the opportunity passes.

To use the example of cutting back on going out, people are always having birthdays or holding parties, or leaving or starting jobs and so on. If you wait a month, the chances are you'll wait another month, and then another.

One way of overcoming these barriers is to imagine the outcome of not doing something immediately. You might be the sort of person who thinks, 'I'm too stressed to start this project now,' but think how much *more* stressed you'll feel if you leave the project until the last minute.

Also, by taking action the emotional barrier disappears by itself. When we arrive late and flustered for work we are more likely to change our mood for the better by getting on with and completing a task than by reliving our terrible journey over a coffee.

5 Action illusion

I'm very busy, so I must be making some progress
No one appreciates quite how much I've got on
There's so much to do, I mustn't stop

Action illusionists, as the name suggests, are the magicians of the procrastinating world. But rather than wave a wand and make people or rabbits or the Statue of Liberty vanish, they use all their sleight of hand to make time disappear. They're the sort of person who, rather than revising for exams at school, would spend endless hours writing and rewriting their revision timetable, and then say 'I

The revision timetable was beautiful

don't know where the day's gone'. The sort of person who'll just pop on the internet to do some research . . . and will still be there an hour later. When challenged, they'll always repeat their mantra – 'I have done so much, honest!' Which, of course, is the biggest illusion of all.

Dealing with action illusion
The curious thing about suffering from action illusion is that we quite often spend more energy *not* doing work than it would take to actually get the thing done. Revision timetables, rather than a practical working guide, easily become a work of art. If only we had that much attention to detail in what we were *meant* to be doing.

If you're an action illusionist, the key to breaking the cycle is to understand that you are not doing what needs to be done.

You may technically be working: you keep checking your inbox; you have another look at the monthly data; you check the provisions in the store cupboard, even though you checked them yesterday. You are busy doing work-type tasks, only they're not the tasks that really need to be done.

Decide what the successful outcome is. Decide what you could do which would do the most to help you achieve this. Do it, and not lots of other stuff that is peripheral to your objective.

Look back at the questionnaire on page 79 and add up your scores for the statements as follows

$(1) + (6) + (9) = \bigcirc$ (Complacency)

$(2) + (11) + (14) = \bigcirc$ (Avoiding discomfort)

$(3) + (10) + (13) = \bigcirc$ (Fear of failure)

$(4) + (7) + (12) = \bigcirc$ (Emotional barriers)

$(5) + (8) + (15) = \bigcirc$ (Action illusion)

For each answer, you should have a number between 3 and 15. The nearer your total is to 15, the more you are leaning towards this form of procrastination. If any total is below 8, then you probably don't need to worry about this type for this situation. But if your score is 12 or more, reconsider the relevant section below. And whatever you do, don't put it off until later.

General tactics

These, then, are the specifics of putting things off, the nuts and bolts of life's nots and buts. It may be that you find you fall into one category for one part of your life, and another in another. Or maybe you are inclined towards a mixture of two or more types. Which is why, as well as understanding why and how it is we procrastinate, it is useful to have some general tactics to fall back on. Below are five catch-all schemes to tackle the five primary types of procrastination (and many minor ones as well). Some will work better for some people than others so it is worth experimenting to find the right one for you.

Strive for five – the five-minute start

Five minutes is nothing: the length of a song, the time it takes to boil an egg, an advert break on TV. So try picking up a project you've been putting off for a while and give it just three hundred seconds of your time. Once the five minutes is up, stop and reassess. Do you want to give it another five minutes? If so, carry on for another five. Stop, and assess again. Maybe continue for another five minutes. Have another assessment. And so on. After a while, the momentum of beginning the task will carry you forward, and you'll forget about all those five-minute chunks.

Back of the net – goals and rewards

Set yourself goals and rewards during the day. Each time you hit a goal, reward yourself, be it with a short break, a leisure surf on the web, checking your personal emails or some other treat. It's important that the goals are realistic (and the rewards are in proportion) – and make sure you select a time to review your progress and adjust your targets accordingly. (Note to action illusionists: put those coloured pens away now.)

Be good to yourself – me today versus me tomorrow

Sometimes, when we find ourselves stuck with a lot of work, we feel cross with ourselves for not having started the work earlier. Try taking this one step further and imagine a conversation between 'you today' and 'you tomorrow'. If 'you tomorrow' (let's call him Saturday Tom) could chat with 'you today' (let's call him Friday Tom) what would he have to say about it? If Friday Tom is leaving all the work for Saturday Tom to do, then Saturday Tom is not going to be best pleased. So be nice to Saturday Tom: make sure that Friday Tom does his fair share too.

Flowers for Simon – unpleasant inaction

Another tactic is to make the thought of inaction so unbearable that we have no choice but to get on and do things. It could be something as simple as writing a cheque to someone or something we really dislike: to a rival team if we are a football fan, or to Battersea Dogs' Home if we are a cat lover. Give the cheque to a friend with strict instructions to send it should we not achieve our goal, be it finishing a project, giving up smoking or whatever. Or be creative with your punishments: you could send flowers to a celebrity you hate, or join the fan club of a pop group you think are awful. The more embarrassing and humiliating, the more incentive there is to get the task done.

I was there – witnessing

In the same way that weddings are public ceremonies, with friends and relatives there to celebrate, but also to reinforce the vows the bride and groom are making, so telling people we are going to do something can give that little extra reason to follow it through. Consider going on a diet: is there more pressure if we don't tell a soul, or if we announce it to all our friends, with strict instructions to refuse if we ask for a chip? It may seem an obvious way of making ourselves feel guilty, but it can also be highly effective.

I TRY If there is a situation that you are procrastinating over, write down the task that you need to get done. Then work through the following questions to see if you can come up with a solution.

_____

A Why is it important to get this done?

_____

B How does the thought of starting to work on this issue make me feel?

_____

C How does the thought of completing work on this issue make me feel?

_____

D Which procrastination attitudes are getting in the way? Why?

_____

E What tactics could I use to get over this?

_____

F When will I get it done by?

_____

G Who will be my witness and when will I review my progress?

The right impression

I'm honest; you're direct; she's rude. I'm creative; you're different; she's weird. I'm decisive; you're judgemental; she's bossy.

One set of behaviour; a whole range of interpretations; a huge potential for making the wrong impression.

So often in life it's not what you do, it's not even the way that you do it – it's the way that other people interpret it that matters. It can seem strange when other people aren't convinced by our compelling argument or won over by our charm and intellect, but there is usually a very rational explanation (and it's not that we have a weak argument, no charisma or are nice but dim).

The reason why we make the wrong impression is that we are used to looking at the situation exclusively through our eyes and not the other person's. Once we have discovered how to see things from someone else's perspective we are in a much stronger position to adapt our behaviour, and so improve our chances of being liked, loved, respected, admired, convincing and engaging.

This section is packed with myriad practical tips, tools and techniques that help us see things from the other person's perspective and adapt the way we behave to

- leave the impression that we want (Impact)

- win people over to our point of view (Influence)

- get on well with people we don't already know (Connect)

- gain the respect and ear of even our most self-confident friends and colleagues (Presence)

I'm great; you're amazing; she's awesome.

 Impact

Why gangsters love their mothers

'He's such a handsome boy, takes after his father. So big and strong, and a natural sportsman. He has to fight the girls off, you know.' A gushing mother's description of her son isn't exactly wrong. It's just a little bit different from how we see our best friend, whose only sporting skill is the speed with which he flicks channels when the football is on the TV.

Anaïs Nin once observed that 'things are not as they are but as we are'. When it comes to people this couldn't be much truer. The same person can seem totally different to different people. No fictional gangster is worth his weight in stolen gold without an adoring mother who thinks that butter wouldn't melt in his mouth.

This is partly because of the way we change our behaviour depending on whom we are with. We probably wouldn't swear or talk about sex in front of our parents any more than our gangster would threaten his mother with concrete shoes and a visit to the bottom of the ocean when the spaghetti is a little late on the table.

However, the different impressions that people have of us are about more than how we adapt our behaviour in different circumstances. It is about how they look at the world and, in particular, at us. Two people come out of a meeting we were in, one of them thinking 'what a relief to have someone who makes decisions on the team' and the other thinking, 'we're going to have to be careful with someone so impulsive on the team'. Our behaviour has been identical but their interpretations are poles apart.

The way someone interprets our behaviour probably tells us more about him or her than it does about us. This may not seem very helpful, but actually this insight is like gold dust (and not stolen either). When we understand how the people around us look at the world then we can adapt our behaviour to get the best from them and help them get the best from us.

In black and white

What do you see here? Some people say that it is a man playing a saxophone. Others are convinced that it's a woman's face. Still others aren't quite sure.

This is just a static black and white picture and already there are different interpretations. It is no surprise that with behaviour, which is infinitely more multi-coloured and complex, the range of interpretations is vast.

Check out your behaviour

When we go the supermarket we have our own individual ways of how we shop. For some people this is an activity that should be done as quickly as possible, selecting items that seem to be appropriate at the time. These people consider a successful shop to be one that has got broadly the right things and has taken as little time as possible.

Others see going to the supermarket as something that should be planned for, lists are made, aisles are visited in a specific order and plastic bags are packed in a way that makes unpacking easier. For them a successful shop is one where precisely the right items have been purchased even if it may have taken a little bit longer.

Another group see the supermarket as a treasure trove to be explored. They turn up without a list and meander up and down the aisles, checking out new products, choosing things on impulse. For them a successful shop is not so much whether they have got the right things but whether they have discovered something new.

If these people go shopping together it's more than likely that there will be cross words. Whilst the first person is halfway round the supermarket in any order, the second person may still be at home making a list, and the third chatting with the assistant offering samples of a new type of cheese.

We choose to do much the same things in very different ways depending on what we find most important. If we can begin to understand each other's motivations (the first person's motive is speed, the second person's is an ideal solution, the third's is discovery) we can begin to change our behaviour in order to have a more positive impact on each other.

Shaking hands or bowing?

Should we change our behaviour? Isn't that dishonest to ourselves? Shouldn't people like us for who we really are rather than a façade we create to please other people? The answer to this question is, of course, that we should be true to ourselves and that people should like us for who we really are, but that doesn't mean we have to exclude being flexible with our behaviour.

An example that is sometimes given is an American meeting a Japanese. Do they shake hands or do they bow to each other? The ideal is that they attempt both – it may be a little clumsy-looking but it gives the indication that both parties are willing to accommodate the other person's way of acting in the world. Managing our impact on others is the same – we are no less true to ourselves but are demonstrating a willingness to see things from other people's perspectives.

Understanding people: the *Sex and the City* way
The key is to understand what motivates people to behave in a certain way.

We may see someone driving extremely fast on the wrong side of the street. 'Maniac', we say to ourselves, only later to discover that his pregnant wife has started her contractions and he is rushing her to hospital. If we understood the motives of the car driver we'd be likely to have a very different impression of them.

Behaviour can easily change to adapt to a given situation but motivations are much more constant. We tend to have a view of what matters and, unless something major happens in our life, we stick to it. If we can understand what motivates people we can adapt our behaviour to fit with their personal priorities. But how do we find out what someone's motives are?

Although we may never come up with a definitive conclusion, a partial answer can be good enough. It is helpful to start with the four basic types of motivation, recognising that no one is simply one thing or another, but that if we are familiar with the main ingredients it's easier to spot the blends. And for those who want to do a little extra research, the good news is that it could be enjoyable; all you need to do is to put on a DVD of the hit comedy *Sex and the City*. The four friends at the heart of the show neatly represent the four different types of motivation.

Type 1: Charlotte, the carer

In *Sex and the City*, Charlotte is the character who is the kindest and the most caring, who likes nothing better than everyone getting on. If there is any conflict, her instinct is to help solve it.

A carer's foremost desire is for harmony with whatever group of people they are in, be it their family, their team at work or a group of friends. They see themselves as people people. They are naturally social, friendly, and they make a real effort to get to know someone. They are also often very effective networkers.

Strong relationships are of paramount importance to carers. As a result, they are keen to express how they feel (in the hope others will reciprocate); they are loyal; they may well give way in a disagreement for the sake of harmony; they like to involve other people in making decisions (and are keen to be involved themselves). They have a strong desire to nurture other people, looking after them in times of trouble and eager to explain or teach to help them flourish. They also want to be liked and appreciated themselves – a few words of praise go a long way.

- Stuck with a problem? Let's ask someone, is their natural response

- At their best: honest, sincere, supportive, friendly, sociable

- At their worst: simple-minded, naïve, smothering, demanding, snooping

- What they hate: deliberate unpleasantness; ignoring people's feelings; insensitivity; bullying; 'the ends justify the means'; rudeness; being ignored or left out; social isolation

- The perfect person if . . . you want something done sensitively.

Type 2: Samantha, the driver

In many ways, Samantha couldn't be more different from Charlotte. Adventurous and easily bored, she is constantly pushing on and through. If Charlotte's behaviour is all about wanting to be liked, then Samantha's is all about wanting to be respected.

Drivers are motivated by challenge, excitement and getting things done. They want to get to the point fast and, ideally, first. And then on to the next thing, and then the next. They like to have demanding goals with clear outcomes and, preferably, a competitive element.

If a situation doesn't have direction a driver can become frustrated but, given a suitable challenge and left to their own devices, they will make things happen and quickly. They consider it generally better to make a decision, even if it turns out to be the wrong one, than put things off. They are more likely to initiate something than complete it – they like to get the ball rolling but will avoid organising and implementing if they can.

- Stuck with a problem? I'll sort it out – in fact I'm almost there, is their natural response

- At their best: direct, competitive, excitable, fast, decisive, challenging

- At their worst: harsh, aggressive, superficial, inflexible, argumentative

- What they hate: being bored; delay; chat rather than action; analysis paralysis; committees (only slow things down); people (or anything else) who get in the way of making things happen

- The perfect person if . . . you want something done quickly.

Type 3: Miranda, the professional

Miranda is a lawyer by trade, and, like any good lawyer, believes that attention to detail is everything. Whereas drivers like Samantha are keen to move on to the next challenge, Miranda would rather finish the one she is doing properly.

Professionals are motivated by doing something very well – they want the best possible solution and, once they commit, they will be inclined to do whatever it takes to get it.

This may be through thinking differently about a problem or being very thorough in the way they do something, or both. The professional's mantra is the saying, if a job's worth doing, it's worth doing properly. The professional's desire for things to be 'right' means that they are often the first to spot gaps or errors and to challenge assumptions about the way things are done. They value being given the freedom and independence to think things through by themselves. Their desire for self-sufficiency, however, means they can also be hard to get to know.

- Stuck with a problem? Let me think about it, is their natural response.

- At their best: independent, original, rigorous, self-contained, thorough, accurate

- At their worst: aloof, nit-picky, cold, long-winded, fussy

- What they hate: slapdash behaviour; delivering something that isn't finished; being rushed into things; being told how to do something; being constantly disturbed; personal questions; big egos; group hugs

- The perfect person if . . . you want something done 'properly'.

Type 4: Carrie, the adapter

Carrie is the character at the heart of the group of friends. Without Carrie, Charlotte, Samantha and Miranda might seem a little disparate. With Carrie, who is in many ways a bit like all of them, it all makes sense.

Adapters are people who are a combination of each of the other three styles. They see the merits in focusing on people, on getting things done and on quality. They value flexibility and taking a balanced approach to any situation.

They can often take the role of peacekeeper in a disagreement as they quickly see and empathise with each of the different perspectives. Adapters like to adapt, experiment, be open to change, make sure bases are covered and options considered. They sometimes feel pulled in many directions by their different motivations.

- Stuck with a problem? I'll work out a way to find a solution, is their natural response

- At their best: flexible, adaptable, collaborative, mediator, jack of all trades

- At their worst: weak, political, all-pleasing, conviction-less, master of none

- What they hate: people who are stuck in their ways; obstinacy; extreme behaviours

- The perfect person if . . . you want to manage all possible eventualities.

What do we think of each other?

Having got a sense of the different kinds of motivation we might have, the next step is to get a sense of what each type might think of others. Here are some suggestions.

What a carer thinks of . . .
- A driver: a bit of an egotist – may mean well but can ride roughshod over other people. Would like to get to know them better but not sure I would like what I found. If they took a little more time to get to know people they would be a lot more effective.

- A professional: a bit of a cold fish. Very good at making sure we do things properly but can take it to extremes – when it's obvious everyone else is bored or wants to get on they just keep going.

- An adapter: open to new ideas. Appreciates that people matter. I rate their flexibility. Never quite sure where they stand.

What a driver thinks of . . .
- A carer: a bit soft. Easy to get round. Deals with the people stuff (which doesn't really interest me). Can be over-sensitive. Good person to go to when I need support and to get others on board.

- A professional: slow. Wants ideals rather than results – wish they'd live in the real world. Always finding fault with things. On a good day stops us making an error and can get us to come up with better ideas (but at a price).

- An adapter: seems to understand the importance of getting things done but changes their view, hard to pin down.

What a professional thinks of . . .

- A carer: asks me how I feel rather than what I need – misses the point. Quite needy. Friendly and means well, interested in what I have to say; they listen even if they don't always understand.

- A driver: an adrenalin junky – always looking for change rather than following things through. Admire their energy but frustrated by their lack of staying power. If you want something left half-finished then they are the right person to ask.

- An adapter: wish they'd get their priorities straight. Muddled thinking. More sympathetic to making sure that things are done properly than the others.

What an adapter thinks of . . .

- A carer: appreciate their sensitive side – good to have someone who cares and keeps the group together. Can fail to understand that other people's priorities are different.

- A driver: admire their drive and energy as without them it would be harder to make things happen. If only they would listen more and be open to different approaches.

- A professional: great to have someone around who cares about quality. Can be a bit set in their ways and a stickler for process. Doesn't always know when to let go and when to stand firm.

All of the above are suggestions. Of course, a professional may admire a carer for their dedication to looking after people; a driver may admire an adapter's surprising (at least to them) ability to build coalitions to make things happen. However, it gives a sense of how they can easily, but unintentionally, rub each other up the wrong way.

It is not difficult to imagine how this group might go about choosing which restaurant to go to for dinner. The carer would be eagerly asking everyone what type of food or ambience they wanted, the professional would be checking in the restaurant guide, the driver might listen to them for a few moments before getting fed up and announcing where they should all go ('let's just go, otherwise we'll still be discussing it when the restaurants are all closed') and the adapter would be in danger of agreeing with the last speaker, or suggesting a process to make a decision.

Not really conducive to a great evening out.

If, therefore, we want to make the best impact, we need to adapt our behaviour to fit with the other person's motivation rather than simply to promote our own.

Making a good impression

The way to make a good impression will depend on the individual. They are likely to be a mix of more than one type, for a start. However, if you can spot their dominant or strongest motivation, then there are things that you can do to make the right impression. Here are some clues on how to spot each type and so how to make the right impact.

How to spot a carer
'Of course I knew it was your anniversary . . .'

Carers will ask how you are. They will remember your birthday, the names of your family and their various pets. They will be keen to connect one person with another, make great hosts of parties and will always make sure people are comfortable.

Carers will also stand up for others. Just because they like harmony it doesn't mean they shy away from conflict – if there is an underdog the carer is more than likely to support them and help them take on their opponent. However, if there is a way of solving a problem without becoming too competitive, that's what they'd prefer.

How to get the best from the carers
'I wondered if you would mind helping me with something . . .'

Involve them, ask their advice and make them feel appreciated and included. The carers love being involved in the emotional and personal aspects of any situation and so if you are able to include them from that angle they will be delighted.

Remember that they feel frustrated when they feel powerless to help, so if you go to them with a problem, help them to help you solve it, otherwise they may feel as though you are simply dumping on them. A carer's desire to keep everyone happy can sometimes backfire in that they find it difficult to juggle conflicting interests. They will hugely appreciate you acknowledging that difficulty and helping them to solve it.

How to spot a driver
'I'll race you . . .'

Drivers see themselves as people who do things and make stuff happen. Ask them what they did on the weekend and you'll probably hear about the seven things they managed to squeeze into an action-packed 48 hours.

Drivers are drawn to competitive activities, so a 'friendly' tennis match has all the hallmarks of the Wimbledon final with serves and smashes delivered with gusto. Often because drivers want to achieve, they are in a hurry or anxious about doing something.

Drivers don't mind a bit of an argument (and may even brew them sometimes) and will stand up for their point of view. Of course drivers will relax, but even that might be done ferociously with just enough time to chill out before the next event makes an appearance.

Getting the best from the drivers
'Do you fancy a challenge?'

Drivers like activity, action and excitement. To get the best from a driver we need to present a situation in an exciting manner. What is challenging about the situation? What is exciting about it? What is the ultimate goal? Drivers' boredom threshold can often be quite low, so challenges need to appeal.

Bear with a driver if they respond competitively to challenges and allow them to enjoy their moment if they succeed. Like carers, drivers like appreciation, but rather than being appreciated for their support they like appreciation for having met a goal or challenge. Where possible avoid over-explanation or hold-ups in processes. They just want to get on with it.

How to spot a professional
'I think you'll find it's better done like this . . .'

For professionals, quality is the best policy. Professionals will believe that there is a 'right' way of doing something. Given that, the professional may well tell you that your apostrophe is in the wrong place, the best restaurant in the area is just round the corner (but don't have the pilau rice), or that a set of shelves needs to be put up with a spirit level ('of course').

You can spot a professional by the fact they will have an opinion, and, while not always said, it will certainly be held. The thing about professionals is that whether their opinion is wildly unorthodox or traditional in the extreme, they are sure it is the right thing to do.

Getting the best from the professionals
'Why don't you go away and have a think about this?'

The professionals like independence and self-sufficiency so give them plenty of opportunity to think things through. They will appreciate the opportunity to explore how to improve or change what currently exists and so will want the opportunity to do something original.

They will not be pleased to have a poorly thought through or overly hurried answer and so need to be given time to arrive at a great solution. Patience with professionals often pays off as they offer interesting and improved solutions.

How to spot an adapter
'That's not everyone's point of view, of course . . .'

The adapter can adopt any of the behaviours above. They may focus on people, challenging or finding the 'right' solution. You can spot an adapter because they will probably understand all the other motivations and think of the one that isn't being represented at the time.

As well as taking account of everyone's opinions, the adapter will be, to borrow an advertising phrase, your 'flexible friend', the one coming up with alternatives and different solutions, rather than just sticking firmly to their original position.

Getting the best from the adapters
'Of course, I'm open to other suggestions . . .'

Let them work through the contingencies and allow them to explain the differences in the others. Give them the opportunity to be flexible and change their minds about how to do something. By doing so, they may well come up with something you'd never have thought of yourself.

And if they are showing signs of behaviour like one of the other character types, then adapt your behaviour accordingly.

What is your motivation?

You have probably made a good guess at what your motivation(s) is/are. The following quiz is not a rigorously tested psychometric that will see into your soul, but you may want to have a bit of fun finding out how accurate your hunch is. Equally, if you want to send it to your friends and colleagues and see if they agree, then go to The Mind Gym Online.

It's best to think about this in context. Rather than thinking about life as a whole, try a particular part of it, say work or being a parent.

You have 10 points to assign to the 3 alternatives depending on how much you think each of the options applies to you, so read all three statements and then decide how to allocate points. You can assign as many or as few points to each statement as you like, as long as the total for each group is always 10. It might look something like this:

---

1 I really like it when . . .

A Things are done right   ⑤
B The other people involved feel good as well   ②
C I've achieved something difficult   ③

Don't worry or think too much about the scoring; put in the circles what seems right to you.

The area I am focusing on:

---

1 I really like it when . . .

A Things are done correctly   ○
B The other people involved feel good as well   ○
C I've achieved something difficult   ○

---

2 I really dislike it when I feel that I am doing something . . .

A Unprofessional   ○
B Unpopular   ○
C Boring   ○

---

3 It would really bother me if I lost . . .

A My independence   ○
B My allies or friends   ○
C My get up and go   ○

---

4 I love having time to . . .

A Do something properly ○
B Get to know people better (or get to know new people) ○
C Take on new challenges ○

5 I like . . .

A Being allowed to get on with things ○
B Being in the middle of things ○
C Being in charge ○

6 I most appreciate praise when it . . .

A Comes from an expert ○
B Comes from the heart ○
C Comes from results ○

7 I am at my best when . . .

A I'm working out the solution to a difficult problem ○
B I'm helping others ○
C I'm under pressure to deliver ○

8 I value . . .

A Freedom ○
B Friendship ○
C Excitement ○

9 The best decisions are made . . .

A Based on the facts ○
B Collaboratively ○
C Quickly ○

10 My motto is . . .

A If a job's worth doing it's worth doing properly ○
B Treat others as you would like to be treated ○
C Just do it ○

TOTALS

A Professional = ○
B Carer = ○
C Driver = ○

If you have scored over 45 in any one category then you seem to be that type (eg, 23, 24, 53 would indicate that you are a driver).

If your scores are all between 22 and 44 then you are an adapter (eg, 37, 35, 28).

If you haven't scored over 45 and one of your scores is under 22, then you are a mixture of two types (eg, 41, 41, 18), say a professional/carer. An explanation of these types is also available at The Mind Gym Online.

 Influence

Most of us know that a cat is supposed to have nine lives, a pregnancy lasts approximately nine months and there are nine planets in the solar system. But we are largely unaware that there are nine primary tactics to influence other people, even though we use these tactics almost every day of our lives.

As a result, rather like the tourist who repeats the same words louder each time the local doesn't understand, we tend to carry on influencing in the same way. We make small tweaks or cosmetic changes but our underlying strategies for influencing remain frighteningly similar, even when they continue not to work (we put it down to the other person being difficult, our powers of persuasion being insufficient for that subject, or some other factor).

In order to change our approach to influencing we need to understand the constituent parts, in much the same way that in order to make Coq au Vin we need to know what goes into it (and it's not just chicken and wine). The nine tactics are a simple yet scientifically grounded way of understanding the ingredients for influencing.

So, whether you want to teach the world to sing, your daughter to tidy her room, your company to give you a promotion or your friends to come on holiday with you to Guadeloupe, mastering the nine tactics for influencing can make the difference between defeat and delight. Your delight for sure, and, if you're clever, theirs too.

Why are you here?

Next time you are in a restaurant, imagine asking each person why they decided to go there for dinner.

Perhaps, for example, a group of four men and one woman are business colleagues with a client whom they want both to impress and to get to know better. A young couple are on a second date and he is pretending to be richer than he actually is (which is why he left his old car at home and took a taxi). A more mature couple are celebrating her birthday (but won't say which one). A German family are on holiday and read in a guidebook that this is the best restaurant in the area. And so on.

What is significant about this situation, and so many others like it, is that everyone has made the same decision, to have dinner in the same restaurant on the same night. But each person has made this decision for a different reason, their reason.

The number one principle for influencing is to understand that people make decisions for their reasons not ours.

When we try to influence it is, therefore, essential that we understand what the other person's reasons might be and so use tactics that will work for them as opposed to tactics that would work on us if we were in their situation.

With this thought front of mind, we are ready to embrace the nine tactics.

What are the nine tactics?

1 Reason

What is it?
'There are three excellent reasons why contemporary art is a worthwhile investment. First . . .'

Reason, at its best, is about using facts, logic and argument to make a case.

Give me an example
You should run the marathon next year. The training will make you fitter and healthier, it will give you something to focus on outside work, which you said you wanted, and you will raise money for a good cause, maybe that hospice you gave all your old clothes to for their car boot sale (let's face it, you won't need to raise much sponsorship to beat that contribution).

When is it useful?
Most of the time. Reason is the bread and butter of influencing. The challenge is to support our views with relevant information and a coherent argument. Although this requires more effort, it is much more likely to have the desired effect.

Warning
Milder forms include presenting a view as if it is a fact ('this problem is going to take a long time to solve') but without any evidence to back it up. Weak reason is the most common influencing tactic but, without the substance to back it up, far less effective.

2 Inspire

What is it?
'Imagine a world where . . .'

Almost the opposite of reasoning, inspiring focuses on the heart rather than the head: it appeals to emotions and suggests what could be, if only the other person would be persuaded.

Give me an example
Some of the most well-known cases are from political leaders' speeches, for example Martin Luther King's 'I have a dream' or Henry V's 'Once more unto the breach, dear friends'. On closer inspection, these examples don't just ignore logical argument but defy it. Take this extract from John F Kennedy's speech about putting a man on the moon with a commentary from a rational sceptic in brackets.

'Before this decade is out, we should go to the moon and do the other thing [we are never told what 'the other thing' is] not because it is easy but because it is hard [yeah, like that's a good reason for doing something; hey, I reckon we should paint the garden wall with a toothbrush and nail varnish because it's really hard], because that goal will serve to organise the best of our energy and skills [how so? Why wouldn't feeding the starving in Africa or increasing world literacy do it just as well if not better?].'

And yet, for all the rational sceptic's backchat, this speech helped mobilise a nation. The magic about inspirational appeal is that it touches our hearts by appealing to our values and our identity. Like falling in love, when it happens nothing can beat it (and certainly not a rational cynic).

When is it useful?

It is especially useful when the rational case is weak or unclear and when we want a high level of emotional commitment. We don't tend to use Inspire much in our daily lives, especially at work, which is a shame because we are missing out on a powerful way to persuade and excite.

Most of us have been seduced by this tactic whether as children ('it'll make you big and strong when you grow up'), when watching TV (advertisements with young, sexy people having wild times drinking a particular cola), or when with friends who are hooked on a new craze (you've got to check out kite-surfing: the surge, the speed, the twists and swirls – it's like dancing on waves).

Warning

It is not just what you say but how you say it – inspiring demands conviction, energy and passion. A downbeat demeanour will leave you floundering. Deliver like it matters more than life itself and you are pretty much invincible.

3 Ask

What is it?

'Would you like to be rich?'

Ask uses questions to encourage the other person to make their own way to your conclusion (or something similar).

Give me an example

I am walking through the airport when a woman with a clipboard approaches from in front of a large advertising board and asks

'Do you have a credit card?'
I utter a dismissive 'Yes' and keep walking.
'Do you get air miles on your card?' she persists.
'Yes, I do,' I reply, slightly irritated, and carry on walking.
'Do you use your air miles?' The truth is I don't but I'm not going to get caught.
'A bit,' I reply but my walk slows.
'Would you rather have cash?'
I stop, turn and look at her for the first time.
'Do you have five minutes to fill in a form to get a credit card that gives you cash?' she asks.

In five questions I have been persuaded to do something I haven't done for over a decade – switch to a new credit card.

When is it useful?
This is a great tactic when it is important that the other person feels responsible for the outcome. In coaching and counselling, for example, a course of action or therapy is much more effective when the other person believes it was their idea rather than when they grudgingly give in.

Ask is also a useful tactic when trying to persuade someone who has more power than you, whether your mother (that buying a scooter doesn't mean that you don't care what she thinks) or your client (that they should sign up for the platinum service).

Warning
This is one of the hardest tactics to use because it is impossible to know how the other person will respond. If the questions are too broad then you are likely to veer off course; if they are too narrow the other person will spot what you are up to and may refuse to co-operate. But while most of the other tactics weaken with excess use, Ask is the long-life battery of influencing tactics: it just keeps being effective time after time.

4 Feel good

What is it?
'You're a smart guy.'

If we feel positively towards someone we are much more likely to agree with them and we almost always feel positive towards someone who makes us feel good about ourselves.

Give me an example
'Hi Sandra. You're looking well. I heard from Mark that you did a great job on the Cosa Nostra case. Not an easy lot to infiltrate – well done.'
'I've got a challenging project coming up in Damascus and am pulling together a top-level team to work on it. Would you be interested?'

When is it useful?
This is a particularly good tactic when trying to influence people with less or the same level of power as you because they are likely to value your views. Many of us use it on our partner ('Darling, you look a million dollars'), our friends ('I know you are someone I can trust') and our clients ('You're the sort of person who will really appreciate this').

The danger with Feel good is that if we're too obvious we'll have the opposite effect (you're only saying that because you want me to do something for you). As a result, some people avoid it altogether. They are missing out. A less risky approach is to leave time, sometimes even several days, between making someone feel good about themselves and trying to persuade them.

Warning
Using Feel good on someone who clearly has more power than you can look like sucking up so, unless you know what you are doing, watch out.

5 Deal

What is it?
'If you pick me up from the airport, I will . . .'

Dealing is when we offer or give the other person something in return for their agreement. This may be explicit but it doesn't have to be.

Give me an example
A 'fake' psychology experiment was set up with two participants and a scientist. At the formal end of the experiment one of the participants (who was actually the scientist's assistant) would try to sell raffle tickets to the other. This was repeated many times. Half the time the ticket-seller would leave in the interval, part way through the experiment, and come back empty-handed. On the other occasions he would come back with two cans of Coke and offer the innocent subject one of the cans, saying, 'I got this for you.'

The subjects who had been bought the can of Coke bought twice as many raffle tickets as the others, which worked out as a 500% return on investment.

In marketing, this is called the 'not-so-free gift'. With psychologists it is an example of the power of the 'deal' as an influencing tactic.

When is it useful?
When you want to increase the odds in your favour and don't mind giving something away in return.

Sometimes it is necessary to be up front ('If you help me paint the bathroom, I'll cook supper every night next week'). Equally, the deal can work better when the connection is only implied ('Sure, I'll introduce you to my sister', and then twenty minutes later, 'Can you really get hold of a pair of

Air Float trainers, size ten?'). Often Deal is at its most effective when the connection is all but invisible, as in the case of the Cokes above.

Warning
Deal works by appealing to a desire for fairness. Some people can 'take, take, take' without feeling any remorse or indebtedness (or they may just think you're a generous fool). Deal won't work with them unless you are very up front about the terms of the exchange.

6 Favour

What is it?
'Can you help me out?'

Favour is about asking for something simply because you want or need it.

Give me an example
'My guest speaker has just pulled out of the club dinner next week. All I can say is that I'd be eternally grateful if you'd be willing to step in and give the talk yourself.'

When is it useful?
This tactic works well only when the other person cares about you or their relationship with you. If used sparingly it is hard to resist.

Warning
They may well feel that you owe them one. If they do, make sure you 'pay' or you won't get such a positive response next time.

7 Silent allies

What is it?
'Everyone who has read this book so far . . .'

Silent allies refers to the views of other people, generally those similar to the person you are trying to persuade. This may be about the sheer number of people who agree or by referring to the views of someone whom the person you are trying to persuade can identify with.

Give me an example
The advertising slogans '8 out of 10 owners say their cats prefer it' and 'The world's favourite airline' are classic examples of using Silent allies. So, on a more everyday basis, are film reviews and quotes from satisfied customers.

In an experiment an actor pretended to have an epileptic seizure in a public place observed either by just one person or by a group of people (many but not all of whom were part of the experiment). When only one person was watching, the actor was helped 85% of the time. But when a group was watching and did nothing, he was helped just 31% of the time. This suggests that we are generally good-natured (the fact that, left alone, almost everyone came to help) but that the effect of seeing other people behave indifferently is, in most cases, strong enough to counteract our good intentions. That is powerful persuasion.

When is it useful?

Where do you shop? Silent allies?

One of the most powerful ways to persuade teenagers to do anything is to show them that their peers, especially the cool ones, are doing it already. Silent allies also works in business by, for example, referring to best practice models or a list of past clients. If the person you are trying to influence is concerned about risk (and most people are, deep down) or is keen to fit in, then Silent allies can be your winning tactic.

Warning

People can be put off by popularity. Would you be persuaded to go on holiday to the Costa Brava because it is the most visited destination in the Mediterranean? And some people prefer to be contrary. Entrepreneurs, for example, are rarely dissuaded from trying something because no one has done it before (in fact, it can have the opposite effect).

The best silent allies are people whom the person you are trying to persuade naturally associates with.

8 Authority

What is it?

'It's our policy not to refund cash.'

Authority is used from a position of power or by appealing to a rule or principle. It doesn't matter whether it is formal or implicit, so long as the source of the power is recognised by the person whom you are trying to influence.

Give me an example

In 1966, a researcher made an identical phone call to 22 separate nurses. He identified himself as a hospital doctor and directed the nurse to give 20 milligrams of Astrogen (a drug) to a specific patient on the ward. There were four good reasons why the nurse should have been cautious: (a) it was against hospital policy to accept prescriptions by phone; (b) Astrogen had not yet been cleared for use on the wards; (c) the 'maximum daily dose' was clearly marked as 10 milligrams, half of what the fake doctor had requested; (d) the directive was given by someone the nurse had never met or even heard of.

Remarkably, on 95% of occasions the nurse went ahead with collecting the drug and was stopped only when he or she reached the patient's bedside. The fact that they thought they were speaking with a doctor put them in an automatic mindset of compliance to an authority figure. All the research suggests that most of us would do the same.

Whatever you say, Doctor

We come across milder uses of Authority as an influencing technique every day: 'Because I'm your dad', 'The customer is always right', 'The boss says so', 'As someone who has worked in this industry for over a decade', and so on.

When is it useful?

The advantage of Authority is that it's quick and it's straightforward. The downside is that it is more likely to lead to compliance than commitment. Better to use authority as a last resort rather than your opening gambit, unless you are in a rush.

Warning

If you try to persuade using this tactic and don't succeed then you don't have many other options left (mainly Force, see below). You are also likely to have damaged a relationship.

And, like Silent allies, it can have the opposite effect from the one that is intended. Think Axel Foley or Dirty Harry being told they're off the case, only to carry on their investigations. Or Julia Roberts in *Erin Brockovich*, refusing to bow down.

9 Force

What is it?
'Do it or else.'

Force requires assertive behaviour such as threats and warnings.

Give me an example
'Finish your greens or you'll be going straight to bed.'
'Love me or leave me.'
'The last person in your job didn't last very long; we wouldn't want you to make the same mistake'.
'The more time you spend arguing about it the less time you are going to have left to do it.'

When is it useful?
In emergencies.

Warning
Because it's relatively easy to adopt and it usually delivers short-term results, ie, compliance, it gets used a fair bit, especially when combined with Authority. However, when relationships break down it can often be traced back to use of pressure.

Almost like smoking cigarettes, the immediate damage appears minimal but the long-term effect can be terminal, and even if you give up it could be too late, so probably best not to start. Using pressure can also be quite addictive as it gives the user a sense of power and it appears to be getting results. Don't be caught out; use this only when everything else has failed.

OK, I've got the nine tactics. Now what?

Becoming familiar with the nine tactics is a great start. Once we are fluent in the language of influencing we can become a lot more 'mindful' about how we influence (and how others try to influence us). Just because you know about the different types of golf club doesn't make you a champion, but without this knowledge it would be almost impossible to improve your game.

Here are four ways you can use your new-found knowledge about the nine influencing tactics to improve your influencing form.

1 Know yourself

There are no right and wrong influencing tactics. Which ones are most effective will depend largely on the situation and the person that you are trying to influence. In overall terms, based on averages from a range of different (predominantly work) situations, the ranking of the nine tactics above is, loosely, in order of effectiveness. This assumes that each tactic is used as well as could be expected. However, this knowledge is of only limited use. You are not an average person and you are not in average situations.

What is worth considering is which tactics you tend to use most and which least. This is likely to vary in different parts (or 'domains') of your life. For example, at home you may use Feel good and Favour whereas at work you may tend towards Reasoning and Deal. Many of the participants of The Mind Gym Influence and persuade workout report that their bosses tend to start with Reason and if it doesn't seem to be working, move directly to Authority and Force. Some even recognise that they do the same and, having discovered Inspire and Ask, have tried out their new techniques with great effect.

So, the first thing you can do with the tactics is decide which ones you use most and least, then consider whether you could try out some of the tactics you are less inclined to employ.

2 Get strategic

We very rarely use one tactic by itself. The skill lies in combining the influencing tactics in the right way for any particular situation. So, before starting, it can help to develop an influencing strategy.

Here are two examples of influencing strategies developed by participants of The Mind Gym's workout and used to good effect.

SITUATION: My husband can't swim and we have recently moved to a house on the edge of a lake

OBJECTIVE: To persuade my husband to learn to swim

Influencing tactic	How to use it
Inspire	Imagine how great it would be if on long, hot summer days we could both take the children into the lake, help them to swim better and play games together as a family
Favour	I lose sleep worrying about you having an accident near the lake. If only for my peace of mind please learn to swim

Deal	If you learn to swim I will organise and pay for a family holiday in Portugal in a private villa by the sea
Force	If you don't learn to swim I won't let you play with the children outdoors

SITUATION:	I am president of the local hockey club and we are short of funds because people aren't paying their subscriptions
OBJECTIVE:	To persuade the club members to pay their subscriptions

Influencing tactic	How to use it
Ask	The club cannot afford to buy any more shirts. This means that we cannot all play in the same colours, which makes us ineligible for any of our cup games. What do you think we should do about this? (Potential follow-up: what would convince you to pay your sub?)
Reasoning	If subs are paid then we will have enough funds to prevent an overdraft and be able to buy enough new shirts for the next cup tie
Silent allies	A number of people have paid up their subs. It would be great if everyone did
Authority	As president I am requesting all members to pay their subs immediately
Force	Anyone who has not paid their sub by the end of the month will no longer be considered a member of the club and will need to pay another joining fee if they want to re-join

As you will discover, there are some sequences that work better than others. For example, Ask usually needs to be used early in the sequence as does Feel good. Once you have used Authority or Force it is difficult to move to any of the other tactics so they are usually best as last resorts. Favour and Deal are often used after other tactics have been tried.

3 In the field
The best laid plans can go wrong. If your attempt at influencing doesn't seem to be working then you can think about which tactics you haven't used and start to try them out. It's much easier to change approach when you have easy access to the alternatives.

4 Keep on improving

No one influences effectively 100% of the time (whatever they tell you). The best way to improve is to observe what is going on and so work out what you could do to be better. Here are some ideas.

(a) For each of the tactics, give yourself a score out of 10 for how good you are at it. Once you have identified the tactics that you are less good at then you can work on improving them.

(b) Reflecting on your influencing strategies, which ones are effective? Why did the successful ones deliver good results? What can you glean from the strategies that haven't worked about how you could develop a better strategy in future?

(c) Which approaches seem to work best on you? How are these people using them and what can you copy or adapt to make you more effective?

(d) Watching other people influence someone that you find difficult to persuade, how are they going about it? What lessons can you learn from watching master influencers at work?

If you are finding that you are still not as good at influencing as you want to be, remember the point at the beginning of this section: people make decisions for their reasons not ours. The most common reason why we aren't effective is that we are looking through our eyes rather than seeing things from the other person's perspective.

Give your mind a workout

I SPY *Influence bingo (1)* – next time you watch a TV drama, pick a character to follow and tick off the 9 influencing tactics as you spot him/her using them; in weeks 2, 3 and 4, pick different types of programme, eg, a sitcom, a current affairs programme (ideally with interviews), a documentary or a soap opera. What have you noticed about how different tactics are used in different types of situation?

Influence bingo (2) – in the next week, listen out for radio advertisements that predominantly use one of each of the influencing tactics. The week after try it with advertising billboards, the week after that with TV advertisements, then in week 4 with salespeople. If you want to make it more challenging, then pair up the tactics, eg, an advertisement with Authority and Reasoning (say, a doctor promoting a new drug) or Inspire and Silent allies (maybe for a car), but do this at the beginning of the week rather than making up the categories after you've seen or heard the advertisements.

I've been influenced – next time someone persuades you to do something, write down the influencing tactics that they used and the order in which they used them. Ask yourself which was most effective and why. Do this four times over the next month.

I TRY Think of someone you want to influence about something and develop an influencing strategy.

SITUATION:

OBJECTIVE:

Influencing tactic   How to use it

Implement this influencing strategy. Afterwards, ask yourself, and write down:

Overall, how did it go?

What was good about it?

What would have made it better?

What one insight can I use to be better at influencing in future?

Think about which influencing tactics you think you use most and least in different parts of your life (domains).

Domain	A lot	A fair bit	Occasionally/not at all
Home			
Work			
Other			

Choose the domain where you would most like to get better at influencing.

Are there any tactics that you use in other domains a lot or a bit but not in the domain that you want to improve in?

Which tactics?

How could you use them more in your priority domain?

Which tactics do you use occasionally/not at all, in any domain?

Could these be useful?

How could you try them out?

(H) Connect

What do you do after you say 'hello'?

The new boss. Your brother's new girlfriend. An alluring stranger at a party. There are times when we desperately want to make a good first impression. And the rest of the time, we just want to be liked.

The phrase 'staircase moment' describes that feeling as we walk away, down the stairs, and think of exactly what we should have said, only five minutes too late. Its first cousin is the toothbrush moment, when we are brushing our teeth at the end of the evening and our partner says something along the lines of, 'Didn't you *like* Sandra?' or 'You could have made a bit more effort with Rob.' Bristles and fluoride muffle the case for the defence, which is probably a good thing.

If there was a magic pill that banished staircase and toothbrush moments for ever and made you consistently attractive and popular, would you take it? Unfortunately it doesn't exist. For the next best thing, read on.

1 Got the drift?

What do you get back as soon as you've realised that it has drifted off? The answer to this brain teaser is simple: attention.

We've all found ourselves in situations where, supposedly deep in conversation, we're no longer listening to the other person, but instead talking to ourselves.

'What on earth was he thinking when he bought that shirt? I wonder if it was a present.'
'Am I making a good impression?'
'Oh my goodness, I almost forgot, I must ring Albert.'
'Sara said he was tall, dark and handsome. She must be going blind.'
'What shall I say next? I know, I'll tell him the story about the antelope and the vase. Yes, that should impress him.'

The most important technique for building rapport with someone is maintaining focus. This means listening to the other person without judging or commenting on what they are saying. And that's not as easy as it sounds, not when we talk at between 120 and 150 words per minute yet can listen at up to 1,200 words per minute. It is no surprise that with all that spare listening capacity we easily get bored and distracted.

Virtually the only common factor among people who are widely liked is that they make the other person feel special, as if they are the only person that matters in the world. But how do we have this effect?

You know you're drifting when . . .

. . .   you start playing 'join the dots' with the other person's freckles

. . .   you think, 'don't those ceiling tiles look like a giant chessboard'

. . .   that song you heard on the radio this morning starts playing inside your head

. . .   you discover the person you've been listening to left five minutes ago

. . .   you wonder if you left the gas on

. . .   you start thinking about which TV personalities the person looks like

. . .   you start to wonder who the person you came with is talking to

. . .   you notice that there isn't any lemon in your drink

Shift the drift

In order to build rapport and 'connect' with people we need to give them our full attention however difficult that may be.

Here are some guidelines that may help.

1 Give them the benefit

'If the first time you meet someone you find them boring, then it's your fault' is a great principle to have at the back of your mind. If we are an interesting person then we will have the ability to be intrigued or excited by new people, new information, stories and characters. Our challenge, which we should choose to accept, is to unlock the interesting side of every person we talk with. If we don't succeed then it's we who have failed, not them.

This will also help us feel more positive towards people, which will almost certainly be reflected in our body language and other micro signals (elbow squeezes and beyond). Above all else we should avoid making negative judgements on the other person. As soon as we think of them critically (stupid, humourless, obsessed with trains) then our chances of building rapport successfully are greatly reduced. If we focus on their strengths and we're much more likely to get on just fine.

2 Listen without prejudice

Real listening requires putting aside our prejudices and preconceptions until we have collected all the information that we want. It is far better to focus on what the other person's argument is than pick it apart as they're saying it.

3 Get involved

One way we can keep our attention up is to get involved in the conversation, by, for example, asking questions about what happened or what it felt like, suggesting analogies or guiding the conversation in a new direction, possibly with a story of our own.

When we're part of the action, it's much harder to switch off.

4 Set a challenge

Choose a task, maybe to summarise their main point in ten words, or capture the three key things that they are proposing. Alternatively, try to separate the facts from the principles, or the implications from the evidence. If we do this effectively we can share our insights with them, which will demonstrate how actively we have been listening and is sure to make them feel great (and great about us).

5 Spot drifting early on

However hard we try to maintain our focus, we all do lose attention from time to time. The challenge is to spot it early and so regain focus quickly. Feelings are a powerful 'alarm'. If we remember what it feels like when we are starting to drift off then each time we experience that feeling we are more likely to 'wake up' and re-focus on the person we were listening to.

2 Strike a match

A group of friends are drinking in a bar. One person takes a sip from their drink and, unaware that they have been prompted, so does everyone else. The managing director clasps his hands behind his head, leans back in his chair and lets out a sigh. All the other directors round the table move in some way.

These scenarios and others like them are repeated millions of times all over the world every day. It has become almost automatic that when two people like each other or one wants to be liked by the other, they will emulate each other in some way. This is known as matching and, like shifting our drifting, is a simple and effective way to help us connect with people.

Matching and mirroring

Matching is, in effect, doing the same as the other person. This may be the same body language – he raises his glass and so does everyone else, she uses her right arm to make a point, and then you use your right arm as you explain why you agree. Usually we do part matching, maybe tilting our head as they do or leaning back at the same time, without necessarily also crossing our legs in the same way, tapping our fingers, and so on.

Sometimes we match one activity with a different one; for example, we might nod in time with their left hand going up and down. The technical term for this is cross matching. It is still a kind of matching but more subtle than the straight matching described above.

Mirroring is like matching only instead of doing the same thing (we both tilt our heads to the right), one person reflects what the other person is doing as if they were looking in the mirror (ie, you tilt your head to your right and I tilt mine to my left).

Matching and mirroring aren't just about body language. We can sigh or make other noises – 'ah', 'uh-huh?' or similar sounds – in harmony with the other person. When someone speaks quietly we lower our voice too, or we start to copy elements of a foreigner's accent.

When the Australian soap *Neighbours* was first a big hit in the UK, fans found themselves echoing the characters' habit of sentences going up at the end as though they were a question, even when they were anything but. 'I like *Neighbours*' came out as 'I like *Neighbours*?'

Matchosoft

An article from *Newsweek*, August 8, 1988, 'Mimic your way to the top', demonstrates non-verbal mimicry or matching at work.

'Here's the scene: the top executives of Microsoft Corp. are in a meeting and co-founder and CEO Bill Gates is talking. As he grows intense he starts rocking and bobbing back and forth in his chair, the rocking and bobbing speeding up as he continues. Seated around him, several of his lieutenants soon are rocking and bobbing, rocking and bobbing. Gates periodically pushes his glasses up on his nose; his associates push their glasses up. Whether done consciously or not, subordinates show a relentless tendency to copy their bosses' mannerisms, gestures, way of speaking, dress and sometimes even choice of cars and homes.'

Why matching should be catching

That any of this matching and mirroring should make the slightest bit of difference to whether someone likes us may seem somewhat implausible. So, here are some facts.

1 When we are matching each other we tend to get along better

There are a great many psychological experiments which show that matching or 'synchrony' between two people shows mutual interest and approval. In one study by Frank Bernieri, young couples spent ten minutes trying to teach one another a set of made-up words and their definitions. Analysis of their interactions showed that those pairs whose movements were in greatest synchrony also felt the strongest emotional connection with each other.

2 Yawning is infectious (so is laughter)

Robert Provine conducted an intriguing study of facial mimicry. He noted that, in humans, yawning is infectious and found clear evidence that, beginning in infancy, yawns are generated by seeing someone else yawn. Six years later, Provine demonstrated that laughter is equally contagious, which explains why TV comedy shows add in laughing cues.

3 When we disagree we are more sympathetic when the other person matches us

In The Mind Gym workout on Rapport building, pairs of participants talk to each other, first about a subject they agree about (the ideal garden is a window box being one of the more eccentric) and then about something they disagree on (blue cheese causes the worst nightmares was another example). In each case, the partners are asked to 'match' each other for half the conversation and then mismatch for the other half. At the end of the exercise each person recalls what it felt like.

Almost everyone who had to match the other person whilst disagreeing on the content said that they found matching and disagreeing at the same time extremely difficult.

In contrast, those on the receiving end, ie, talking with someone who disagreed with them but matched them, said that it didn't feel like there was any significant disagreement at all. Extraordinarily, the fact that they were being matched tended to mean that they felt that they were in agreement even though they knew, once they thought about it, that they were in total disagreement.

Once the mismatching started, their view changed completely and it felt like they disagreed (which, indeed, they did).

Whether consciously or not, and it is usually 'not', when we are connecting with someone or keen to get on with them, we adopt similar postures and movements. And when this happens the other person is more likely to assume that our thoughts and emotions are similar so they tend to feel warmer towards us, almost regardless of what we are actually saying.

The Woody Allen film *Zelig* was about a character who would turn into the person he was talking to. He would meet an Hassidic Jew and would suddenly sprout long hair in ring curls. He would talk to someone with a high-pitched voice and his voice would become squeaky. This is matching taken to extremes. However, most of us do a milder form of it every day.

A few non-verbal behaviours to look out for when matching include:

1 Posture
Are they sitting upright or slouched? Are they leaning to one side? Are their legs crossed? Are their shoulders tense or relaxed?

2 Movement
Are they shifting from one leg to another? Are they twiddling their fingers? Are they blinking their eyes?

3 Breathing
Is it fast or slow, regular or irregular, deep or shallow?

Spot the friends

4 Speech
Do their speech patterns change or stay the same? Research suggests that people are more attracted to and comfortable with people whose conversational rhythms are predictably sequenced and closely co-ordinated with their own.

Powerful voices

Communication researchers have discovered that we unconsciously shift our speech patterns to match those of people in positions of power and authority. One study used *The Larry King Live* TV show for its material. The psychologists found that when Larry King was interviewing a high status guest (eg, Bill Clinton) his voice changed to become more similar to theirs. However, when he was dealing with lower status guests his voice didn't change, but their voices started to match his.

That synching feeling

Leading and following

When you are next on a bus or train, look around for people who know each other. Watch how their movements and, if you can hear them, voices fit together and contrast this with all the strangers whose movements and posture are unrelated (and if they're not, well you know what that suggests).

Often one person leads and the other follows. The person who is doing the 'following' is likely to be the one who

1   cares most about being liked

2   is keen to make a good impression

3   agrees with/respects the other person.

Is this weakness? Not at all. It is simply a way of increasing the chances that someone will feel connected with you and so feel positive towards you. This may be for wholly good reasons (making the world a happier place) or there may be an ulterior motive (the saleswoman eager to befriend us so that we buy her insurance). The motivation is independent of the technique's effect.

Five top tips on matching

1   Be subtle. Overdoing it is embarrassing for everyone

2   Practise with one element at a time, say head movement or voice tempo

3   Matching when you disagree will feel uncomfortable at first but is well worth pursuing

4   Watch other people doing it; once you start to spot it automatically then you will find it easier to do yourself

5   Try switching from 'following' to 'leading' in a conversation – and notice the difference.

In synch
Rock 'n' roll dancing, or other forms of activity that require partnership and picking up each other's cues, are similar to the great state when two people are in synch, each both leading and following during the conversation. This is a very comfortable place to be and a sign of a strong relationship.

Swapping roles
Sometimes we start as the 'follower', eager to make a good impression, move into synch as we get on famously and can then, having made such a positive impression, switch to being the leader.

This can be a useful sign when we are selling, dating or trying to convince someone. Once our prospective client starts to follow us then they are more likely to be seduced by our offer.

3 Common ground

'Captain Dalton, Herefordshire Regiment.'
'How do you do? My mother's family is from Hereford.'

Later:
'A good man. Family's from Hereford.'

Often a feeling of human warmth comes from shared connections and so, when we want someone to like us, we try to find something in common.

If we assume that the other person likes himself or herself then he or she will usually like someone who is in some way similar.

Broadly, there are three areas in which we can search for common ground: beliefs, enthusiasms and experiences.

Experiences

'Have you been on holiday recently?' asks your hairdresser as he settles down to the task in hand. If there was an international curriculum for hair stylists this universal opener would surely be in the first lesson. Why? Because it works. The chances are that you will recall some trip ('I went on a long weekend to Prague back in the spring') which will give them a range of different ways to find connections: long weekends away; travelling in the spring; cities that are used to shoot films; maybe even Prague itself. And if they can't find any immediate connection, there's always the next thing, 'Have you got a holiday planned?'

Experiences are a great place to start the search for common ground because we all have them and we usually have quite a few that are shared. Whether it is people we both know, places we have visited, subjects we have studied, films we have seen, sports we have played or books we have read, you and I have thousands of experiences in common.

The trouble is that not all common experiences are equal.

In a scene from the film *Diamonds are Forever*, James Bond is smuggling diamonds in a coffin. He is picked up at the airport by the bad guy's muscle men, who drive him away in their hearse.

'Who's the stiff, I mean the deceased, is that your brother?' asks one of the flunkies of the coffin.
'Yes, it is,' Bond replies.
'Oh, I got a brother,' comes the reply.
'Small world,' retorts Bond.

The flunky's awkward effort to build rapport fails not just because it is wholly insensitive but also because the shared experience is irrelevant. A shared experience that is shared with millions of other people is not a shared experience that will help build rapport. We all breathe air, eat food, talk, sleep and pay taxes. These are universal experiences and so not much good for building a connection. Sure they say 'I am like you in this respect' but then so is everyone else.

When it comes to finding common ground, the more exclusive the shared experience the more likely it is to help us build a connection. This is one of the reasons why discovering that we know people in common is such a powerful connection (another is that it suggests we live/work in similar worlds and so are likely to share some beliefs, of which more later).

What happens when the shared experience is a negative one? You and I might discover that we have both been dragged through the courts as part of an ugly and drawn out divorce. This would be a relatively exclusive common experience. However, as a way of building a connection it is risky. We may connect very strongly by sharing a common adversity but, equally, the negative emotions I feel as I remember the battles over custody and rights of access may outweigh the milder positive feelings I have towards someone who has had a similarly harrowing experience.

By contrast, new parents can talk for ever about the miracle of childbirth and the joy of their children and build strong connections with each other as a result, not because this is a particularly exclusive connection but because it is an overwhelmingly positive one.

And so, while any common ground can help to make a connection, the more exclusive it is to the two of you, and the more positive an experience it is to recall, the greater the chances that the other person will feel warm towards you as a result.

For those who like a visual way of looking at this:

	Negative	Positive
Exclusive	Unpacking at the beginning of a rock climbing expedition to discover I had picked up the wrong rucksack at the airport	Seing dawn break at Machu Picchu on New Year's Day
Universal	Delayed plane	Going on holiday

The hairdresser's question is more effective than, say, 'Has anyone been angry with you recently?' (arguably, a much more interesting question) because it works on the hypothesis that travelling abroad is a good experience. Whether a holiday, an important business trip or a break from daily routine, they are betting on the assumption that it is something we will enjoy recalling. Whether or not they are handy with the scissors, when it comes to building support hairdressers tend to be true professionals.

Enthusiasms

Most of us have something that we are enthusiastic about and that we could talk about for ages. When we find someone who shares our interest, or at least is eager to find out more about it, we are inclined to get excited and to feel good towards the other person. As a rule of thumb, people are generally more positive when they are talking and being listened to than the other way round. And even better when they are talking about a subject close to their heart.

'I started reading the sports pages so that I would have something to talk about with my clients other than work. It was a great way of breaking the ice and being accepted on their terms,' explained a workout participant from a consultancy.

Beliefs

Above all else, we like people who see the world as we do. A bit of challenge is fine, maybe even a good thing, but first and foremost it is good to know that we are starting from the same principles.

Some of our beliefs are weakly held. I might believe that Arsenal will win the league and Janet Jackson has an amazing voice. If you agree with me then you are clearly a bright person with great foresight and insight (like me). If you disagree and think Manchester United will win and that whilst Janet Jackson has many fine features her voice isn't one of them, that is OK too, so long as you can give me good arguments and you are happy with a difference of view.

Direct disagreement with any of my stronger views carries a serious risk that I won't like you. A healthy challenge on who will win the league may be fine. But if you disagree with me about whether we should/shouldn't have gone to war or whether it's our duty to protect the environment, then I am much less inclined to feel a connection with you. And so, when we do disagree with someone we want to like us, it can pay to keep our views covert.

There is an exercise in one of The Mind Gym workouts where one person comes up with an outrageous suggestion, eg, you should dye your hair purple, and the other person has to reply with three things they like about the suggestion and three things they wish were different. For example, I like the idea of standing out from the crowd, I like the colour purple and I like the idea of improving my hair; I wish that my colleagues would still take me just as seriously, that I wouldn't get funny looks from people on the train and that my mother would still speak to me.

This is going too far (deliberately) but next time you are about to say 'No but . . .', try, instead, 'Yes and . . .' You may well find some of those difficult conversations become much easier.

① Presence

The twelfth-floor meeting room, midday. Two employees of the prospective client are giving me some background as we wait for their boss to arrive. Ten minutes after the meeting is due to start, he walks calmly through the door.

His colleagues stand up. The most senior one, herself a senior vice president, changes her demeanour completely. A moment ago she was telling me in clear ringing tones how things work around here and her views on how they could be improved. Now her voice is quieter, her back no longer straight but slightly hunched, almost as if she is in abeyance.

'Hello, I'm Nick, you must be Mark.' His voice is distinct and clear, neither loud nor quiet. He offers his hand and I shake it.

Nick sits down at the head of the table (the seat has clearly been left for him), and, looking straight into my eyes, asks, 'Now, what is it you want to sell me?' It's not interrogating, just direct. I'm a busy man, is the implication, so let's cut to the quick.

I start telling him and, as I'm talking, he stands up, turns round and walks over to the table with the teas and coffees. He starts pouring. Do I continue or do I stop? Nick is the decision-maker: it's also clear that he is going to make a decision based on whether he thinks I'm his equal or his inferior. If I can match him for presence he may well buy.

I stop talking. There is a brief moment of silence.

'It's OK, go on. I'm listening,' Nick says, from behind his back, which is all I can see as he continues to pour.

Do I disobey his direct instruction or do I carry on fighting with the clatter of teaspoons?

'Don't worry,' I sit back, 'best to get the coffees and teas out the way first.'

For the first time there is a slight hint that Nick isn't entirely comfortable with the situation. He asks who would like a cup, acknowledging his colleagues for the first time since we started talking. They gush their thanks but refuse. I thank him and say that a fresh cup would be nice (I won't drink it but that's not the point).

Nick sits back down, again looking directly at me. 'So, you think you can teach my people to be more persuasive?'

'Among other things, yes.'

'Are you using any of your techniques on me now?' he asks without even a glimmer of a smile. This is a very clever question. If I say 'no' then why ever not, if they are so effective. If I say 'yes' then all he has to say is, 'They're not working on me, can you do any better?' and I'm stuffed.

I hold his stare and without blinking or pausing reply, 'Yes. And we'll see if they work at the end of this meeting.' I offer the hint of a smile to suggest that I know we're playing a game and that I'm enjoying it too.

The conversation continues for another ten minutes. Nick then stands up. Everyone else does too.

'That's very interesting. We'll get back to you in the next couple of days.' He looks briefly at the senior vice president to confirm that it is she who'll be doing the getting back. He looks me in the eye again, shakes my hand, 'Thank you', nods to the others and walks calmly out of the room.

That afternoon I got the call to say that we had won the work.

This (true) story is very typical of a shorthand people use every day to decide if we're up to it. It may not be a good way of judging but it's one a lot of people adopt and so if we don't know how to play the gravitas game we're going to miss out.

It's not just in business. When we first meet our partner's mother and father, when we are introduced to a new group of people in a bar or at a party, when we are negotiating with a builder or we meet the headmistress of our daughter's school, our presence will dictate how seriously they take us.

And if anyone tells you that you don't look old enough (or senior enough) then you could almost certainly do with gaining a little gravitas (better than grey hair dye, anyway).

What is it?

Everyone else stops and listens when you start to speak.
You get attention from the people around you without apparently trying.
Your views are often quoted.
People want to know what you think.
You are talked about though always with respect.

What have you got?
Presence.

Although it is easy to see when it's there, presence is hard to define. Perhaps the best place to start with is what presence isn't. It isn't, for example, being invisible and it certainly isn't being arrogant, but perhaps somewhere in between. The following may help explain this elusive characteristic.

In my mind

No/little presence	Presence	Arrogance
I'm not sure what to do	Calm – it will all work out well	I need to show who's boss
They are so important/ impressive	I know what I'm doing (or, at least, where I'm going)	I'm right
I'm worried I'll make a mess of it		Attack is the best form of defence
		I'm nervous but I don't want to show it

Others' perceptions

No/little presence	Presence	Arrogance
Walkover	Respect	Pompous
Ineffective	Worth listening to	Doesn't listen
Who are you talking about?	Wise	Loud
I don't remember them	Knows what they are talking about	Aggressive
Inexperienced/ junior		Irritating
		A bore

Not liked

The other thing presence isn't about is being liked. In some senses having presence is the opposite of building rapport. When we want to be liked by someone we may go out of our way to demonstrate similarities and adapt our behaviour to increase their approval.

Presence is often about mismatching or doing the unexpected. Our presence may irritate people, at least in the short term, and leave them unclear where they stand. This is why we don't want to have presence all the time. Just sometimes, at the right times.

When do you want it?

Higher presence is helpful when we want respect. For example when

- we are being judged based on how authoritative we are, say, trying to sell an intellectual service (consultancy, advertising, project management) or convince someone older or more senior to change their mind.

- the other person has decided to play at presence, for example the demanding father who wants to see if you're good enough for his daughter (or son).

- what we are proposing is likely to be unpopular.

- we are talking with a large group who may easily be distracted, say, telling a story to a whole table of people or making a speech at a wedding.

Low levels of presence, by contrast, are particularly helpful when we want the focus of attention to be more on the other person or people. This could be when

- we want other people to talk openly. A journalist eager to uncover secrets in a celebrity interview, for example, or when a close friend is telling us something important and personal and we want them to share fully.

- we want others to shine and enjoy the limelight. It's your son's birthday, your whole team's achievement.

- we want others to feel that they are in control of the situation – a boss, a client, a nervous lover.

- we need to calm things down. We're stuck in the middle of a heated row and another ego would only make things worse. Instead, empathy and sensitive questions to find out what the disagreement is really about are a far more effective antidote. However, we may need to raise our presence so the two warring parties give us their attention in the first place.

- it is very important that the other person likes us. This can be true when dating, asking for a favour, meeting someone new or working with colleagues with whom we need to have a strong relationship. Sometimes, though, they may like us more if we are not too eager to impress.

In many situations we may raise and lower our level of presence as we go along. For example, if we are interviewing someone for a job we may choose to have very low presence at the beginning as we encourage them to share as much as possible about themselves. Once, however, we have decided that we do want to hire them, we may well increase our presence if we suspect that this will help convince them to accept our job offer.

If you are the person being interviewed you might well start with rapport, so they like you, move to presence, so they think you are worth hiring, and then gently ease back to rapport so that you leave on good terms.

How much presence have you got?

Think of a 'domain' or type of situation where having presence is important. Ideally, it will be a situation that you have experienced already a few times and are likely to experience again. It could be client meetings, when you are with a particular group of people (old college friends) or when you are in a particular place (the bridge club?). Write it down.

The situation where I want presence:

With this situation in mind, tick the most appropriate box for each of the following questions.

	very rarely/never	rarely	often	almost always/always
1 People interrupt me in the middle of what I'm saying	○	○	○	○
2 People make eye contact with me when I'm talking	○	○	○	○
3 I raise my voice to emphasise a point	○	○	○	○
4 People make eye contact with me when they're talking	○	○	○	○
5 Other people do most of the talking	○	○	○	○
6 I repeat myself to make sure that I am understood	○	○	○	○
7 When I'm angry it is clear to others	○	○	○	○
8 I am considered up to date on current affairs	○	○	○	○
9 When someone else is talking I am completely focused on them	○	○	○	○
10 When I have finished any point I stop talking, even if there is silence	○	○	○	○

Before you start scoring, remember that the results are only for the particular situation that you chose and are likely to be very different for other occasions. You can fill in the questionnaire as many times as you like for different types of situation and you will probably get very different results.

Given what you have ticked for the situation that you have chosen on this occasion, allocate yourself the following points based on the table below.

	very rarely/never	rarely	often	almost always/always
Questions 1, 3, 6, 7	4	3	2	1
Questions 2, 4, 5, 8, 9, 10	1	2	3	4

Add up to make a total that will be from 10 to 40.

34–40 Respect

In this situation you have a great deal of presence and are likely to get all the attention you need. Your views will be valued and the people you are with may often refer to you and what you have said when you are not around. Don't worry, what they say is likely to be polite. And they won't forget you.

If you want to gain gravitas in other situations, consider what you are thinking and doing in this situation and see whether you can copy some of it.

Watch out that you don't come across as a little too pleased with yourself – see Arrogance alert, below.

26–33 Up there

You do have presence. There is no fear that you are going to blend into the wallpaper. Equally, you probably don't have the undisputed gravitas that you would like and may well be competing with other people operating with a similar level of presence.

There are probably some relatively simple things that you could do which would give you that extra presence to mark you out from the rest of the crowd without coming across as an oddball or as arrogant.

18–25 In the game

In this situation you are one of the crowd. You aren't invisible but you aren't particularly noticeable either. The chances are that people will remember your contribution if they are prompted but may not give particular weight to anything you said without a nudge.

In the domain you have chosen – you have made a start but there is much you could do to gain gravitas.

10–17 On the sidelines

Your presence is very low in this situation and you are in danger of being ignored or dismissed as irrelevant. If having presence is very important, you may want to avoid this situation. Alternatively, you can rethink how you see yourself and the other people who are there and take significant steps that will help you gain gravitas. It won't be easy but the effect may be remarkable. 'You're a different person these days' could well be the reaction if you get it right.

Arrogance alert

The challenge with gaining gravitas is that it can easily veer into arrogance. How did you score on questions 3, 5, 7? If you scored 1 or 2 in any of these then watch out.

Is your mind on it?

It's all very well getting a gauge on how much presence we do (or don't) have. The challenge is what to do to get more of it when we want it.

The key to having presence is being in the right state of mind. If our thoughts and feelings are where they should be then we will gain gravitas almost automatically. Equally, with the wrong thoughts and feelings all the practical tips and techniques are likely to be close to worthless. Even if you have all the right steps, you won't be a great dancer if you are worried about what everyone else is thinking. As with dancing, so with presence.

1 Confident uncertainty

I am going to meet with the bank to get a loan. There are some things I know for sure. I know what my monthly commitments are; I know what my average expenditure has been for the last six months; I know what I want the loan for (a holiday in the Maldives). There are some things I don't know: the bank's policy on loans, for example. But I'm not bothered. The bank manager will tell me these things, if they are relevant. So, whilst there are things I don't know or am not certain about, I have dismissed these as either unimportant or something I will learn on the way. The fact that I don't know about them, or about a range of other things I may be asked, doesn't matter. I am, therefore, confident in my uncertainty.

An expert takes questions at the end of her lecture. She is asked about a complex, technical issue. Unflustered, she replies, 'That's a very good question and I'm afraid I don't know the answer. Let me think about it and if you give me your email I'll get back to you.' The lecturer has not been worrying about being asked a question that she doesn't know the answer to. Instead, she is confident that whatever she is asked she will be able to deal with, even if this includes admitting that she doesn't know the answer.

Confident uncertainty is the essential part of a mindset that will help give us presence. But it is not the whole story. There are four other aspects that will also help.

2 Purpose beyond pleasing

When we want to be liked our primary purpose is to please (at least, to make a pleasing impression). When we want to have presence we have something more crucial on our mind, a 'purpose' which is more important than making a good impression.

Our purpose may be to encourage new talent, to treat people fairly, to make the neighbourhood safe, to stick to a code of ethics, to do what we professionally consider to be correct. The key point about this purpose is that if it came to the crunch we would always choose the purpose over pleasing the people we are talking with.

So, ultimately, if you don't agree with me or like what I am saying, it's not my problem. I might find it a shame or disappointing but it isn't a show-stopper as my purpose is greater than pleasing or convincing you (though, of course, I'd rather you agreed with me; if I didn't then I would be likely to come across as arrogant).

Beat the bouncer

Whether it's walking into a posh hotel to use their lavatory or jumping the queue to get into a popular club, presence can make the difference between easy entry and no entry.

A good start is to think in a high-presence way.

Please come straight in

Confident uncertainty: I will be allowed in. I can stare them in the eye without blinking, act assured and deal with whatever barriers are put in my way

Purpose beyond pleasing: I am on a mission to get in and stay in, not to make the doorman my best friend (though if that's what's needed then I will do that too but only as a means to an end)

Equals: I will not beg, plead or look desperate. Equally, I will not act like I own the place. Only that I should be inside, and as a sensible man (or woman) with the establishment's best interests at heart he (or she) will think the same

Positive energy: Determined but in a delightful way

Generous thoughts: The doorman wants to get it right and he will realise that letting me in is part of getting it right

3 Equals

When we meet someone we respect or who has significant power over us, we tend to change our behaviour dramatically, as the senior vice president did in the example earlier. When we want to have presence we need to feel that we are acting as normal – there is nothing special about this situation. So it's Nelson Mandela we're talking with; no big deal.

Many celebrities admit enjoying the experience of fawning fans but don't claim to respect or like them. Celebrity etiquette dictates that, if you meet a famous person, you should treat them much as you would treat anyone else. Let them mention their latest song, show or series if they want to but don't be the one to bring it up.

Two candidates turn up for a job interview with a busy, senior director. The first is very nervous, desperate to make a good impression and not waste the director's time. The second is calm and, though keen to position herself as well as possible, considers the meeting more as a discussion to find out both if she is right for the role and if the role is right for her, than a formal interview. The senior director's needs are, in the second candidate's mind, no more important than her own.

No prizes for guessing which candidate has the most presence and so is most likely to be offered the job.

Those with presence don't patronise or look down on the people they are with. But they don't look up to them in awe either. You may be my boss, my client's boss, a famous pop star, the president of the golf club or a professor, but as far as this conversation is concerned we are equals, each with our own strengths, neither superior to the other.

4 Positive energy

People with presence tend to have energy. It may not be the ra-ra, in-your-face kind of energy (in fact it probably isn't) but there will definitely be the sense of a force waiting to be unleashed. Apathy and presence don't tend to go together.

Usually the energy is linked to the purpose: I am eager to make the neighbourhood safer; I am passionate about maintaining high-quality standards. Although it can be more general – full of excitement; keen to get on with things.

The energy can be destructive and still increase presence. Sean is charming and almost everyone likes him as soon as they spend a few minutes in his company. Toby is the opposite with a sharp but dismissive humour and a slight sneer. On first meeting, people tend to dislike Toby, often intensely and for reasons they can't quite understand. Toby could be described as having negative charisma. He still has presence (would you forget someone to whom you took an instant dislike?) but it is based on a negative energy.

Presence requires energy. Whilst the energy doesn't have to be positive the impact is more predictable and often more powerful when it is.

Don't interrupt

As a general rule, don't let other people talk over you or have side conversations. If other people start talking at one side then stop. Remain silent. Look at them, not aggressively but calmly as if you have all the time in the world and are happy to wait; it's just that you don't want to interrupt them or, by implication, be interrupted yourself.

They will usually then stop and apologise, which you can choose to recognise if you want. And then you can continue where you left off. It is unlikely that anyone else will interrupt. Much the same if they stand up to pour coffee as in the earlier example.

5 Generous thoughts

Generally, when we want to increase our presence we want to avoid thinking too much about the people we are with and how they might be reacting. But sometimes we can't.

As we imagine that the other person is bored or waiting to be impressed, we are more likely to panic and as a result dilute our state of confident uncertainty, or lose it altogether.

In these circumstances it can help to 'endow' the other person or people with the characteristics that we would most like them to have. For example, we might endow an audience with an appetite to discover or a desire to be challenged.

Some people actually say to themselves about the people they are going to meet, 'I endow you with enthusiasm' or 'I endow you with trust in what I have to say'. They then assume that their audience is thinking or feeling this way even if their arms are crossed and they are frowning.

Unlikely though it may sound, by believing the other person or people have certain traits, we behave as if they do; they can pick this up from our micro signals (small, often unnoticed bits of non-verbal communication) and unconsciously adopt the mindset that we want them to have. It's not foolproof but it can make a significant difference. It's certainly a lot better than imagining that they are out to get us.

Time to talk

Imagine a conversation with a group of people. You may be sat round someone's kitchen table discussing what to do about the Council's proposal to reduce the frequency of buses or you're in a conference room with the company's top executives considering how to react to a takeover bid. Either way, you want your views to be listened to and you want to be taken seriously.

What can you do to increase your presence?

Listen in
Non-evaluative listening can be an effective way to gain gravitas without actually having to say anything particularly clever.

When other people are talking we need to give them our undivided attention, at least to start with. If we are the person who is always listening attentively then people will increasingly address their comments to us (after all, they want to know that they are being listened to) and so it will look, to the rest of the group, as if we are the person who needs to be addressed. This, in turn, will increase our level of presence.

When we are listening, and this applies to only one other person as much as to a group, we need to do so as much as possible without 'filters', ie, not judging or evaluating what they are saying as they are talking. If we express emotions these should be only to show that we have heard and understood what they have said and not our opinion on what they are saying.

Talk up
The 'less is more' axiom is particularly valid when it comes to talking. A few well-chosen words delivered with a measured voice (no gushing) can generate far more presence than a long but unfocused rant. Though not if that is what everyone else is doing.

The types of content that tend to increase presence include:

1 Adding new information that materially alters the nature of the conversation: 'I've been analysing some more recent research and the results suggest something rather different . . .'

2 Summarising where the conversation has got to: 'It seems to me that there are in fact three options that we are considering, first . . .'

3 Giving a view based on experience: 'In both the gardens I created in Berkshire I found that azaleas and rhododendrons were the quickest to take in peaty soil.'

4 Using what has been said so far to explain our view: 'The merits of Dave's argument are . . . but the factors that haven't been considered are . . . so, on balance, I think we should go ahead with the plan.' In effect, this is selective summarising to back up our opinion.

Presence often requires mismatching, ie, behaving differently from the other person or the rest of the group. If everyone else is emotional it pays to play calm. If everyone else is as cool as ice then let them know that you really care. And when you've made your point, stop. If there is silence then fine, you don't have to fill it.

Tales of the unexpected

Much of gaining gravitas lies in doing the unexpected. It is a fine line between going against the norm and doing something unacceptable: eccentric versus insane. Equally, without taking a risk we are never going to gain gravitas, or deserve it.

A different role
One way to surprise is to take on a role that is different from the one that is expected of you. For example, as a guest, taking on some of the habits of the host by helping pour drinks (without, of course, upstaging them).

The grand gesture
Big gestures are high risk. When they work they definitely create presence. Nikita Khrushchev, a former Russian premier, in a key address to the

United Nations used some shock tactics. 'I even took off my shoe and pounded on the desk. Nehru said that I shouldn't have used such an unparliamentary method. It became a widely publicised incident which outraged the sensibilities of many Westerners,' he explained.

Grand gesture: the university interview

Interviews are never the most relaxed of occasions, but university ones can be among the most stressful. We've all heard the horror stories of arrogant professors reducing prospective students to tears but one (apocryphal?) tale shows a way out.

In this story, the professor doesn't even look up when the interviewee enters the room. Instead, he opens his newspaper, blocking himself from view, and says, 'impress me'. The student who got the place was the one who took out his cigarette lighter and set fire to the newspaper.

It doesn't always work. Another story tells of the applicant who, taking a university entrance exam in late November, realised he had no idea how to answer a particular question and so wrote, 'God knows, I don't, Merry Christmas.' Six weeks later he received a letter from the college which read simply, 'God passes, you fail, Happy New Year.'

There are milder versions: tearing up your notes as a sign that you have changed your view or are speaking from the heart; rolling your sleeves up to show that you mean business; switching your phone off to show that you are giving your full attention. None of these gestures are grand, but in symbolic terms they can count for a lot.

Manners
It sounds old-fashioned but one way to maintain and often build presence is to have very good manners. This is different from etiquette (knowing which fork to use). Good manners includes listening, not cutting across people, offering coffees and biscuits to others before helping yourself, being considerate, thanking people when they have done something for you and, sometimes, standing up when someone comes into the room.

No one can find fault with good manners, though others will be quick to find fault if we are ill-mannered or rude. And if we have good manners we can feel equal (ie, not inferior) in at least one respect with anyone else.

Are you sitting comfortably? A story about presence

This story illustrates many of the points above about presence, why it matters and how to get it. It is from an account director at a small agency who was trying to win a piece of work with one of the most highly respected consultancies in the world.

First they told us to meet them in Sydney, then it was New York, then it was London and then it was Chicago. Each time the meeting got cancelled, sometimes before we'd bought the airline tickets and sometimes afterwards (we are a small agency and went bucket shop so there was no refund – but we certainly weren't going to ask for expenses). Finally, they arranged for a meeting in Milan.

Two of us took the very early flight (to avoid hotel costs) to be there for the meeting. We waited for it to start, which it did, an hour and a half late. There were six of them there, three of whom were partners. I asked what it was they thought they wanted. They each gave their view and then built on and changed each other's views. As the discussion continued it became increasingly clear that they didn't really know what they wanted.

I changed role and started to facilitate them to help them define the requirement. I listened intently to what each of them said and an hour later we reached a summary that everyone (meaning in practice the three partners as the other people barely spoke) was happy with.

'That's great,' I said, 'so are you going to use us?'

The lead partner looked at me in shock. 'This is a briefing meeting. The pitch is in New York in three weeks' time. Anyway, how on earth could we hire you – we don't even know what you've got to offer?' Then pre-empting what I might say, 'And we've got another meeting immediately after this.'

This was no good. We were going to spend the next few months flying round the world (or at least buying tickets to fly round the world) at the beck and call of these unfocused partners just to earn the right to pitch for a piece of work we would end up having at best a 20% chance of winning. They may be big but it didn't mean that they shouldn't respect our time too.

'What are you doing this evening?' I asked.

They looked perplexed. Each looked at the other for an idea on how to respond to this unexpected question. Finally the most senior of the partners said, 'We're having dinner here.'

'And before that?'

'Why?' she asked.

'I tell you what I'll do,' I replied. 'If you come back here at six o'clock we'll pitch to you on how we can help you with the requirement that you've just agreed. I don't mind whether you give us the work or not. But I do have one condition: you let us know definitively whether or not you want to use us or not within twenty-four hours.'

There was silence. Once again the group looked at each other in search of a lead on how to reply to this unusual request. The senior partner took control. 'That's an interesting idea. Would you like to leave us for a moment while we discuss it?'

Half an hour later we were summoned back and told they would return to the room at 6pm to hear our pitch.

Now what to do? It had become increasingly clear that while our ideas would help influence their decision the real issue was whether we could advise them as equals. In the battle for presence we had, at best, a score draw. If we were going to win the work, we had to do better.

My colleague and I looked around the meeting room in a hotel in the outskirts of Milan (it could have been anywhere) and knew that if they came back and sat in the same seats they had been in this morning they would assume all the same attitudes that we had already witnessed. We didn't want that. The whole experience had to be as unexpected as possible.

The first thing we did was remove the furniture. All of it. The next thing we did was handwrite our ideas on large sheets of paper with multi-coloured pens. This up-to-the-minute, Masters of the Universe consultancy had certainly never been pitched to with anything so low-tech in their working lives.

At six o'clock there was a knock at the door. My colleague opened it and welcomed them, like a host at the front door. When they walked in they were slightly dazed to see the room looking so different.

'Do sit down if you like,' I offered. They looked around for chairs. 'The floor's fine,' I added as if there was nothing unusual about it. The senior partner decided, perhaps because there was no alternative, that this was rather fun and sat on the floor. Everyone else immediately followed and tried to look happy about it.

Standing above them my colleague and I talked them through our story. At every moment, even the questions at the end, they were looking up to us. The last time they had been in this position they were at school and the person standing up was their teacher.

Twenty-four hours later I received a phone call. No pitch, no New York: we had won the work.

Give your mind a workout

I SPY Exercise 1

The above story shows many of the different techniques used to gain presence. Read it again and see how many you can spot used by (a) the consultancy and (b) the account director of the small agency.

Exercise 2

Next time you are in a restaurant waiting for someone, look around for a table with a group, ideally a selection of friends or a collection of business people.

You probably won't be able to hear what they are saying (best if you can't). See if you can spot the relative levels of presence amongst the group. Try to identify the specific behaviours behind your assumption that one person has more or less presence than the others, and the behaviours of the other people in response to them.

Which behaviours do you tend to show in a similar situation?

I TRY Exercise 1

A technique used by actors can help us increase our presence in everyday situations.

In a moment, close your eyes and think about your personal space. Personal space is the area around us that we consider our own, and if someone comes into it we feel that they have 'got too close'.

Then imagine that your body space is double what it is. And then double it again. And then imagine your body space fills the whole room. And then the whole building, and maybe even the whole street.

Open your eyes and hold that thought. The way you move and behave will suggest presence. And when people start reacting as if you have presence your confidence will grow which will help make your presence self-sustaining.

Exercise 2
Next time you are about to go into a situation where you want greater presence, 'endow' the other person/people with the thoughts and feelings that you would like them to have.

Maintain those thoughts (or assumptions) for as long as possible during the encounter, ideally until it is over.

Did the experience feel a little better?

This technique is unlikely to make a dramatic difference the first time but keep practising and it may make all the difference. Although best of all is when you don't even consider what they may be thinking.

Tough conversations

We've been in conversations where we wish the ground would swallow us up. This section examines three different kinds and suggests ways to make each of them if not exactly enjoyable then a whole load smoother.

First, arguments. It's all too easy for these to go toxic. A few poorly chosen words, a simple misunderstanding, and suddenly all hell breaks loose. When Duran Duran sang the unlikely lyric 'You're about as easy as a nuclear war' they may well have been thinking of the kind of explosion that can occur when we say the wrong thing. But it's also very possible for these conversations to go very right. In Conflict detox, we explore the ten main toxins that turn a disagreement nasty, how to avoid them and what the antidote is when they start to poison a relationship.

Next, what we think of each other. From putting the top back on the toothpaste to making them better at their job (or a better lover), there are loads of ways we'd like to change people. But even if we told them what we thought they should do differently, it doesn't mean that they'd follow our advice. My honest opinion, shows how we can give our views so that other people are more likely to accept them, change for the better and put the top back on the toothpaste.

Finally, Bad news. This chapter uncovers techniques that make sharing unpleasant truths both easier and more palatable and goes a long way to protecting the life of the messenger. A kind of psychological flak jacket.

(J) Conflict detox

'It was the end of a wonderful evening,' recalls Chris. 'I'd cooked my girl-friend's favourite meal to celebrate our second anniversary. As I was clearing up I made some joke about the washing up, about how Anji could leave it and for once I wouldn't mind, and before I knew it we were having this full-scale row. The funny thing was that after half an hour of shouting at each other, neither of us could remember what the argument was about in the first place.'

The time comes in all relationships when we disagree. And while some disputes are resolved amicably, we've all been in situations like Chris and Anji's where an off-the-cuff comment ends up spiralling out of control. The danger is that these non-conflicts can end up having very real effects: the cooling of relations, the building up of misunderstandings, the potential for grave long-term consequences.

The strength and sustainability of relationships, be they marriages or friendships, boss to colleague or parent to child, depend on how we cope when we get into conflict.

The skill lies in spotting the early warning signals and knowing what to do to prevent a disagreement going toxic.

We have a choice

The most important thing to remember when we get into disagreement is that we have a choice, in fact usually a whole range of choices. This is easy to forget in the heat of the moment. It seems like there is only one way to react and we usually go head first into it – 'But I never said that.' The trouble is that the 'one way' quite often raises the temperature and makes the situation much worse.

So, if we want to keep the storm in the teacup, we need to be able to spot what makes a point of view turn into toxic conflict. Below are ten ways in which we, to borrow the title of Toby Young's bestselling book, can lose friends and alienate people. And, with each one, that all-important anti-dote: how to conflict detox.

1 The caustic opener

'What's up with you?'
'So, what are you actually saying?'
'What on earth gives you that idea?'
'Don't you know me better?'
'Are you going out of your way to be unhelpful?'
'Are you trying to be ridiculous?'
'Are you trying to upset me?'

When you've stuck the knife in, a caustic opener is the linguistic equivalent of twisting it. It is an unnecessary phrase or comment whose sole impact is to raise the temperature. They are 'openers' in that they can initiate the conflict, but they are also openers too like can openers, the can being filled with worms.

Caustic openers can be questions, as above, and they can be statements too. The statement itself might be perfectly innocuous, but the way it is said leaves no doubt as to the ulterior meaning.

'The car hasn't got any petrol in it.'
'It's six p.m. and I still can't see the report.'
'I thought we came here to enjoy ourselves.'
'I'm trying to help.'

Not all caustic openers are so succinct. Another classic technique is known as the 'splurge'. Here, rational argument is crossed with an echo of teenage tantrum, with perhaps the 'martyr card' thrown in for good measure.

'Fine. You want to spend Sunday relaxing in the garden? Splendid. That's right. Great idea. I'll just make sure that the children are with their friends, the laundry for next week is done, the food has all been bought, the lawn's been mown, the car washed, the appointment with the plumber booked and, while I'm at it, shall I phone your mother too?'

How to detox

However tempted you are to reach for a pithy one-liner, or respond to one, the best rule here is simple: avoid them. The sarcasm or innuendo may make you feel better briefly but there is an inevitable downside, setting off a whole set of triggers in the other person (or people) that will make you feel a lot worse in a few moments' time.

Instead, stick to the facts and address the issues you have directly.

2 Mind-reading

Sarah and Marco come out of a meeting with their boss in which he found a series of errors and omissions in their presentation and sent them back to do more work on it.

SARAH: What were we thinking? We should have asked someone to go over it with a fine-tooth comb or postponed the meeting for another week.

MARCO: Hey, don't go blaming me. You were just as keen to get the meeting out of the way as I was.

SARAH: Calm down, Marco. Who said I was blaming you? I'm just as much at fault. I thought we were in this together. Now let's get on with making these changes . . .

MARCO: Hang on: 'together' I thought you said. So let's discuss together whether we're going to make the changes rather than an executive decision . . .

Sarah's exasperation has led to a chain of reactions that is making it less likely that the two of them will ever get their report in a fit state.

What has happened is that Marco and Sarah have each made assumptions from what the other has said. Marco is assuming that when Sarah says 'we' she means 'Marco' as he was the one who suggested getting the meeting in the diary early and dismissed her suggestion that they could postpone. Sarah hadn't thought this at all but when Marco reacts as he does she thinks he is in danger of giving up on the project and decides to focus them both on doing something to improve the situation. Marco reads this as Sarah thinking 'I'd better take control from now on as you messed this up' and so responds as he does.

In both cases their assumptions about each other's beliefs have caused the conflict to go toxic.

How to detox

Spot when you are making an assumption (usually when the facts aren't there to support your belief) and then check with the other person.

'When you say "we" do you actually mean me?'
'Of course not, Marco. We went into this together. We made all the decisions together and I value this relationship very highly. I said "we" because I meant "we".'

3 Everywhere, for ever

'Technology is always a disaster.'
'I've never had to do something so impossible in so little time.'
'I'll never be able to cook.'

When things go wrong our frustration and disappointment can lead us to believe in our own anti-Midas touch. One unfortunate incident (overcooking the fish) can apply to everything, for all time (I can't cook). As a conflict toxin this one isn't too serious by itself (though it might do unfortunate things to our stress levels and our confidence, not to mention leaving us hungry). It can, however, act as a trigger, which leads others to respond negatively.

Vicky's computer freezes when she is in the middle of writing something that she hasn't saved.

VICKY: I can't believe I've lost all that work. Computers are useless: I'd have been better writing the report by hand.

MARTIN: They're not *all* useless, are they? If it wasn't for computers, life wouldn't be half as simple.

VICKY: But they never work for me, always against me. It's like I've got some sort of computer curse.

MARTIN: Nonsense. All you need is a little patience.

VICKY: Why are you always attacking me?

MARTIN: I'm not attacking you. I am just trying to point out a few simple facts.

The conflict started with a fairly innocuous 'Everywhere, for ever' but led into a more serious conflict about identity where the 'Everywhere, for ever' is repeated and then combined with 'That's you all over' and 'The blame game' (see next page). That's when it gets uncomfortable.

The conflict sequence is easier to understand when we know what each of the characters is thinking.

VICKY: I can't believe I've lost all that work. Computers are useless: I'd have been better writing the report by hand.
This is really annoying; I've wasted a whole morning's work; I want sympathy.

MARTIN: They're not *all* useless, are they? If it wasn't for computers, life wouldn't be half as simple.
Vicky's over-reacting; she'll stress herself out if she carries on like this. I'll help her to get things back in proportion.

VICKY: But they never work for me, always against me. It's like I've got some sort of computer curse.
Martin doesn't seem to care; let me try again.

MARTIN: Nonsense. All you need is a little patience.
She really is over-reacting. If she carries on with these gloomy fantasies she'll end up believing them.

VICKY: Why are you always attacking me?
He is mean and heartless; when I most need a little TLC he goes in for the kill.

MARTIN: I'm not attacking you. I am just trying to point out a few simple facts.
I didn't ask to get involved; I just try to help and this is the thanks.

How to detox

The best way of dealing with negative events is to consider them as one-offs and temporary (for more on this see the section on attentive optimism in Lucky you). So if the laptop crashes, think this is annoying but I've dealt with worse. If the fish is overcooked, think this may be challenging (to get it onto the plate in one piece), but the dinner party is recoverable.

Keep it specific and if you want sympathy make it clear. 'You won't believe it, I've just lost a whole morning's work.'

Equally, if someone does an 'Everywhere, for ever' on you, don't take it too literally. In moments of high stress and conflict people rarely mean what they say (of which, more later).

4 That's you all over

'Look, the washing up is just left in the sink. That's typical of you – you don't care what state we live in.'
'Eating another piece of cake? No wonder you're such a fat slob.'
'Why can't we just relax and enjoy ourselves? You're such a worrier. It doesn't do any good, you know.'

If the buzzwords in 'Everywhere, for ever' are 'never' and 'always', then in this fourth category of toxin the key word is shorter and far more personal: you. Here we take a specific instance and extrapolate it to attack someone's character. It may be about their universal view or it may be about the type of person they are. It is often combined with an 'Everywhere, for ever' as in 'You never listen to anything I say', 'You are a hopeless map-reader', 'You always think you're right about everything'.

Like many of the other conflict toxins, it's designed to get a reaction, no matter what that reaction is. And unsurprisingly the reaction isn't a very helpful one.

'I wish we hadn't agreed to go out tonight.'
'It was your idea. Why are you always complaining?'
'I'm not always complaining. I just said that I'd rather have a quiet night at home with you, especially if you weren't so grumpy.'
'There's nothing grumpy about me.'

How to detox
Stick to specifics.

Instead of 'You're lazy' try 'I thought you said you would take out the rubbish this morning but it's still there', or replace 'You don't care about anyone but yourself' with 'It's Flo's birthday tomorrow and you haven't bought her a present'.

And when someone does 'That's you all over' on you, don't get taken in. They probably don't mean it and if you're unsure ask them. 'Do you really think I'm useless around the house or is it just my skills with shelves that aren't up to much?' Say it in the right tone and you will usually get a smile, a clarification, and it will feel like you're both on the same team again.

5 The blame game

'You're a hopeless map-reader' or *'The directions are pretty useless'*?
'What have you been doing to the CDs?' or *'What a shame, that CD's scratched'*?
'You've made me late' or *'I should have started preparing earlier'*?

When things go wrong it's very tempting to blame the other person. Tempting but unhelpful. It may be their fault or, more often, a bit their fault and a bit something or someone else's fault too. And, maybe, they had nothing to do with it.

How to detox
Whatever our views on where the blame should lie, it usually pays to be generous.

Blaming inanimate objects is a good policy – they can't argue back (though, if you kick them, they can hurt your foot). Failing that, try abstract bodies of people (academics? traffic wardens? Unless, of course, you are an academic or a traffic warden) or institutions (local government?). Alternatively, take the responsibility on the chin. Who knows: the other person may feel guilty and own up to their share of the blame.

6 Exaggerate? Me?

'This is a catastrophe!'
'This is the worst thing that anyone has done in this bank since it was founded in 1783!'
'I'll never be able to show my face in the neighbourhood again. We'll have to move.'

Exaggerating and over-reacting fuels any conflict by unnecessarily raising the stakes: it's the old saying about making a drama out of a crisis. Not only does it have a negative effect on an argument, but it has the potential to really irritate other people (no exaggeration, honest).

Just as dangerous as the exaggeration is the dismissal, when we minimise the importance of something. A final demand for a bill tossed into the rubbish bin with, 'So what? Let them come round here if they want it that bad', or reacting to the loss of a major client with, 'It's only one client and it's not as if they knew what they wanted in the first place', can be just as inflammatory.

There are three areas where we tend to exaggerate when we're in the middle of an argument and where this makes the situation only worse.

A We exaggerate the causes
The reason why something happened may or may not be relevant to the discussion but exaggerating is likely to bring it centre stage.

'No one could be expected to perform at their best after being kept awake half the night by some million-decibel car alarm.'

B We exaggerate the consequences
As with some of the examples earlier, it is easy to make more of the consequences in the hope that it means that our view will be treated more seriously. It often has the opposite effect.

'If you don't stop pulling a face, the wind will change and it will stay that way for ever.' (To which the tempting retort is, 'Well, you can't say you weren't warned.' A highly caustic opener.)

C We exaggerate the conditions for resolution
This is where we put extreme conditions on what we need from the other person to resolve the conflict.

'The only way I'll ever marry you is if you win the lottery, grow your hair back and change your name to Hugh Grant.'

How to detox
Resist the temptation. Focus on the outcome that you want from the conflict (eg, a resolution) rather than your immediate need (eg, to be heard) or what's really upsetting you (eg, they aren't taking me seriously). When we stick with the facts and a reasonable assessment then our chances of resolving a conflict amicably are much greater.

7 You say potato

'We're running late for the party, how rude is that?'
'We're going to be late arriving at the party, as any in-the-know person would . . .'

There is no disagreement on points of substance but there is the potential for a full-scale row simply because each of the players looks at the world through a different lens and so uses a different type of language. Neither is right or wrong, just different.

How to detox

There are many ways in which we choose to look at the world. Some are explained in Impact and others in Connect. The way to prevent this toxin from gaining influence is to spot how someone is presenting their view and try to understand the issue from their perspective.

Conflict toxin

8 Yesterday's hangover

I am SO angry. I have just wasted twenty minutes. After pressing endless buttons and listening to an interminable series of recorded voices, I still can't get to speak to a human being in the insurance claims department.

Like the cartoon character with the cloud over their head that follows them wherever they go, we sometimes take our bad moods with us, wherever we go.

I walk into the meeting and I'm trying to concentrate but the fury and frustration I feel isn't far below the surface.
'So whose idea was this?' Naomi asks, holding up my report.
'Mine. Why? What's wrong with it?' I bark back. Here I am assuming that Naomi is critical not because of what she said or how she said it but because I am still furious and have decided that the world is conspiring against me.
'Take it easy,' Naomi replies, 'or am I supposed to walk on egg shells around here?' Naomi had an argument with her husband, Simon, as she was rushing out of the door and she is still smarting from his over-reaction, as she sees it. My outburst confirms to her that all men are hyper-sensitive.
'Well, a bit of sensitivity would be nice instead of holding up the sum total of my last six months' work as if it was dirty washing.'
'I only asked, in all innocence, whose this was. I'm sorry that I haven't been giving your work schedule my full attention. I have had one or two minor things to do myself . . .'

Any questions?

If there is any doubt that there might be a misunderstanding, then we should ask the other person to explain their views. If we are still unclear, then we can ask more questions to clarify. But not all questions are good questions. As a general principle, we should keep the questions open and neutral if we want to avoid escalating the situation.

This will help because the other person will tend to disclose their views, which will make it easier to find common ground and, because we have listened to them, they are now more likely to listen to us.

Open and neutral	Closed and neutral
Given the situation as you have described it, what do you think we should do next?	Do you think that it would be best to accept Nicky's offer?
Almost any answer could be given (except 'yes' or 'no') and it is difficult to guess what the questioner would like the response to be or what they think themselves	The question asks for an answer that is either 'yes' or 'no' – almost anything else would seem odd
Open and loaded	**Closed and loaded**
OK, tell me, what actually would make you happy?	Are you really saying that, after all that has happened so far, you back Mike's option?
Whilst almost any answer could be given (except 'yes' or 'no'), it is also clear what the questioner feels, ie, that the other person is being unreasonable or difficult	The question asks for a yes/no answer and it is clear what the questioner thinks, ie, that Mike's option should not be supported

If you want the other person to focus on the substance of the disagreement, then closed neutral questions can be more useful. To improve the reception it can help to 'hedge' them up front, ie, precede them with some slightly self-deprecating conditional statement.

'I am probably being a bit thick here, but are you in favour of . . . ?'

'Please correct me if I'm mistaken, but do the views of the . . . ?'

'I think I may be missing something. Can you give me a little more detail on why you think . . . ?'

It's not hard to see how this conversation could escalate. The conflict is, however, totally unnecessary and has occurred only because two people are carrying with them emotions from a different situation (though once in full swing, 'Caustic openers', 'That's you all over', and a whole range of other conflict toxins will keep the temperature up). In effect, we are behaving as if we are still suffering from yesterday's hangover.

How to detox
The first thing, as with all these toxins, is to recognise that it is happening. The next thing is to 'park' the old emotion – if you need to screw up a sheet of paper and hurl it into the bin then do so; much better than getting into a pointless argument. But if things boil over, then apologise and maybe even explain why: 'Naomi, I think I owe you an apology. I'd just had the most infuriating phone call before the meeting and took it out on you. I'm sorry. No egg shells needed, honest.'

9 What I mean, not what I say

'Wow, you look so much older than your photograph. Sorry, I mean sophisticated. Not that there's anything wrong with being over forty, of course. You're thirty-three? Ah . . .'

Conflict can be a little like awkward first dates – we often don't mean exactly what we say. Caught up in the momentum, what comes out of our mouth is what first comes to mind rather than what would do most to help the situation. The other person or people are likely to be doing the same. The conflict toxin kicks in when we take what they say literally and react accordingly.

How to detox
The antidote is twofold

1   Let it pass. Often we hear someone say something and we half know that they don't mean it. We can ignore it or not interpret it literally and it is usually best to do so

2   Ask. The best way of knowing what they really mean is to ask them, ideally using neutral, open questions that give them plenty of room to re-interpret what they have said. 'How do you think that happened?', 'What have you experienced that makes you describe Mike as "the most incompetent vet in Britain"?', 'Other than being "cold, heartless and uncaring", could there be any other explanations for Rachel's no-show?'

10 Irreconcilable differences

'I can't work with music on.'
'I need music in the background in order to work effectively.'

These views from two colleagues who share a studio sound like they are irreconcilable. It's certainly possible to imagine that this could turn into a fairly fierce disagreement.

But what if there is a solution? For example, perhaps it's words that distract the first person, but if the music were classical or chill tunes without lyrics they would be fine. Perhaps the second person just needs some background noise and having the window open with the sound of the traffic will be enough. Perhaps they could listen to the music through a pair of headphones.

A prime reason for disagreements to continue is that we focus on positions rather than interests. You want to go on holiday to Tuscany. I want to go to Ibiza. These are our positions, ie, what we say we want. On the surface it looks as if we are going to find it difficult to agree. However, when we delve a little deeper, your heart is set on going somewhere pretty with good food and I want to be able to relax on a beach all day. We could go to Sardinia, or Sicily, or any of a myriad other places that would meet both our needs. When we examine our interests the conflict is easy to resolve.

How to detox
To understand someone's interests (including our own) we need to ask why we have the position that we do. What is it about my position that really, really matters to me?

For example, I may want a pay rise for any of the following reasons:

- I want more money

- I feel I deserve it

- I want to be appreciated for what I have done

- Other people doing the same work are getting paid more

- I want my loyalty to be recognised

And no doubt many more. Some of these will be more important than others and some of these may have deeper interests behind them. The reason why I want more money may be to pay off a debt or have a smarter car.

You might be thinking that you can't meet my needs because there is a pay freeze in our company. However, if you know that my real interest is in the car perhaps you can organise for me to get a company car or the company to provide security so I can buy one on hire purchase.

Understanding motives, ie, why an individual is getting into conflict, is often the best initial step to resolving it. The position people take in conflict (ie, what they say they want) may be different from their interests (ie, why they want it). If we understand why someone disagrees and what their motives are we can begin to identify their interests and so resolve the issue. The challenge, then, is to look for points of similarity rather than points of difference.

Getting hooked

You are busy. I ask you to help me with something. You could snap back 'Can't you see I'm busy?' or you could pause, ask yourself what you think my motives are and, having decided that they are benign even if I am being a little thoughtless, reply, 'I am right in the middle of something at the moment, could it wait until later on this afternoon?'

Imagine I don't co-operate. 'Humpf,' I snort. 'Yes, I've got a lot on too, you know.' Your mood temperature is beginning to rise. Tempted though you are to say something along the lines of, 'Well then, why don't you just get on and do it and stop interrupting me?', you stop yourself from getting hooked by my (unconscious) game and respond in an even tone, 'What is it you want help with?'

You have chosen your words carefully. Not 'What do you want ME to help you with?', which could turn things unhelpfully personal, or 'What do you want help with NOW?', implying that I ask for your help too often or that I am putting an unnecessary time pressure on your help, but a neutral question seeking information.

'I need to change the light bulb and I was wondering if you could hold the chair while I stand on it?'

It will take you at most a couple of minutes, it will help me get on with my things, I will owe you a favour and I am unlikely to disturb you again in the near future. You agree. And by not letting yourself get hooked our relationship is as strong or stronger than it was before. In fact, by remaining calm when others might have reacted emotionally, you have probably gained stature and respect.

The most useful conflict toxins to spot are the ones that happen when the same person hooks us in the same way, again and again. My boss asks if I've briefed the team for the meeting with the head of department; 'But you never asked me to', 'Oh, I didn't realise I needed to ask', 'I have done all the things that you did ask me to do', 'Oh well, I suppose that's OK then'.

How to avoid getting hooked

1 Learn to spot the triggers, say, a comment with an implied meaning (a caustic opener, for example), a loaded question, an unusual reaction of surprise or irritation to something you've said. If you've been here before, be doubly cautious.

2 You may be in your rights to respond forcefully, but before you do, ask what is in your best interest? Invariably it pays not to get hooked.

3 What are the other person's motives? If they are good then allow them a little insensitivity; if you are unsure then ask open, neutral questions to find out more (and if their motives are undoubtedly thoroughly bad, then you might as well walk away).

4 Focus on the facts of the issue rather than the emotion that may lie behind them. So long as you stick with the substance, the game can't start.

5 Avoid interpreting what they say about the issue as what they may or may not think about you. Equally, make sure that you don't say anything which could be misinterpreted as declaring what you think about them.

Parents and their grown-up children can repeat patterns that started many years before: 'You're always interfering', 'When will you let me run my own life?', 'You're just like your father'.

If you always argue with your mother about clothes or with your best friend about who was the greatest footballer, and you'd rather not (some of these arguments we actually enjoy and are part of building intimacy), then look out for the hooks they are putting out and find ways to avoid taking the bait.

Real conflict

This chapter has focused on what gets us into unhelpful conflict and how to avoid the traps. There are, of course, also disagreements over substance rather than the way that something has been communicated. This conflict can be highly creative and lead to better solutions. The tension between Mick Jagger and Keith Richards, or Liam and Noel Gallagher, is what makes the Rolling Stones and Oasis such successful rock bands. Conflict detox is the way to keep such conflicts productive and helpful rather than allowing them to be sidetracked or hijacked.

Give your mind a workout

I SPY Rank the conflict toxins in the order of the ones you use most to the ones you use least.

Type of toxin	Ranking – my estimate	No. of times used this week
The caustic opener		
Mind-reading		
Everywhere, for ever		
That's you all over		
The blame game		
Exaggerate? Me?		
You say potato		
Yesterday's hangover		
What I mean, not what I say		
Irreconcilable differences		

Spend a few days counting how many times you use (or are about to use) each one and see how close your initial estimate was. Have a look at the top three that you actually use and decide what you could do to detox with each of them.

I TRY Decide on a particular person with whom you tend to have unhelpfully emotional disagreements and you're not quite sure why.

Next time you are talking with them, listen out for the toxins they use (often unknowingly) and try to react in almost any way other than the way that feels most natural, ie, what you would normally do.

If you tend to cut across their sentences, let them finish and pause before replying. If you tend to raise your voice, make a conscious effort to keep it at the same level. If you tend to make sweeping statements, use questions or stick to specifics. As soon as you are about to react in an automatic way, do something else.

Breaking the auto-responses is the first step to preventing those same old unhelpful arguments.

This will help. The next stage is to look out for the specific toxins that *you* use, and stop. Persevere and you will find that the rows become less frequent and the relationship deepens.

(K) My honest opinion

Always turning up late for everything. Leaving the used tea bag on the side. Trying out all the different mobile phone ringtones on a packed train. Changing the way other people behave may be immensely desirable but it is also notoriously difficult. We want to give them our honest opinion but, for all sorts of reasons, we don't.

'Are you saying I smell? Who do you think you are? And while we're on the subject, I've got a thing or two about your personal habits that I've been meaning to tell you as well.' Quite often, telling people what they could do to improve their lives backfires: rather than improving theirs, they make ours more difficult.

This is a shame. The consequences of this apathy are far wider reaching than the brief decision to 'let it drop this time' suggests. When relationships break down, people get passed over for promotion, friends drift apart and teams turn in on themselves, the root cause is often something relatively insignificant that could have been dealt with ages ago but, instead, has been left to fester.

Fortunately, there is a technique that, though not guaranteed, has a very impressive hit rate when it comes to changing the way people behave. It is a technique that has been around since the beginning of time, one that we all use occasionally, usually not that effectively, and something that everyone can master. Not only that, it is an option with an abundance of scientific research to support its potency. The technique is praise.

Praise indeed

Should you be praised for the amount of praise you give out? Look at the questions below and consider your answers to them.

1   When was the last time you congratulated someone for something they had done well?
    In the last hour; today; yesterday; in the last week; more than a week ago

2   In a normal day how often do you praise someone (not necessarily the same person) for something they have done?
    Once at best; 2–3 times; 5–10 times; 10–20 times; more than 20 times a day

3   When you last praised someone did you
    Say 'well done' and leave it at that; tell them what they did that was good; outline the impact of what they did

4   Thinking about someone close to you (colleague, partner, etc), for every ten times you praise them, how often do you criticise them?
    Never; once; 5 times; 10 times; 20 times; 50 times; 100 or more times?

There are no definitive right answers to the amount of praise we should give, but one simple wrong one: not enough. If any of your answers have given you pause for thought then, like most of us, you could be in need of a bit of praise appraisal.

Why didn't you say anything?

In one of The Mind Gym workouts on Great feedback, a vice president of an investment bank (let's call her Val) admitted that she never told people when they had done something well. Her reason? 'That is what they're paid for.' If they were doing a satisfactory job, Val's argument went, it seemed unnecessary to tell them so.

Perhaps the vice in Val's job title referred to her bad habit of not praising. Because the view from the people who worked for her was likely to be quite different. They don't know when they've done a good job as no one tells them. In search of approval, they keep trying new approaches, often jettisoning successful ones for others that have less chance of working.

The number one reason why we don't praise people is that if someone is doing something well, we assume they already know and so there is no point in telling them.

A second significant reason why we don't praise people is that we somehow imagine it undermines us. Val, for example, thought that her team might think less of her if she congratulated them. It would suggest, she felt, that she had lower standards and was easily impressed. In fact, many highly respected people are very generous with their praise, largely because they don't feel threatened by the people around them. Praising is a sign of confidence not weakness.

The third significant reason why we don't praise people is perhaps the most British: it can be embarrassing. Part of us is worried that we might make the person praised feel embarrassed. And if they get embarrassed, then so do we. Certainly, praising people can be awkward if we do it badly: for example, it's best not to shout 'You were a *tiger* last night' as your partner squeezes into a crowded train. What we really need to do is learn how to give praise effectively.

The rest of this chapter is devoted to this, as well as some techniques for using praise's alter ego, wise counsel (also known as constructive criticism) – all so we are less likely to offend and more likely to make a helpful difference.

Raising the praising

Time to praise
Choosing the right moment to praise someone makes a significant difference to the impact we have. Ideal times to give praise are

- **At the time or soon after**
  Broadly, for praise on minor matters we should give it straight away, otherwise it will look like a bigger deal than it is (*thanks so much for making me that delicious cup of tea a week last Thursday*). For more significant matters, the praise will tend to have more weight if we choose a moment a few hours or days later: this suggests that we have thought about what they have done and aren't just giving an automatic response.

- **When you aren't asking them for something**
  If you are expecting something in return then the praise is greatly devalued and may even have a negative effect.

The power of praise

Here are four reasons why we should praise more people, more often.

It works: There is a strong correlation between telling people that they have done something well and them repeating that behaviour. There is nothing else that we can do that has such a predictable impact on how someone else will behave in future. And not only that, but telling them what not to do can have all sorts of unpredictable consequences. So if you want to change something about someone, this is by far the best way of starting out.

Absence makes the heart grow weaker: Some people have sufficient confidence to know when they've done something good without anyone telling them. The rest of us need some guidance on how well, or badly, we are performing: otherwise we become confused about what we should and shouldn't be doing. While in some things, like sport, our performance can be easily measured, in real life – being a parent or a good friend – it's more difficult to assess. Praise is a powerful way of setting solid co-ordinates about how we are doing.

Love is in the air: An environment where people give each other appropriate and authentic praise is usually a good one to live and work in. People tend to feel warmly towards each other and when things go wrong they are more likely to help out than to criticise.

Give and you shall receive: One of the other advantages of giving praise is that you are more likely to be liked – we tend to think well towards people who are positive about others and even more so if they appreciate our strengths.

And praise is infectious. If you start giving it you are likely to find that other people start congratulating too, and some of their positive comments are likely to be directed to you. What goes around tends, with praise, to come around.

- **When you have their attention**

  A passing remark that they haven't heard or can pretend to ignore is a waste (when they are watching their favourite TV programme, for example, or leaving the house in a hurry).

- **When they are alone**

  This isn't essential but it does reduce the chance that they (and you) will be embarrassed. Equally, if the praise will increase with the approval of others then a more public forum, be it Sunday lunch or a team get-together, might be better. (*You might not have noticed her efforts, but Samira is our unsung hero . . .*)

5-star praise

There are times when a quick 'nicely done' is sufficient. However, if we want to praise someone so that the impact lasts and there is a good chance of changing the way the other person does things in future, then we would do well to follow the 5-star model.

Give yourself one star for each of the following that you include.

- **Context**

  If the feedback isn't given immediately then it will help the other person if we let them know up front what we are talking about. 'That supper we had in your kitchen, when was it? Last Thursday, yes, that's the one.'

- **Explain specifically what went well**

  The more specific the praise, the more effective it is. By just saying, 'Thanks for the report – it was great', we are not giving the other person anything they can use and apply in future. Was the report great because it was long, had pictures, started with a succinct summary, included questions for the reader to answer, or what?

  The best praise focuses on specifics. Again there is a balance to be struck. 'Great food', could be too little, but 'I particularly liked the infusion of rosemary that seeped through the succulent lamb like the soft scent at early dusk in the savannah of my adolescence' is clearly over the top. Unless you're the food critic for *Gourmet*, perhaps.

- **Describe the impact it had**

  This is the part that motivates. The good consequences that came as a result are a big incentive to repeat this behaviour, and try others like it. Again, a balance needs to be struck. Overstating the impact ('Your supper saved my life') will sound false; omit it altogether and the praise will have significantly less impact.

- **Reinforce their identity**

  Or what it tells you about them as a person. This is the part that makes the other person feel really good: 'I've got to say, not only was the lamb delicious, but to get that many interesting people together and make sure they all got on, that's the sign of someone who really knows how to make a Sunday lunch exceptional.'

- **Congratulate**

  This is usually the beginning, middle and end of praising. It has a role but if it's all we do, we get only one star.

5-star praise	Example	Situation
Context	The other day when I had so much on that I didn't know what to do	
Specifics	You were great both at helping me think straight about what mattered and for checking the prices for me on the web	
Impact	As a result, I managed to get everything finished by the deadline	
Identity	That you helped me out even though you had lots on yourself is the sign of a really good friend	
Congratulations	Many thanks, I really appreciate it	

Think up a couple of situations where you might praise someone, and think about how to give them the full 5-star praise effect. Jot down the suggestions: does the praise seem real? If it feels false, think about another way of making the points.

What if there is nothing to praise?

If you can't find anything to praise then of course it's possible that there really isn't anything the other person is doing well. But far more likely is that you simply aren't looking hard enough.

If someone is usually late then praise them on the one occasion that they arrive on time, or when they deliver something when they said they would, or even, possibly, when they are less late than usual. And don't forget to mention the beneficial impact that this punctuality has.

Counsel

If we want to change someone's behaviour for the better then praise is more likely to work than criticism. Equally, there are some situations where we need to point out what is not working well and what we want them to change. For this, we turn to praise's constructively critical alter ego: counsel.

'I think I've done enough on this project and I should move on to something new.'
'You know, I wonder if you've got staying power.'
'Of course I've got staying power, what are you saying?'
'Only that you've been on this project for less than a month. If you can't stick with a client you'll find it much harder to build the relationships and revenue needed to get promoted.'
'Yes, I know that. Obviously.'

The above example is a high-risk approach to constructive criticism. On this occasion it did work (the restless person did stay on the project, which they then grew and they were, indeed, promoted as a result). It succeeded only because the person whose staying power was in question had a strong relationship with and respect for the person giving the counsel. If the counsellor's relationship was less strong, then they may have had a response such as 'I have staying power when I think the project is worthwhile and this one sucks', which would, of course, have sent things spinning off in very much the wrong direction.

Giving good counsel can greatly help by allowing you to share your concerns and the other person to do something about them but it can also backfire with disastrous consequences. The challenge is to do it effectively. Here is how.

Start in the right frame of mind

It is painful receiving criticism. The only way to sweeten the pill is if we believe that the person giving it has our best interests at heart. And so, if we want to prove a point, put the other person firmly in their place, show how patient we have been so far, or to criticise for any reason other than wanting to help the other person improve, the chances are the conversation will turn pear-shaped. Don't think they won't notice our motives, because they will: if we're lucky, they'll retire hurt; if we're unlucky, they'll bite back.

So, before we offer unsolicited advice, we must make sure we know that we are doing it first and foremost to help the other person. There may be a knock-on benefit for us too but, for the duration of the conversation, any thoughts of personal gain must go firmly on the back burner.

5-star counsel
Like the 5-star praise approach, the 5-star counsel system offers the best way to offer help and support and keep the risk of messing up to a minimum.

- **Context**
  The first thing to do is to set up the scenario we want to talk about. If we are confident the other person has a good idea what we are about to say, we may choose to start with a question: 'What do you think the other guests thought of you at last night's supper?' It is better if we can get them to come up with the issue as it will make the conversation feel more like collaboration than an attack.

  The risk, of course, is that rather than replying 'You're right, I think I got a bit tipsy and may have overstepped the mark', they say 'They loved me; I was tremendously funny, the life and soul of the party.' If we think the latter response is more likely it's better to give the context up front: 'I want to talk about what happened last night at supper.'

- **Specifically and objectively state what went wrong**
  Giving someone unsolicited advice on what they need to do differently means challenging their identity, ie, how they see themselves. This is something we all protect vigorously. Telling me I missed the turning is specific and not up for argument: either I missed the turning or I didn't. Telling me I'm a bad driver, however, is general and liable to provoke a confrontational response. The second star is for being specific about what happened on this occasion.

  The more specific and objective we make our argument the better. Saying 'When Siobhan told us about her trip to Egypt, you tapped your spoon repeatedly against your glass, saying, "I've got a *far* more interesting story to tell"' is more likely to get you listened to than, 'You rudely cut across Siobhan and ruined her story by shouting and banging on your glass like a crazed chipmunk.'

- **The impact and the significance**
  For our counsel to have the right effect, we also need to be clear about the impact this behaviour had. For example, one person might consider turning up ten minutes late as being pretty much 'on time'. It's only when the impact this might have at work is explained (irritating

clients, looking lazy in front of the boss) that the point about lateness may be appreciated and treated more seriously in the future.

'The danger is that it will put people off inviting us over for dinner, and then you'll be stuck with me every night.'

- **Reinforce their identity**
  However delicately the counsel is expressed, it can feel like a personal attack. So it is important to make sure we encourage them to think positively about themselves and so bolster their identity. 'You are a great host', 'You are loved by your friends', 'You do tell the best stories of anyone I know', 'You are usually so entertaining at dinner'.

5-star counsel	Example	Situation
Context	So you want to move off this project?	
Specifics	You've been on five different projects in the last four months and you've been on this one for only a few weeks	
Impact	Do you realise that if you don't stick with a client you will find it much harder to build the relationships and revenue needed to get promoted? Also the clients don't like a constantly changing team	
Identity	You are highly rated by the clients and they will be delighted if you do decide to stay on the project	
Solutions	What do you think we should do? What would make you want to stay on this team?	

Fill the above table with examples of the five steps of counsel to an everyday situation. Maybe try some of the same ones as in the 'praise' table on p. 171, to compare the differences between the two approaches.

- **Seek solutions together**
  This is the time to discuss what to do to recover the situation and reduce

the chances of it happening again or improve it in future. For example, 'It only goes wrong when you have been drinking on an empty stomach and we did have to wait ages for the food to arrive. What if you didn't drink anything until the meal begins, or if you decided to drive?'

If we can get them to come up with the solutions themselves then there is more chance that they will follow up and do what we have agreed, but a few suggestions may ease the path.

If the conversation has gone well, then it may be worth praising them for listening and having a good discussion. If we want them to change then, for sure, we want them to feel good about it.

Click not clunk

If we focus on following the 5-star counsel sequence in this order there is a risk that we will come across as quite clunky and so not all that sincere. It is better, therefore, to see these as a list to cover as part of a conversation. This will help reduce the 'clunk'.

To make the counsel 'click' we need to make it feel like we are both on the same side. This requires empathy. If the person to whom we are giving counsel feels that we empathise with their situation then they are much more likely to listen and agree with everything else we have to say.

'I completely see why you want to keep moving projects.'
'I know how Siobhan can bang on and how tempting it is to interrupt her.'
'My mother drives me up the wall as well.'

Sleight of mind: implicit praise and counsel

Giving praise or counsel explicitly greatly reduces the chances of a misunderstanding. Sometimes, however, it can feel like we're making too big a deal of the situation. We want to say something but we want to be subtle. On these occasions we can share our views implicitly. The predictability of this approach is less certain and the risk of it going wrong is much higher, but when a gentle nudge is all that is needed, a more low-key technique, deftly applied, can have the right effect. Here are four ways to give implicit praise and counsel.

What's the story?

Nursery rhymes are a traditional way of telling a story to children to warn them about what to avoid or how not to behave. Hilaire Belloc's *Cautionary Tales* introduces a collection of characters each of whom gives us counsel – Matilda who told lies and ended up getting burnt to death; Jim, who ran away from his nurse and was eaten by a lion; and George, who played with a 'dangerous toy' and suffered 'a catastrophe of considerable dimensions'. Aesop's Fables are designed to do much the same for adults.

Stories are a very underused communication tool and a singularly powerful way of making a truth acceptable without having to address it straight on: 'I remember when a new recruit arrived, fresh from college, all full of enthusiasm and determination to make a good impression and get promoted fast; anyway, this guy, Bill, found it really hard when he didn't move up straight away. But you know what, he stuck at it, and ended up getting a far more interesting job which came up later . . .'

The third way

Third-party endorsement is a fine way of praising someone with less risk of embarrassment for them or you: 'Anne told me that she's really impressed with how your timekeeping has improved.' Best of all, everyone's a winner: it makes it easier for the person in question to accept the comment, Anne comes out well and, as the bearer of good tidings, we're likely to come out smelling more fragrant too.

Aesop's fable: the sun and the wind

Here is a story that implicitly promotes the power of praise over criticism in persuading.

The sun and the wind are having a competition to see who can make someone take their coat off. The wind goes first, and blows as hard as it can, lashing a gale around the man, using all its power to blow the coat away. But the harder the wind blows, the tighter the man wraps his coat around himself. Eventually, it's the sun's turn. Rather than turn the weather nasty, it creates a beautiful day. In fact, so beautiful and warm is the weather that the man gets too hot and takes his coat off. Wind nil, sun one.

Play the joker

'That's great, I can walk to the kerb from here.'

Woody Allen's admonishment of Annie Hall's parking abilities in his classic comedy of the same name is a great example of the power of humour. Where the relationship is well established and the motives are understood and unquestioned, humour can be a gentle way of letting people know what we think. It makes light of things and so can deflect from an earnest conversation. In the above example, Annie Hall's response is to laugh and agree that her parking could improve. Would her reaction have been the same if Woody's comment had been 'Unbelievable! Your parking is so bad I can't imagine how you ever passed a test.'

Humour is the most high-risk of techniques for praise and, more frequently, counsel because it can go so horribly wrong. What was meant to be funny can sound to the person on the receiving end as deliberately mean or nasty.

'What are you saying? That my parking is terrible?'
'Nothing. I was only joking. Relax. You're a bit sensitive today.'
'That's rich coming from you. At least I see the kerb, unlike some people I could mention . . .'

In short, handle humour with care.

Body talk

The young kid stumbles into the saloon. Yul Brynner carries on playing cards. The young kid fires his gun. The bar goes silent and everyone looks up. Yul Brynner slowly puts his cards down and looks at the young lad. 'I want to ride with you. I am good enough to ride with you,' the lad slurs at Yul. Yul looks down again, picks up his cards and continues the game.

In this scene from *The Magnificent Seven*, Yul Brynner doesn't need to say anything to make his view clear. Simply by returning to his card game he is making his point: 'I don't think you are good enough to ride with us.' Similarly, we all use non-verbal communication to give counsel implicitly. The raised eyebrow, the silent response to a question and the shrug are all ways we can implicitly convey that we think the other person would be better off behaving differently.

Saying it without words

The danger with using non-verbal communication is both that it can be over-interpreted

(I could tell from her look that she really hates me) and it doesn't give the other person much to work on. The young kid knows Yul doesn't think he's good enough but doesn't know what he can do about it. That's fine in the Wild West but may not be what you want in your kitchen.

All in the mix

Sandwiches are bad for you
There is a technique commonly referred to as a feedback sandwich. What this means is giving praise ('You've done a great job with the project plan'), then counsel ('You have upset several people in the team who feel that you are not listening to them') and then more praise ('That email with the progress report was well written'). The idea is that by cushioning the blow, the counsel is more likely to be well received and acted upon.

In reality, however, if we use the feedback sandwich we will probably have the opposite effect. The praise is either devalued because the other person believes we are giving it only to dilute the counsel, or ignored, as all they hear is the criticism. In performance reviews at work, people will often nod away to the list of things they are doing well but only start taking notes when it comes to the things that they should improve on. If the praise and the counsel are given at different times each is more likely to resonate and be remembered.

Stamina over sprint
The challenge with praise (as with so many things) is keeping it up. If you give someone lots of praise and then suddenly stop, they are likely to infer that they aren't doing so well when in fact it may just be that you have forgotten or your attention has gone elsewhere. A little and regularly is better than a lot and then silence.

Comparisons
There is a story of a middle brother who felt throughout his childhood that his parents preferred his elder and younger brothers. The brothers and all the boy's friends assured him that he was being overly sensitive but he still felt he was the least loved. When an aunt died and left the boys some family heirlooms, the parents had to divide the objects up between the three of them. The middle brother, even though objectively he had just as fine and valuable pieces as the other two, shouted at his parents, 'You always preferred both of them to me', and burst into tears. The mother looked in shock to the father and then turned back to her son and said, 'Oh darling, has it really been that obvious?'

The mother's reaction shocks us (how could she? we gasp, whilst also per-haps fearing it is a trap we too could fall into). But it is also very pertinent to the challenge of getting the right mix of praise and counsel.

The middle brother had picked up that he was the least favourite despite his parents' efforts to hide this. A significant factor is likely to have been how and how often the parents praised their sons and how and when they criticised them. When there is a group of peers, be it your children or members of your team, treating them on equal terms is vital. It is not enough to give praise and counsel effectively to each one, you also need to be consistent across the group.

Hot and cold
As mentioned earlier, the number one condition for praise and counsel to have a positive impact is that we are doing it for the benefit of the other person rather than for ourselves. The more this is at the forefront of our minds, the greater our chances of being consistent and predictable in our praise, and when it comes to telling people what we think of them, pre-dictability is a very good thing.

There's many a macho manager who believes that by blowing hot and cold they are keeping their team on their toes. But when feedback is dependent on the mood of the person giving it, we stop trying to improve and focus instead on anticipating their reactions. What's more, we take what they say with a pinch of salt: 'He's only saying that because he's in a good mood.'

Different strokes
Different folks, as the saying goes, require different strokes. In order to get the right ratio of praise to counsel we need to understand the needs of the people we are talking with.

All of those who deliver The Mind Gym workouts quite rightly want recog-nition. Some require more praise before they feel ready to listen to insights that will help them deliver more effectively, whilst others are happy to have some praise but really want to focus on how they can get better, ie, have as much in-depth counsel as possible.

In research in a primary school (for children up to the age of 11) in the UK, the ratio of negative comments (don't do that, that's wrong, be quiet) to positive ones (very well done) was 19:1. This is not a good ratio for any-one. As a rough guide the lowest we should go is 1:1 and, in most cases, praise should be significantly more frequent than counsel.

I SPY Every day for the next week listen out for someone praising you or praising someone else, either in your life or on radio or TV (in which case, presumably, they will be praising someone else). On each occasion give them a ranking based on the 5-star approach to praise, ie, which of the elements they include. By the end of the week you will find it much easier to tell why some praise is more effective than others.

Repeat this exercise for counsel, allocating up to 5 stars each time you hear someone giving constructive criticism, based on the steps outlined earlier.

I TRY Praise
Every day commit to praising someone when you wouldn't normally have bothered. On the first day, 1-star praise is good enough but, each day, add an extra star to the praise that you give so that by the end of the week you have given someone 5-star praise.

In week two, give 4- or 5-star praise to someone every day.

By now, you should have got into the habit and it will become easier. Enjoy the buzz and watch how people repeat the great things that they are doing, getting better and better (as a result of your influence).

Counsel
Write down all the things you've wanted to say to people but have never managed. Commit to, at least once a week, telling someone what you want to say but doing so only when you think it will help them. Probably wise to start with things that aren't too tightly linked to their self-perception; it may be easier to get someone to put dishes inside the dishwasher rather than leave them on top than make a mean person generous.

Before you start to give your (unsolicited) counsel you may want to complete the table opposite.

Preparing

What do you want to
tell them?

How will they be better
off as a result?

When are you going to
tell them?

Where? Who else if anyone
will be around? Are you likely
to be disturbed?

The conversation

What are you going to say
to set the context for them?

What specifically went wrong?
How can you express this
objectively?

What were the implications?
How can you explain these
without appearing to put your
own slant on things?

What are some of the things
they could do (a) to recover
the situation and/or (b) to
prevent repeating the same
unhelpful behaviour?

What questions are you going
to ask to help them decide on
their own solutions?

If you feel unsure about this then find someone you can practise with.
Explain the situation and give it a go. Often when you say the words out
loud they seem quite different from writing them down. The person you
practise with can also respond in a variety of ways so you can prepare for
a range of possible reactions.

Ⓛ Bad news

When Rik Mayall, Adrian Edmondson and the rest of the Comic Strip came up with the idea of a spoof heavy metal band, they thought long and hard about what the worst possible name for a group could be. They eventually settled on Bad News, the joke being that bad news, of course, is the one thing that no one ever likes to hear.

Sharing bad news is something most of us dread doing and we tend either to do it badly, in a rush, or put it off, which only makes things worse.

But though giving someone bad news is unlikely to be easy, there are things we can do to soften the blow without pulling any punches. In this chapter, we will focus on when we want to share new information or decisions which we anticipate the other person will be unhappy about, and how to do so in a way which achieves the best possible outcome. At a minimum, we want the other person to believe that the news was delivered sensitively and effectively; ideally they will feel good about it and about the person who delivered it too.

The good news about bad news

'I'll do it tomorrow.'
'It's not that bad.'
'Do they need to know right now?'

A staple of the romantic comedy film – Julia Roberts in *The Runaway Bride*, Hugh Grant in *Four Weddings and A Funeral* – is the jilting at the altar scene, the dramatic last possible moment to end a relationship.

While we may not have gone this far, when it comes to giving bad news we are all guilty of stalling and putting off the dreaded moment until later.

Discovering how to share bad news well means we are more likely to get on with it and so avoid the consequences of inaction. Mastering how to share bad news can also improve our relationships. When we bring clarity to confusion or disclose bad news with sensitivity, our tact and understanding can be appreciated long after the impact of the news has disappeared. The people whom we love or admire most are often the ones who did the right thing (by us) when the chips were down.

Why bad news comes in threes

When delivering bad news, we need to consider three main components: the facts, the emotions caused as a result and, finally, how the other person sees themselves, which is called identity.

Different types of bad news will require different amounts from each area. Simply telling someone that their tea is cold only requires the facts (unless, of course, they're *really* thirsty) while explaining to someone that you want to leave them (and keep the house) will need a mix of facts, emotions and identity. As a general rule, the more significant the news, the more we need to tend to the emotional aspects and protecting the other person's identity.

Face the facts
There are many different types of fact to share and we need both to get them right and in the right order.

1 **The context**
   They won't know what the conversation is about unless we tell them. 'I want to talk with you about the safari you've been organising for the last few months.'

2 **The headline**
   This is the essence of the bad news. It is usually best to get it out of the way early on. 'The bad news is that I'm not, after all, going to be able to come.'

3 **More detail**
   Occasionally all the news is in the headline, although usually there is more that needs to be shared. 'It's not that I'll never be able to come on safari, just not this year.'

4 The reasons behind the headline

We tend to find it easier to accept difficult messages if we understand the reasons behind them. 'I have been checking my finances and they are a lot worse than I had realised. I simply can't afford to go on an expensive holiday at the moment.'

5 The process that led up to the headline

This helps explain both the bad news and why it is happening now. It can also show that this is not a snap decision that can easily be changed. 'After you told me about the plans, I was really excited and said I would come. Then I spoke with Angela who told me how much a safari is likely to cost and then I went on the web and looked into the prices for different safaris and . . .'

6 The consequence of the headline

The consequences may be obvious. If they aren't it can be useful to bring them to the surface. 'I appreciate that you need an extra person to cover the cost and that it is only six weeks until you plan to go.'

7 Alternative courses of action

Sometimes there is nothing we can do as a result of the news or it is so devastating that we don't want to even start thinking about possible courses of action. On other occasions, the best way to deal with the situation is to consider what the other things are that we could possibly do. 'If you did decide to switch the safari from Kenya to the Lake District, I might be able to come.'

Second: that emotion

Bad news can unleash a whole range of emotions – anger, sadness, disgust, self-pity, shock, relief, distress and many more. There is nothing wrong with this. Almost the opposite: it is entirely natural and expressing these emotions can be an important part of dealing with the situation.

Equally, as the giver of this bad news we need both to empathise (or even sympathise if we have been in a similar situation ourselves) and to give them a chance to share how they feel if they want to. It is important that we don't take the easy option of getting caught up in the facts, but consider and discuss the other person's feelings as well.

Whatever we may feel about actually giving the news we should keep it under wraps. It is bad news for them not us and so comments like 'You don't know how much it hurts me to say this' are somewhat selfish and more than likely to be self-defeating.

Why people always turn to the BBC in times of crisis

Whether it is a political coup, a terrorist scare, or an apparently fixed election, our behaviour across the world has been fairly consistent. We seek out the BBC to find out what is really going on.

The BBC World Service has, over the years, built up a reputation for impartiality, informed opinion and telling us the truth. Unlike newspapers, which tend to colour the news with their masters' political leanings, the World Service, we feel, remains spin-free.

When we have bad news to give out, we should try to follow this example: to give the news straight, not in a sensational or biased way. The person to whom we give the bad news may not buy us a bunch of flowers to say thank you, but they'll be grateful for our honesty all the same.

The identity card

The really bad damage from bad news is less in the facts and the immediate consequences than in what it does to my image of myself, ie, my identity. It is bad enough to be dumped by a long-term partner, made redundant from a job or left out of a family will. It is, however, far worse if we then conclude that we are unattractive, unemployable or unloved.

The third element, and often the most vital part, of sharing bad news effectively, is reinforcing the individual's identity.

Below are some examples of how a piece of bad news can easily become, in the mind of the person on the receiving end, a profound blow to their self-esteem.

It is often the identity component that drives the rest of the conversation – how we feel and therefore what we say. The most pivotal part of sharing bad news, therefore, is how we deal with the other person's identity.

Situation	Impact on my identity if not handled correctly	How to handle identity better
1 You've lost the contract	I'm terrible at selling	You have been extremely helpful and patient, it's just that the type of service we need has changed
2 We've decided not to keep you on	I'm terrible at selling	The role is no longer needed but I can think of a number of people who would leap at the chance to have someone with your skills
3 I want to end this relationship	No one fancies me, I'm unlovable	You would be the perfect partner for someone with the same passions (it's just that they aren't mine)
4 We're reorganising the department	I'm as important as the paperclips	You have shown how efficiently things can be done. We couldn't have got through without your commitment
5 I can't come skiing with you	No one likes me	You are a great person to go on holiday with and I'd love to go on another trip with you another time
6 The order is going to be late	I'm not valued as a customer	I am sorry that you have been treated in this way. You are a very important customer to us and I will do everything possible to get your goods to you as quickly as possible

Stages of bad news

There are four stages to sharing bad news effectively. These are preparation, declaration, discussion and conclusion.

The first stage: Preparation
As the old cliché about school exams puts it, failing to prepare is preparing to fail. We are much more likely to share bad news effectively if we are well prepared. Here are some things to consider as we start to plan.

- **Situation, timing and environment**
  Where to share the news? What medium to use? What environment to create? Dumping someone by text message is unlikely to leave the other person feeling good about the experience however carefully the message has been crafted (*Wnt b 4evr. Plnty mre fish n th C!*) Nor is it a good idea to tell someone that their pet project has been rejected whilst we're hovering around the coffee machine ('Did I get the coffee on your trousers? I'm *so* sorry . . .'). Instead, it's best to set aside enough time to have a thorough discussion and do everything possible to make sure there aren't any interruptions – turning off the mobile is the minimum.

There are other ways

- **The opening words**
  It's good to know what we are going to say to start with. We may stop short or adapt at the time but if we have a script in our mind then we are more likely to get going on the right track.

- **Rehearsal**
  Running the opening piece through in our head is good, doing it aloud is better and doing it with someone else who can tell us what it felt like on the receiving end is best of all. In a 'live' rehearsal (ie, with someone else present) it suddenly becomes much more obvious what works and what does not.

The second stage: Declaration
Having prepared it is time to actually deliver the message to the other person.

- **Give the 'headline' and supporting facts early on**
  This means that once the person is sat down, rather than building rapport, 'How has your day been?', or hoping you can get them to guess the bad news by asking questions, 'How do you think our relationship is going?', it is best to give them the facts up front. If we prevaricate first, we will not only be wasting time (theirs as well as ours) and increasing the discomfort, but they will resent us for not coming out with the headline at or near the outset.

- **The way the news is framed makes a huge difference to its impact**
  'In comparison to most men your age, other than your high blood

pressure you are in good physical shape' will have a totally different effect from 'I'm sorry to say you are suffering from hypertension which often leads to heart disease and can prove fatal'. There are also different ways we can give the same headline. Compare 'The bank won't be authorising your loan' with 'As is the case with many first time applicants, we won't be able to give you a loan on this occasion. However, most people find that by better understanding how we make loan decisions, they are much more likely to get approval in future.'

- **Show you can care**
  It is always good to recognise that the other person will have feelings about the news. Where feasible, eg, with bereavement, it is worth showing that we understand what these feelings are. It helps the other person to regard the sharer of bad news as an ally rather than as an adversary. However, if the emotions are unclear, it is best to ask rather than assume. And judging or evaluating how another person feels ('You're right to feel angry' or worse, 'You shouldn't be that upset') can make bad news turn ugly.

- **Reinforce positive aspects of the other person's identity**
  One of the most important parts of giving bad news is to get across that it is about a specific set of circumstances and not about the person as a whole.

  Imagine telling a chef friend that you have gone with another catering company for your wedding. Your friend might have a number of identity issues which arise from this such as 'I'm not a good cook', or 'I'm not a good enough friend'. To counteract some of these thoughts we need to reinforce their identity by saying such things as, 'You're clearly an experienced chef with a reputation for coping brilliantly with large numbers of people and everything we tasted was delicious. For the wedding, however, and knowing our friends, we are looking for something more ostentatious.'

- **All bad**
  The last thing someone will want to hear on the death of their husband is that at least they have more space in bed. Equally, however dark the cloud there is always some silver inside. The challenge is working out what the silver is and suggesting it at the right moment. If it is appropriate you can help the person see the positive side of the event – 'I'm sure you will get a catering job that will play much more to your strengths.' Try imagining yourself in their situation, and think what positive comfort you could take.

The direct or indirect approach when writing?

When sending bad news, which is better: a direct approach with the headline up front, or an indirect approach, with the message somewhere inside the text?

Some psychologists suggest using the indirect approach. If we put the bad news first, they claim, there is a danger the person will stop reading and start thinking about their reaction or getting angry. By starting with a neutral statement, a 'buffer', the reader is more likely to stay engaged and take notice of the reasons behind the bad news.

There is however a camp who believe that the direct approach is better. Smith, Nolan and Dai asked 90 students to compare two very similar rejection letters, except that one used the direct approach and the other used the indirect approach. The students then rated the letters on scales such as sincerity, considerateness, tact and courtesy. The direct method fared much better than the indirect approach.

- **Share the options on next steps**
  With some bad news it is clear what needs to happen next, whilst at other times the options are open to interpretation in terms of whether to do anything and, if so, what. If there are possible options or a pre-determined sequence of subsequent events then we should explain them, either up front or later on, after the news has been fully digested and discussed.

The third stage: Discussion
It can help to have some time between the 'declaration' and the 'discussion'. This gives the other person a chance to reflect and take in what they have just heard. Alternatively, when the bad news that has just been declared is very final it may be that the other person doesn't want to discuss anything at all and instead wants to get out of the room or off the line as quickly as possible.

When the time is right to discuss the bad news, we can help by asking open-ended questions. The essential ingredient for a successful discussion is quality listening: we do this by focusing our attention entirely on the individual. During the discussion we should aim to talk for less time than them.

It's not you, it's me: what those rejections really mean

However you try to reinforce someone's identity, be careful not to go too far. We can all read between the lines, as the following examples show:

What they say	What they mean
I'm not sure we're good for each other	You are driving me mad
I'm just not ready to settle down	I fancy your brother
I don't want to feel that I'm holding you back	I'm seeing your brother
Maybe we just need some space	I need to be a long way away when you find out about your brother
It's not you, it's me	It's you

The fourth stage: Conclusion

When the discussion has gone on for as long as the other person needs or until you think they are ready, it is time to agree what next (if the options weren't declared or discussed earlier then now is the time to do so). We should finish off by confirming what has been said, what has been agreed, what happens next and when.

Bad news: tough reactions

Sometimes, even when we have planned effectively, delivered the messages sensitively, shown empathy and reinforced their identity positively, people can still respond in unexpected ways. The best way to manage a tough reaction is to be prepared for it. Here are some common responses and suggestions on how best to deal with them.

The outburst

'This is a catastrophe; it's going to ruin my life, you know.'
'This is an outrage.'
'You're not going to get away with this.'

An emotionally explosive reaction, from anger through to tears, is wholly understandable. The best way to deal with this is not to take it at face value (they don't really want you to jump under a bus) but to listen and express empathy with how they feel. Only when they have done as much shouting or crying as they want should we ask if they'd like to discuss this further, or try correcting any facts they may have misunderstood or mis-represented during their emotional explosion.

Be patient. Stay calm. Listen. And if necessary, duck.

The freeze

'. . .'

One of the most difficult reactions is when we get no reaction at all. The other person sits there in silence staring out of the window or at the floor. We may even wonder if they have heard anything we've said.

One technique is to ask open questions that are easy to answer ('What are you thinking?') and then give them time to reply – share the silence. If the response is one word close-down ('Nothing'), pause and then probe further ('Nothing at all or just nothing you want to share?'). When we keep going we are likely to get one of the other tough reactions. By chipping away, we can deal with the stony silence.

Ask questions. Share the silence. If all else fails give the other person some space and resume the conversation later.

The denial

'This isn't happening.'
'You're joking, aren't you?'
'Come on, tell me the truth.'

Here the person simply refuses to believe the facts. The best approach is to empathise ('I can completely see why this must seem incredible'). When you think they might be listening, reassert the facts. If it helps, re-explain the process that led to the decision and how/why the decision is final. It can also help to reinforce their identity ('You are still the brilliant project manager that you were this morning').

Empathise. Repeat the facts. Reinforce their identity.

The plea

'Please, I'll do anything to make it work.'
'What can I do to undo the situation?'
'Just give me one more chance.'

Some people will claim they'll go to any lengths to change the situation. This can be a big challenge as we may feel sorry for them and want to give them another chance. Here we need to acknowledge their willingness to accommodate, but explain that the decision has been made and will not change. Next we should reframe the situation so that they can see the potential positives ('You'll be so much happier with someone else') or the long-term negative consequences of staying in the old situation ('We'll end up back the same as it always is – fighting and not talking to each other').

Confirm the decision is final. Focus on the positive consequences.

The self-blamer

'I knew this was coming – it's all my fault.'
'I'm useless.'
'If I were you, I'd dump me too.'

This person personalises the news, believing that the reason the situation occurred was entirely due to their behaviour and not because of circumstances. In this instance we might reinforce the individual's identity, re-explain the reasons for the situation, and reframe the situation placing much of the blame externally ('You're still a great guy. It's just this job in Outer Mongolia is too good to turn down').

Reinforce their identity. Explain what else has contributed to the news.

The attack

'It's all your fault.'
'You're the reason why I'm in this mess.'
'I bet you're really enjoying this.'

A verbal attack happens when the person who has received the bad news sees us as the reason why they are in that position. Here we need to remain calm and listen to what they have to say. This can be very difficult as we may disagree with it entirely, and may even be hurt or insulted by their comments. But it is important that they are able to express their view (even if they see us as a low-down, two-faced good-for-nothing). If we can make sense of the motivations behind their attack, we can take steps to address them. And if things become heated, remember that what someone *wants* to say could be very different from what they actually come out with. They've just had some bad news to digest, so give them leeway.

Remain calm. Listen. Don't answer back.

Burying bad news

Bad news can be like a vampire – just when we think it's safely underground, it's back, alive and eating, if not us then someone else we care about. The equivalent of the stake through the heart is to get on with sharing the facts whilst making sure we cover off the emotions and the identity too. It's always a bad day when we bury bad news. And it could be a good day when we share it effectively; no garlic necessary.

Stress and relaxation

Along with morning coffee runs and 'hilarious' email circulars forwarded round the office, stress has become something of a given in our modern working lives. When a recent survey asked Londoners if they found work stressful, 87% said yes. Certainly, there is plenty to get the blood pressure rising: the journey in in the morning, be it 'sardined' on a train or stuck in a traffic jam; the ever-groaning inbox of emails waiting for us when we arrive; the lunchtime rush to get to the gym before everyone else does; the photo-copying machine running out of toner *just* when we need to use it; the person on the train home ringing every five minutes to say he's on the train. No wonder, then, that tomes such as *The Little Book of Calm* sell by the truckload.

But here's the intriguing thing. Although 87% of Londoners found work stressful, 50% of the people surveyed said that they enjoyed what they did. Even taking into account the 13% of Londoners who don't find work stressful – what do these 13% do? – that still leaves 37% who enjoy their stressful jobs. Sure, there are a few workaholics around, but even factor-ing those in, that still leaves a good percentage of normal working people who are fine with being stressed. What do they know that we don't?

The answer may sound surprising at first but the more you think about it, the more it makes sense: stress can be good for you. Of course there are times when it can be bad for our health and our lives but stress is also, in different forms, essential for our happiness, success and fulfilment. If we eradicate stress we will become less able to deal with, let alone enjoy, the thrills, pressures and challenges that make life worthwhile. No stress, in other words, no joy.

So what kinds of stress are 'good' for us, and which types are 'bad'? That's what the first chapter in this section, The joy of stress, is all about. It describes how stress can be both positive and negative, and offers ways to help us work out which sort we are feeling. The more we know about our own stress, the better equipped we are to deal with it.

Stressbusters, meanwhile, is all about getting down to business and offers sure-fire strategies to deal with the 'negative' kinds of stress. This is the place to go when we know we're experiencing bad stress and want practical advice about coping with it. As well as the general tactics, there is also a stress 'early warning system', and a mental 'alarm bell' for when stress is about to occur.

The remaining chapters in this section, Deep breath and Tranquillity, offer two very practical techniques for instant relief from negative stress that can be used anywhere, at any time.

(M) The joy of stress

Round the bend

Alice is taking her final driving lesson before the test. She arrives and chats to her instructor. After 15 lessons, Alice is feeling pretty confident. She gets in the car and starts to drive. Two minutes later, while talking about what she was watching on TV last night, Alice fails to spot a van coming out in front and she has to jam on the breaks. Then she starts to concentrate. Without even thinking, Alice checks her rear-view mirror, depresses the clutch, changes gear, gently releases the clutch, uses her indicator with plenty of warning, steers smoothly round the turning and, altogether, drives like a professional.

Reversing round a corner proves a little trickier and, even though she's done it perfectly on the last three occasions, Alice hits the kerb this time. But she recovers and even though it's a little jerky, she makes the rest of the manoeuvre without incident. She's back on the road, but then she gets to a roundabout – her worst part – and she stalls the car. Alice tries starting it again but she's left it in gear and it isn't working. She slams the palms of her hands on the steering wheel in frustration and her instructor has to calm her down and help out.

If we wanted to plot Alice's driving lesson then it would look something like the chart on the next page (Fig. 1).

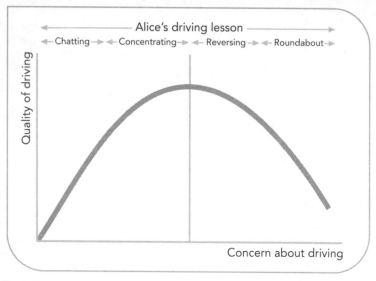

Fig. 1

Stress ain't what it used to be

A hundred years ago, two psychologists called Robert Yerkes and John Dodson created a similar-looking graph to show how our level of 'arousal' affected what we achieved.

In the same way that the quality of Alice's driving increased once she stopped chatting and started concentrating, so Yerkes and Dodson suggested that as our arousal goes up, so does our performance. It's fair to assume that double entendres went unnoticed when Yerkes and Dodson were writing at the beginning of the 20th century.

But only up to an (optimum) point: like Alice tipping from confidence to concern as she struggled with reversing round a corner, so more arousal can lead to a decline in performance, and, ahem, excessive arousal may lead to no performance at all.

This model was developed further by the Austrian-born Canadian psychologist, Hans Selye. Selye devised names for the different stages of stress: the section of the graph where performance is improved by increased arousal he called eustress (or euphoric stress). An example might be the increased adrenalin rush we get when playing well in a game of squash. The area beyond this, where extra arousal starts damaging our performance, he called distress (Fig. 2).

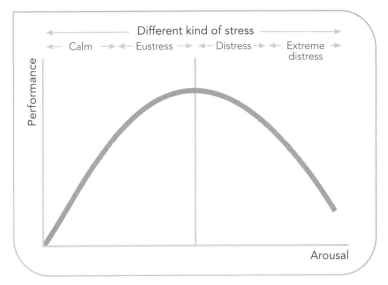

Fig. 2

By separating out these different types of 'arousal', Selye pinpointed the key message of this chapter: not all sorts of stress are negative. Yes, the types beyond our optimum point do have a negative effect on our performance, but if we can keep to the left of it, increasing our 'arousal' levels produces a positive result.

Somewhere along the way, however, Selye's impressive findings got lost in the mix. As our working lives have sped up, so his subtle definitions have been left behind: the term 'stress' has become a single catch-all term to encompass both eustress and distress; distress now refers to what Selye would call 'extreme distress'; and the section of the graph where we are not stressed is reduced to the small section on the far left of the curve. See Fig. 3 on page 201.

All of which creates a problem. By merging Selye's two definitions together, we have lost both the language and the understanding to distinguish between positive stress (eustress) and negative stress (distress). Without these, we are left with the (false) assumption that all stress is bad for us. And if we can't diagnose the problem correctly then we are highly likely to prescribe the wrong solution.

Stress: what happens when we get confused

Sally is an actress and auditioning for a part in a musical. If she gets the part it would be her big break and she could quit her job as a waitress. She's been rehearsing hard for the audition and is firing off the adrenalin. Her performance piece is good. In the diagram on the next page she is on a stress curve, 1, and her current arousal/performance position is at point A in Fig. 4.

Here, however, is where our modern 'one size fits all' definition of stress comes into play. If you asked Sally if she was stressed, she'd probably reply 'yes'. And as she assumes, like most of us, that stress is a bad thing, her response is to relax, in the hope that this will reduce her stress levels and so improve her performance.

Assuming she is on the downward rather than upward slope of her stress curve, Sally has mistakenly, therefore, drawn her curve as curve 2. Sally's response is to reduce the level of stress so rather than rehearsing again that afternoon, Sally decides to go shopping to calm her nerves.

Sally's mistaken analysis of the situation (she is stressed) leads her to carry out the wrong action (relaxing), which has the opposite effect to what she intends (worsening rather than improving her performance). In fact, Sally is coping well with the adrenalin of rehearsing, and by continuing to work she can improve her performance. In other words, she is actually on curve 1 rather than 2, and by increasing her 'arousal' can move towards her optimum performance.

And it doesn't necessarily stop there. If Sally can redraw her stress curve to the left once, then she can do so again (to curve 3) and again, until her resilience to stress is negligible and even waiting at tables during the quiet periods could prove too much.

But there are two pieces of good news. First, if we can identify where we are on the curve we can take the right steps to improve our performance. And second, just as we can mentally redraw our stress curve downwards, so we can also redraw it the other way and therefore become more resilient. Sally is on her way to Hollywood.

Welcome to club stress
The number one key to coping with stress, then, is to work out where we are on our stress curve. In order to do so, it is useful to consider the curve as having four distinct zones, rather like the different rooms within a club, each with their own ambience and atmosphere (Fig. 5). By looking at each in detail, we can come to a decision as to where we are and where we want to be at any particular moment.

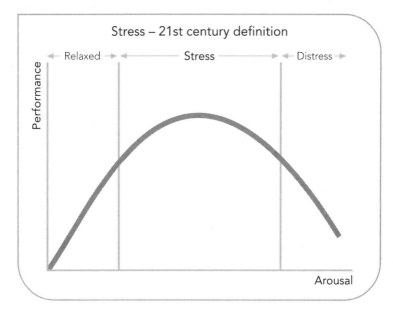

Fig. 3

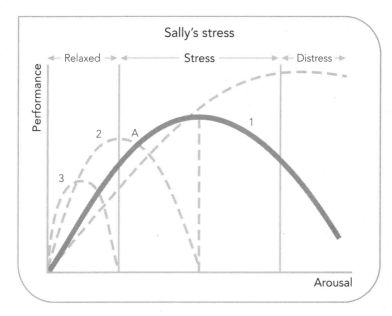

Fig. 4

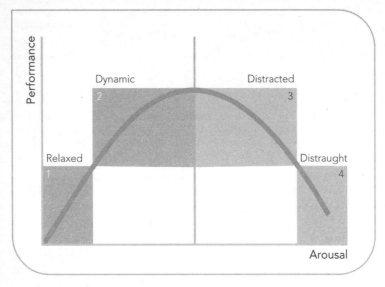

Fig. 5

1 Relaxed – The Chill Zone

Currently playing: 'Easy Like Sunday Morning' – The Commodores

There's no doubt about it: The Chill Zone is a great place to be. The music is smooth and gentle. The lighting is soft. Everyone's talking rather than shouting to get heard. There are spongy sofas and soft chairs to sit on. The hustle of the rest of the world seems a million miles away. Everyone is happy, unwinding, laid back and relaxed . . .

The people hanging out in The Chill Zone are pretty much at their lowest level of arousal. If they are thinking at all, then the sort of thoughts might be:

- It's not that important; not my problem

- Life is good

- Yeah, whatever; not bothered

- Isn't the world a beautiful place?

- No need to worry, it'll all work out in the end

- Bored, bored, bored

Some people spend most of their lives in this zone: take James, a participant at one of The Mind Gym's Sorted for stress workouts. He never really experienced stress, he explained, the only thing he felt even remotely stressed about was the fact that his peers had all progressed further than him at work.

All of which, when we think about it, makes perfect sense. In order not to experience much stress of any sort, James must spend most of his time in this zone. As a result, his performance rarely reaches that of his peers who spend more time in zone 2 and, possibly, zone 3. They had experienced stress that had improved their performance and had been promoted as a result.

The majority of popular advice on stress implies that this zone is our ideal default position. In fact, this isn't quite true. People who spend most of their life here, like James, are in danger of letting the world pass them by. Far better to view The Chill Zone as a good place to be every now and then: when away on holiday, for example, or at the end of a heavy day. Everyone needs time and space to unwind. But to do so, there needs to be something to unwind *from*.

2 Dynamic – The Thrill Zone
Currently playing: 'Hot Stuff' – Donna Summer

Thrill zone?

If The Chill Zone is cool, then The Thrill Zone is hot. The music's upbeat without being in your face, the lights are sharp and everybody's dancing. They're some good-looking people here, but you show them some moves and they like what you've got. This could be your night . . .

Remember Hans Selye, the Austrian-born Canadian psychologist from earlier in the chapter who came up with the idea of eustress? This is his room. It's the place to be when we are feeling up for it, the adrenalin's pumping, we're on top form and are giving things a go. This is the zone where high-flyers reside, people who are fulfilling their potential at work and are pushing for promotion. People here feel these sorts of things:

- Excited or exhilarated/enjoying ourselves

- Nervous

- Under pressure/being tested/being pushed to our limits

- Determined

- Every moment counts

- Time is distorted with longish periods of time feeling like a few seconds

Another person in this room is the doctor who told The Mind Gym, 'I'm bored of people coming to me and telling me they're tired. In my opinion, if you're not tired you're not living.' She's right: don't be put off with all the advice from the stress scaremongers; The Thrill Zone can be a great and rewarding place to be. If we want to achieve challenging goals and aren't satisfied with just 'getting by', then we need to spend considerable time in this zone.

3 Distracted – The Spill Zone
Currently playing: 'Disco Inferno' – The Trammps

At first glance, this doesn't look too different from the previous zone. But while that zone was hot, here things are just starting to boil over. It's a little bit competitive at the bar. People keep on bumping into you and spilling your drink. There is still a lot of talent on the dance floor but you're trying to impress too many people at the same time. Whereas the last zone felt fun, this time you're starting to feel hassled . . .

If we spend a lot of time in zone 2 we will, almost inevitably, slip into zone 3 every once in a while. It's not a fantastic place to be. When we are in this zone, we tend to spend a lot of time worrying. We focus in on ourselves and think about the situation and how impossible it is rather than what we can do to get out of it. These are the sorts of things people in this zone might be thinking:

- I don't know where to start

- No one appreciates the pressure I'm under

- This is going to be a disaster; I'm not sure that I can see a way out

- I have got SO much to do; how on earth am I going to do it all?

- Or, quite simply, argghhhh!

The trick is to make our visits to this zone occasional and short: that's what the following chapters are all about.

4 Distraught – The Kill Zone
Currently playing: 'Le Freak' – Chic

Now things are going from bad to worse. It's too hot, the lights are too bright, the music is too noisy and the dance floor is too crowded. You've been waiting half an hour at the bar but no one will serve you. Your head is starting to thump and the taxi you booked is still two hours away . . .

Where is happiness?

Mihaly Csikszentmihaly isn't just a potentially award-winning Scrabble score. He's also the former Chairman of the Department of Psychology at the University of Chicago. Csikszentmihaly (said chick-sent-me-high) has spent thirty years conducting research with thousands of people across the world to find out what happens at their moments of greatest enjoyment. What he discovered was that one, two or up to all eight of the factors below are involved:

1 We confront tasks that we have a chance of completing

2 We can concentrate on what we are doing

3 There are clear goals

4 There is immediate feedback

5 There is a deep and effortless involvement that is all-embracing

6 We have a sense of control over our actions

7 We don't think about ourselves during the activity but think better of ourselves after we have completed it

8 The sense of the duration of time is altered

In each case the people involved are experiencing significant amounts of eustress; they are firmly in zone 2. However, he also says that if you are satisfied with passive pleasure, which he rates as a much weaker contributor to happiness, then you can find that in zone 1. So where is happiness? Somewhere on the left-hand side of the curve, depending on what sort of person we are.

One of the big differences between zone 3 and zone 4 is that when we are in zone 3 we recognise that it is the specific situation that is worrying. We don't tend to think it will apply to everything and go on for ever. In zone 4, however, it seems like it will. Everything is getting on top of us and we can't see a way out. The situation is so grave that it will stretch out across our forseeable future – there is no escape.

Here are the sort of things we might be thinking if we're in this zone:

- My life is a mess/disaster

- There's no way out

- The world is out to get me/I am useless

- I just can't cope any more

- Everything I touch goes wrong

- I can't concentrate on anything

- Even simple tasks take ages

Many of us have been in zone 4 briefly but usually we see some hope or relief and we get out quickly. The danger occurs when we are in zone 4 for extended periods of time. It can be like quicksand, dragging us into a sense of hopelessness from which, after a while, it is not easy to pull back.

Which zone are you in?

Have a look at the questions below and decide which option best describes your thoughts for each situation.

---

1 You are stuck in traffic and so will arrive late at your destination. What do you think?

a So, what's a few minutes? There's not much I can do about it anyway

b Let me see if there's another route. I'll call to warn them

c This is so unlucky; if only I'd left earlier

d I can't believe it, I'm going to be really late. This is a disaster

2   You have an important deadline that is fast approaching and no idea how you are going to deliver good quality results on time.

a   I'm sure it will all work out somehow or other

b   This is an exciting challenge – let's get going

c   I don't know where to begin

d   This is impossible – it's going to be a catastrophe

3   Someone asks you to do something urgent which means that you will need to change your plans significantly.

a   Yeah, sure

b   I'll rise to the challenge and make it work

c   I can't believe you're doing this to me – I've got my own things to do too, you know

d   This is the final straw; I can't possibly do it as well

4   Your flight was delayed, the villa is nothing like the picture in the brochure and it's raining.

a   We're on holiday, it doesn't really matter, let's just enjoy ourselves

b   This is no good. I'll get on to the tour operator to sort this out

c   The airline is incompetent, the holiday company are crooks. I am furious

d   This is the worst holiday of my life. I wish I'd stayed at home

5   You check your bank balance and it's looking much worse than you thought.

a   Who cares about money? At least I've got my health

b   I'll sort this out. Not quite sure how yet, but I'll get on the case straight away

c   And that's before I pay the bills at the end of the month; what am I going to do?

d   Everything in my life is going wrong – I'm a walking disaster zone

6   Which of the following best describes your view on life?

a   Life's a breeze (though it can be a bit boring sometimes)

b   My life is a constant stream of exciting, fresh challenges

c   I've got too much on at the moment and I don't know how I am going to cope

d   My life is a mess

Which zone are you in: the answers

Mostly As: Zone 1 – Relaxed
For people who spend most of their time in zone 1, the question is whether or not you are happy. If you are, then great, though you might wonder if you are fulfilling your potential. If you would like to spend more time in zone 2, you may want to set yourself some challenges that really stretch you.

Mostly Bs: Zone 2 – Dynamic
People here are definitely experiencing stress but have nothing to worry about and potentially lots to celebrate – this is a great place to be, provided there is the occasional dip into zone 1 to relax and recharge. High performers who spend a lot of time in zone 2 may well sometimes slip into zone 3 now and again. As long as this is spotted and acted on there is no reason for concern.

Mostly Cs: Zone 3 – Distracted
People here feel stressed quite a lot and it isn't the good stress. Anyone who spends a lot of time here might want to have a rethink about how their life is structured. The tips and techniques in the following chapters will be a great help in reducing negative stress and moving back to zone 2.

Mostly Ds: Zone 4 – Distraught
People here are likely to be suffering from stress. They should stop, smile (the physical action automatically makes us feel better) and remember when life was more enjoyable. It may not be easy but there are definitely ways to make life good again, or better. It might be wise to talk things through with someone – family, friends or a professional.

Choosing a zone

Who's responsible?

The good news is that the person who can do most to affect our level of stress is ourselves: rather than being stuck in a situation of someone else's making, we can always take action and do something to sort out our stress.

Just by knowing that, we are already better equipped to deal with distress. And if we can combine that knowledge with the tactics and techniques in the following chapters then we can go a long way to being sorted for stress.

(N) Stressbusters

Fred is sitting in solid traffic on his way to his brother's wedding. If it doesn't clear soon he will miss the start of the service. It's a very small gathering at their local church – he is going to be in so much trouble. Why didn't he take the train or leave half an hour earlier? He feels completely helpless and the more he realises that there is nothing he can do the angrier he gets. Fred then imagines his father's reaction when he discovers that Fred isn't going to be there – Fred's anger turns to dread and his dread turns to panic.

Fred's brother Chris is in a car about 50 metres behind Fred in the same traffic jam. He is also going to the wedding and not only that but he is also giving one of the readings. Chris decides, however, that as there is nothing he can do about the traffic, there is no point in worrying. Meantime, he is better off doing something useful. He sits back and starts to practise his reading.

Chris and Fred's half-sister Anne is three cars ahead of Fred, also stationary. She's not sure about the person her brother is marrying, but is always happy to have an excuse to wear a hat. Anne has spent the last ten minutes on the phone to a traffic helpline to try and find out how big the jam is. She's left a message for her mother to tell her the situation and to see if the service can be put back. Then it occurs to her that Fred might also be stuck in traffic, so she picks up her phone again and dials . . .

Three people, all in the same situation. And yet, three very different approaches to dealing with stress. Fred's way of dealing with it is not really dealing with it at all. He is working himself into a state that will only end up making things worse. This is not good for him or his steering wheel, which he keeps on slamming in frustration. Chris, meanwhile, has taken a very different approach. His reaction is to think about things differently, and relax rather than stress about the situation. Anne has taken a problem-focused strategy. She has worked out what she can practically do given her circumstances and has started to implement her plan.

We have all, at different times, experienced each of these reactions. At some stage or another we have freaked like Fred, chilled like Chris and acted like Anne. Probably, however, we didn't think about what the best approach would be but leapt into doing whatever felt right at the time.

If our intuition was good then this would have helped, but if not then we would have become more distraught. The purpose of this chapter is to help our intuition out, by giving us more choices about what to do when we are about to become, or already are, negatively stressed.

There are nine ways of tackling stress in this chapter. Each has its own strengths. There will be some situations where one stressbuster will be more useful than others. And, as often as not, we may need to use a combination of them to help us out.

The nine tactics are ordered, roughly, from those that require thinking about the situation differently, like Chris in the example above, to those that focus on taking action, like Anne. One thing is for sure, though, if we master these tactics and discover how to combine them to the best effect, we need never freak like Fred again.

Different types of stress

In the previous chapter we discussed how to differentiate between different types of stress. To recap briefly, stress can be divided into both positive and negative kinds. Positive stress is known as euphoric stress or eustress. This occurs when we thrive on the adrenalin of the situation to boost our performance. A good example in our wedding scenario is Anne. She is 'on form', aroused, busy and focused on productive activity. Negative stress, meanwhile, is where our level of stress inhibits our performance and is also known as distress. In our wedding example, this is what Fred is feeling.

1 Play it down, part one: reducing the importance

Distress occurs when we believe not only that we aren't capable of dealing with a situation but also that the situation itself is important. One simple way of reducing our level of stress is by changing our assessment of the situation to make the outcome seem less crucial.

Quite often, of course, the opposite is the case. The more we think about the thing we're stressed about, the more important it feels. *Missing your brother's wedding? Fred's mind might be telling him. Well, don't worry about being late for the next family gathering: you won't be invited. Your father's will? Forget about it: he'll probably just leave you his watch to remind you what an idiot you've been . . .* Such a runaway train of thought is known as a catastrophic fantasy. We all create them, when we're running late like Fred, or last thing at night when we can't get to sleep and are worried about that meeting first thing tomorrow.

So here's what to do. The first point to remember is that a catastrophic fantasy may sound catastrophic but it is also just a fantasy. So dismiss it. If we can pause and listen to ourselves, we will realise how ridiculous it is. Secondly, rather than paint the most negative version of events, we can go the other way and give the situation the most positive twist possible.

Here, for example, is what Fred could be thinking: *I'm going to be late for the wedding but I am not the first person to be late for a wedding and I won't be the last. They can either delay things until I get there or they can get on without me. My brother will be annoyed but, at the end of the day, he is my brother, he knows I want to be there and he'll forgive me. And if he does bear a grudge because I'm a few minutes late, well, then that's his problem not mine. I know I've done my best. If being late for my brother's wedding is the worst thing I've ever done to him, then I guess it shows what a good relationship we've got.*

By playing the situation down, reducing the importance and impact of being a few minutes late, Fred would avoid becoming so distraught.

(For more on catastrophic fantasies, see New chapter.)

How you see it, how you don't

If we went skydiving, most of us would find the situation fairly stressful to say the least. However, if a skydiving instructor was about to make her 300th jump the chances are she would barely be stressed at all.

Richard Lazarus and Susan Folkman suggested that the way in which we view a situation makes just as big a difference to our level of stress as the situation itself. They called this concept cognitive appraisal.

Amongst the most influential factors in determining how stressed we feel are our personal beliefs (eg, jumping out of planes is dangerous) and situational factors like how familiar or predictable the event is (the first vs 300th jump).

This is one of the main reasons why in identical situations, some people remain totally calm whilst others become highly distressed.

The joy of this theory is that we can alter our level of stress simply by choosing to think about the situation differently.

2 Play it down, part two: reducing the likelihood

As well as exaggerating the importance of an event, we also tend to exaggerate the probability of the negative outcome happening.

Marie, a participant at a Sorted for stress workout, recounted a horror story about sending out a company newsletter. When the copies came back from the printers, Marie realised she'd made a major mistake: the graphs on the front page were the wrong way round. Rather than explaining a company success, it suggested a massive failure.

In a state of panic, Marie offered to pay for a printed retraction out of her own salary. But rather than ask for her bank details, her boss told her not to worry. 'To be quite honest,' he continued, 'I'm not sure how many people will notice.' He was right: out of the 20,000 people who received the newsletter, not one mentioned it.

Marie was correct in her view that it would be extremely bad news if everyone had thought that the project was a failure (ie, the impact is important). But she was wrong to assume that everyone, or indeed, anyone, would notice her error (ie, the probability that this outcome will happen).

Playing down the probability of a bad outcome is a very powerful way to counteract distress.

3 The frame game: thinking things differently

Imagine someone is trying to rent their house out but is having problems attracting interest because of the small size of the bedrooms. By repainting the walls in a lighter colour and removing some of the furniture and clutter, the seller can make the rooms feel bigger and more attractive. In a similar way, a stressful situation can appear much less daunting if we think about it or 'reframe' it in a different way.

You are trying to organise a holiday to Rome but everything is going wrong. The cheap tickets that you spotted on the website but didn't buy immediately are now twice the price. The hotel the *Time Out* guide recommended is fully booked. Your neighbours have just come back from Italy and said they had a terrible time. A close friend has announced that they are having their birthday dinner in the middle of the proposed holiday. And just when you thought nothing else could go wrong, you discover that your passport is due to expire in three weeks.

Your initial reaction to all this may be to give up: everything's getting too stressful and is conspiring against me. But by 'reframing' the situation things could look far more positive (and therefore far less stressful).

The cheap tickets have gone? Flying normal rather than budget might be more expensive but at least we'll land at an airport near the city centre rather than an hour away. The hotel is fully booked? We can stay somewhere quieter that isn't full to bursting. The neighbours who had a terrible time? They can tell us all the places to avoid. The close friend having a birthday dinner? We can do something separately, without having to put up with his mad sister all evening. The passport's due to expire? We can finally get rid of that dreadful photograph even our mother always sniggers at.

The technical term for all this is reframing – thinking differently about the external facts and focusing on what is good about them rather than what is not. Take a football team whose key striker is injured just before an important tournament: rather than worrying, it could be the opportunity to let someone else show what they can do (think Geoff Hurst and the 1966 World Cup). Or imagine someone made redundant in a restructure at work: the three months' pay-off gives them the time and money to do all that travelling they've been talking about for years.

Using reframing to rethink a stressful situation

Traditional	Reframe
I have got so much to do, it's impossible to do it all	I've got so much to do because there is so much that I can do that will make a difference. I'm so lucky to have this opportunity to show people what I can do
Why is everyone resisting these changes that I have to introduce?	The best changes are those that have been challenged and revised as a result; if I can convince the sceptics then I know I'm doing the right thing
I'm trying really hard but I don't seem to be making any progress – I feel like giving up	Now that I have eliminated a large number of possibilities I know what not to do and so am more likely to succeed from here on in
I am never actually going to get a holiday	When I do go on holiday I am going to appreciate it all the more for all the challenges I've had to overcome to get there

4 Celebrating

Feeling stressed leaves us feeling low. One way of tackling this is to think of all the good things that are going on in our lives at the same time.

So the offer on the house fell through and it seems that finding a decent place to live in is as far away as ever. But what are the good things in life at the moment? Get a piece of paper and write them all down. Close friends? Interesting job? Nice car? In love? Seen a good film recently? Got enough money to buy a new house? Chances are that the list will be longer than expected. And thinking about these things will take the attention away from the negative stress, which in turn makes us feel better.

Equally, when things go right, don't be afraid of celebrating. Rather than dismiss it as 'done' and start worrying about the next thing, patting ourselves on the back will help boost our energy levels and give us eustress ready for the next challenge.

At the end of a busy day set aside a couple of minutes to think through what you have achieved rather than what you have to do tomorrow. This will reduce your level of anxiety and you will almost certainly sleep better too.

5 Use mental energy wisely

If the stress tactics above don't appear to be enough, then try asking the following question: 'Is worrying about this helping me? Is there something better I could be doing with all this mental energy?'

We each have only so much mental energy to go round. If we're using it all worrying and working ourselves up, then that doesn't leave much to address the issues that are causing all the grief in the first place. If we save our energy for something more worthwhile than worrying we're more likely to get the situation sorted and we'll feel better about ourselves in the process.

6 The great escape

Sometimes the best way of dealing with excessive stress is to escape from it. We could try to literally walk away from it – a change of scenery and getting some oxygen into our brain might just help us see things differently. We can also choose a mental escape – making a pact not to think about the situation for a while. Or it may involve taking time out: an evening off, or a night out on the town, so that when we return to the situation we look at things afresh.

Of course, escaping for too long can be dangerous as the causes of distress may have increased while we were away thereby making our level of distress even greater. But a short break can also help to put things into perspective and so bring long-term benefits.

7 Friends united

Sometimes the best way of dealing with a stressful situation is to share our thoughts with someone else: rather than carrying the burden alone, talking it through will help us feel better.

Most of us have played at least some of these support roles for friends, colleagues and family. There is no reason why they wouldn't be delighted to do the same for us. But remember, few of them are clairvoyant. We will need to ask them for support if we are going to benefit from their help.

Here are some ways a friend or colleague can offer support.

Wrong number

- Listen and empathise – 'He really called you that? No wonder you feel terrible. They don't know how lucky they are to have you there . . .'

- Challenge our assumptions about what is happening – 'Are you sure that is what he meant? Things written in emails can sound far more aggressive than they actually are.'

- Help facilitate a solution to the situation – 'Why don't I ask him if he wants to join us for a coffee or a drink after work to clear the air?'

- Help come up with solutions – 'Let's get together and see if we can think up some more creative alternatives.'

- Actually do things on our behalf – 'I'll make some posters and put them on trees around the area. Does he answer to anything else apart from Foo Foo?'

- Lend or give us the physical or financial support that would alleviate the cause of our distress – 'I've just done my expenses, so I'm fine for money at the moment. I'll pay to have the red wine stain removed and you can pay me back when you want. He'll never know it happened.'

This is what friends are for (well, one of the reasons), so don't be afraid to ask for help.

8 Ask the right questions: and act on the answers

When we get distressed we tend to ask ourselves the wrong questions, if we ask any questions at all. By asking the right questions, however, we can get to the heart of why we are distressed. And once we know this, then we can take the appropriate action to reduce it.

So, what are the right questions? Well, they're not the ones where we start beating ourselves up about the situation: How could I have been so stupid? What made me think I could cope with this? Instead, the questions to ask are the ones that are straightforward and involve doing something practical. Questions like these . . .

- What is the real cause of my stress? That I might miss the wedding (as opposed to being a few minutes late).

- What could I do to reduce the demands of the situation? Ring ahead and try and get the wedding delayed.

- What alternative ways are there to address the cause of my stress? Look at the map and see if I can turn off at the next junction and find another route.

- What can I do to increase my resources? I could call a traffic hotline to find out what is causing the delay and how long I might be waiting here.

- What can others do to help? While I am listening to the traffic hotline, someone at the wedding can alert the vicar that people are going to be late.

- What should I do and in what sequence? Ring my father, explain the situation and see if there is any way the start of the wedding can be delayed. Ring the traffic hotline to see how long the delay is likely to be. Phone Fred and Chris to see if they are in the same situation.

In our original wedding example, Anne discovers one of those perfect circles in order to cope with stress. By getting things done, she is able to keep calm. And by keeping calm, she is able to get things done. But however smart Anne is in coping with the situation, she could be smarter still by asking herself two further questions, once the wedding is over.

- Is this cause of stress, or something similar, likely to happen again?

- If so, what can I do to prepare for it?

By learning from our experiences, we can start to build up our stress immune system, which means that we are less likely to experience distress in future and better equipped to deal with it when we do.

9 Confronting

We can accept the demands and pressures that people put on us or we can challenge them. Sometimes, confronting the issue head on is the best way of reducing the distress we feel: 'I know I said we'd meet this afternoon, but I'm afraid I can't any longer.' And by doing so, quite often we discover the situation is not as bad as we first thought.

A common situation where this helps is our relationship with our boss. There is a desire not to look weak in front of him or her and so we try to carry on as if nothing is wrong. But it's far better to let them know how we feel: nine times out of ten, they will respect us more for being honest.

Turning stress tactics into successful strategies

These, then, are our nine tactics to deal with stress:

1 Reducing the importance

2 Reducing the likelihood of the nightmare scenario

3 Reframing things in a positive way

4 Celebrating

5 Using mental energy wisely

6 Escaping

7 Seeking support from friends

8 Asking the right questions

9 Confronting the situation

Within the nine Stressbusters, there are two distinct types. Numbers one to seven are all to do with looking at the situation differently: they are emotion- or assessment-focused strategies. Tactics eight and nine, meanwhile, are to do with working out what action to take and then taking it. These are problem-focused strategies.

In order to bust stress effectively, we often need to use a mixture of these techniques.

Imagine the following situation:

There's a letter from the bank that I've put off opening for a week. I finally decide to look inside and see how bad the situation is. Oh my God, they

must have made a mistake! I know I've been spending a lot on the credit
card, but this is crazy. It can't be right, can it? What am I going to do?
They'll stop my card. I won't be able to keep up with my mortgage
payments. They'll repossess the flat and I'll be declared a bankrupt. It'll
be virtually impossible to borrow ever again . . .
I should have opened the bank statement when it arrived. By not
responding quickly, I've made the situation even worse. And I'm late for
my class at the gym. Not that I'm going to be able to concentrate
properly, not while I'm worrying about this . . .

So that's the situation. The question is, what is the best way to deal with
it? Before reading on, it might be worth skimming back through our nine
tactics, and deciding which you think would be most useful here. There is
no 'right' answer, but here are some suggestions.

First, I need to stop myself from panicking. So, on the way to the gym I'm
going to take the following steps.

- Play it down – reduce the importance
  Let's be realistic: I am a long way off having the flat repossessed. The
  worst scenario in the short term is that I can't withdraw cash or write
  cheques for a week or so. Well, I never write cheques anyway and I'll
  just use one of my other credit cards if things get tight.

- Always look on the bright side – celebrate
  It's not all bad. I've got a good job that is relatively secure, I'm healthy
  and fit; fit-ish anyway. The sun is shining, and I've just come back from
  a fantastic holiday.

- Reframe
  And it's not like I haven't been in this situation before. I was really badly
  in debt when I left university and I managed to pay that off eventually.
  If I can do it once, I'm sure I can do it again.

- Escape
  While I am at the gym I am going to lose myself totally in the class and
  not think about my debts until afterwards. After the class, I'll think
  through the following steps.

- Ask the right questions
  What is my real cause of stress? In the short term that I might not be able
  to cover my round in the bar; in the medium term that I won't be able
  to pay the mortgage and my flat will be repossessed. What if the bank
  has made a mistake? I should check the statement thoroughly and call
  them if I have any questions.

What can I do to cut my costs? I could stay away from the pub for the next couple of days; I could not renew my subscription for cable TV.
What can I do to increase my income? I could always rent out the spare room if the mortgage becomes a problem. I also think I have got some Premium Bonds – I could cash some of those in.
What can I do to keep the bank off my back? I could write to them and let them know what I am doing to address the situation.

- Friends united
  I'll call Jim. His wife works in a bank and he may be able to find out how these things work.

This is just one suggested strategy: there are many others that would be equally applicable in this situation. And what each of them should show is this: the nine stressbusters are great in isolation but they are most effective when combined to deal with the stress of the situation.

Trip wires and alarm calls

This chapter is filled with tactics and strategies to cope with a situation once our stress levels are already up. But there is another way to look at dealing with stress: before it actually occurs. If we can teach ourselves what the tell-tales signs are of getting stressed, then we can take pre-emptive action and stop the stress before it starts. There are two kinds of early warning system for distress: trip wires and alarm calls.

Trip wires
My shoulders are getting tense. I can't sit down for more than a minute before I am up again, pacing around. I keep on boiling the kettle without actually making a cup of tea. I chew the end of the pen until it, like me, is in a bit of a mess . . .

Whatever our mannerisms or habits when stress is on its way, we can work out what they are and learn to spot when we're doing them. We should then pause, think about our situation, and take the necessary steps before the distress occurs.

Alarm calls
We all recognise things that our partner, colleague or children do which means there's a mood or a strop or some other emotional reaction on the way. And if we can recognise it in them, they can do the same for us.

Alarm calls are like trip wires except, instead of recognising our own sensations or habits, it is other people pointing them out. The people who know us best can warn us when we are about to get into a dangerous or distressed state. We may have to ask nicely to get them to tell us. After all, tapping someone on the arm and saying, 'Be careful now, I think you are about to lose it', may be exactly what tips someone over the edge.

We make best use of our alarm calls when we not only ask our friends, colleagues or family to warn us when they think we are heading into emotionally troubled waters but also when we suggest how they can tell us: perhaps they could make a cup of tea, or give us a neck massage. If we can agree on a simple way of warning without prompting an overreaction, everyone will benefit.

Give your mind a workout

SPY To find out the extent to which you are using assessment- or emotion-focused stressbusters (tactics 1–7) and problem-focused ones (8 and 9) in any particular situation, answer the following questions.

Think about a stressful situation you experienced in the last month or so. How did you cope with the situation? Circle the appropriate number based on the following:

I didn't do this at all 1
I did it a little bit 2
I did this, for sure 3
I did this quite a lot 4
This was a very significant part of what I did 5

1 I shared how I felt about the situation with friends and/or sympathetic colleagues	1 2 3 4 5
2 I thought about what good things might come out of the situation	1 2 3 4 5
3 I remembered that I had coped with similar situations in the past and this helped me feel more confident	1 2 3 4 5
4 I took action based on what had worked for me in the past	1 2 3 4 5
5 I challenged my view of what could go wrong to make sure it wasn't an unrealistic exaggeration	1 2 3 4 5
6 I tried to keep my feelings from interfering with what I was doing	1 2 3 4 5
7 I worked out what needed to be done to make the best of the situation	1 2 3 4 5

8	I did things that made the situation better	1 2 3 4 5

9	I tried to make myself feel better by eating, drinking, going for a walk or some other activity	1 2 3 4 5

10	I talked to someone who I thought could help me with the problem	1 2 3 4 5

11	I looked at the situation optimistically	1 2 3 4 5

12	I looked at all the good things that were happening around me	1 2 3 4 5

13	I asked someone for more information about how to deal with the situation	1 2 3 4 5

14	I broke the challenge into more manageable pieces	1 2 3 4 5

15	I decided that the situation wasn't as bad as I had first thought	1 2 3 4 5

16	I knew what had to be done, so I doubled my efforts to make things work	1 2 3 4 5

17	I took a chance and did something risky	1 2 3 4 5

18	I went to someone who was involved in the situation and challenged some of their assumptions, eg, about what needed to be done and when	1 2 3 4 5

19	I looked at the situation differently and it felt easier or better as a result	1 2 3 4 5

20	Almost immediately, I did some relatively simple things which eased the situation	1 2 3 4 5

Scoring

Total up your scores and place them in the appropriate box in the grid below:

		Total
Problem-focused	4, 7, 8, 10, 13, 14, 16, 17, 18, 20	P =
Emotion-focused	1, 2, 3, 5, 6, 9, 11, 12, 15, 19	E =
Difference between P and E	P - E or E - P depending on which is longer	

Before you look at what these scores suggest, remember that you have filled in the questionnaire with one particular situation in mind. In another situation you might react quite differently.

Which was the highest scoring *type* of stressbuster? That gives you your letter: P or E.

What was your total score for this type? That tells you which column you are in in the grid overleaf.

What is the difference between your score for this type and for the other type. This tells you which row you are in.

(Eg, if you scored 23 for P and 12 for E, then your letter is P, your top score is 23 and the difference is 11 and you are in the middle row and the middle column.)

Find the appropriate box in the grid overleaf.

Score / Difference between P and E	20–40	41–70	71–100
5 or less	You don't appear to be doing very much to bust your stress in this situation. There are many more options available and it would be worth considering using a few of them next time you feel too much stress.	This is good. You are using both types of stressbuster in fairly equal measure. If this is working, then there is no need to change anything. If you still feel too stressed then there are other techniques available – give them a go.	Well done. You appear not only to be using a wide range of stressbusting tactics but also to be using different types of stress-buster in tandem to deal with excessive stress. This is usually the most effective approach. Keep it going.
6 to 30	E: Thinking about the situation differently helps but it is not a substitute for action. You may find that you ease the situation only temporarily before it returns in the same or a similar form. Try identifying the real issue and deciding what you can actually do to make the situation better. P: The situation is likely to be emotional and managing your emotions (and those of the people around you) can be as important as doing things that will help. You are likely to be missing out on powerful tools to make the situation a lot easier, particularly around how you choose to look at the situation.		
More than 30	N/A	If you are having difficulty dealing with excessive stress then this could well be why. You are relying on one type of stressbuster to the virtual exclusion of the other. Both bring benefits so try using more of the kind that scored lowest. For more detail on the implications of being P or E see the box above.	The good news is that you are doing a lot to reduce excessive stress. But watch out. You may be in danger of relying on one type of solution rather than using both because one kind comes more naturally. Look at the one with the lower score and consider what you could do to use more of this type of stressbuster.

(O) Deep breath

Breathing is something we all do, otherwise we wouldn't be here. Yet this banal observation belies a fascinating truth: we may all breathe but very few of us breathe as well as we could. Research shows that unborn babies are more efficient at breathing than adults. Indeed, we breathe best when we are least aware of it – when we are asleep.

Learning to improve our breathing is a brilliant way of coping with stress. It's less fattening than eating a large bar of chocolate, it gives less of a hangover than a bottle of wine, it is less exhausting than a session in the gym, and less expensive than an afternoon shopping. It's free, simple and can be used instantly to calm us, whenever we feel unable to cope.

Consider the old adage 'Take a deep breath and count to ten'. The general reading of this saying is that it's all about pausing before we do something that we might later regret. What often gets forgotten is the 'deep breath' part of the sentence, yet this is of equal, if not greater, benefit.

This chapter explains the different ways in which we breathe and offers practical ways to improve our breathing to help us relax.

Breath freshening

When we get distressed, we breathe in a manner called chest breathing. The focus, as the name implies, is around our chest: our breathing becomes shallow, irregular and rapid. Less air is able to reach our lungs and this in turn leads to an increased heart rate and greater muscle tension.

As well as in distressing situations, chest breathing is also common when we are inactive. The essentials of office life – sitting at a desk, working at a computer – necessitate the sort of posture that pushes us towards such breathing. Office work encourages a breathing style that increases stress rather than helps us to unwind.

The alternative form of breathing is known as **diaphragmatic breathing.** Rather than the emphasis being on our chest, we breathe with our diaphragm – a membrane that separates our lungs from our digestive system. The membrane is naturally taut and expands when we breathe in, gently moving back into place to help us breathe out.

Whereas chest breathing is shallow, irregular and rapid, diaphragmatic breathing is deep, even and loose and allows the respiratory system to work as effectively as possible (it does this by using the full amount of oxygen to oxygenate the blood stream, which helps waste products like carbon dioxide to be removed). As chest breathing leads to increased heart rate and muscle tension, diaphragmatic breathing lowers our heart rate and normalises our blood pressure.

Breathing: the ins and outs

The goal is to learn (and remember) to breathe using our diaphragms. If we do that, we can put our bodies into a state closer to relaxation rather than closer to stress. And the first step to doing this is to be aware of the way we breathe.

To do this, you will need to lie on the floor or sit in a relaxed posture in a chair, legs uncrossed, arms by your sides. Place your right hand on your abdomen or stomach, just above your waistline, and your left hand on your chest. Close your eyes and notice how you are breathing. Which hand is rising and falling as you inhale and exhale?

Most of the time adults breathe with their chests (so our left hand will move more than our right hand). Now try pushing out your stomach as you breathe so that you feel your right hand moving instead.

Can you feel the difference between the two types of breathing? At first it might seem strange to be pushing out your stomach to breathe but after a while it will become more natural and less forced. Try not to make the breathing jerky, or use your stomach muscles too much in the breathing, instead allow the diaphragm to take over. Get a gentle rhythm going: do this for a couple of minutes.

Diaphragmatic breathing: a summary

- Lie down or sit in a relaxed posture (not with crossed arms or legs).

- Close your eyes.

- Be aware of the way you are breathing and if you want to place your hands on your abdomen and chest.

- Breathe through your nose.

- Breathe in such a way that the hand over your diaphragm rises and falls and the one over your chest gently follows the movement of your lower hand.

- If you are finding it difficult breathing using your diaphragm then you should press your hand down as you exhale and let your abdomen push it up as you inhale.

- Do this for a couple of minutes – gently breathing in and out.

To show the effect that distress has on our breathing, now think of something stressful, like being stuck in a traffic jam when you are late for a date. Which hand is moving now? In The Mind Gym's Relaxation techniques workout most people find that their breathing automatically reverts from diaphragmatic breathing back to chest breathing: in other words, their left hand starts to move.

Over the next couple of days, catch yourself breathing at different times. Are you breathing from your chest more than your diaphragm? Once we know how we are breathing, we can focus on how we make it better. Below are two ways of doing so and thus helping us to relax.

Better breathing 1: suggestive breathing

The key to better breathing is to focus on our diaphragm rather than our chest. But we can make it better still by adding in a mental as well as a physical process.

The ideal number of breaths per minute

People tend to breathe more than they need to. Most of us, on average, take a breath every six to eight seconds, but in a recent survey, doctors found that the optimal breathing rate was significantly slower.

In the study published in *The Lancet*, one of the medical community's highly respected journals, researchers working with patients with heart disease investigated breathing rates. They discovered that patients using breathing techniques were able to increase their blood oxygen and perform better on exercise tests. The researchers wrote that low blood oxygen may weaken 'metabolic function and lead to muscle atrophy and exercise intolerance'.

The researchers found that a breathing rate of about 6 breaths per minute, or one every 10 seconds, was around the optimum level.

Along with your diaphragmatic breathing, try saying or thinking 'breathe out tension'. Bizarre as it may seem, it will help you relax. It's the same principle as used in visualisation (see the next chapter, Tranquillity): our brain reacts in much the same way if we imagine an event as if it was actually happening. By imagining ourselves 'breathing out tension', we can make our brain have the same response as if we really *were* breathing out tension. After all, it doesn't matter whether the situation is real or imagined, the important fact is that it helps us relax.

In this exercise, as we inhale we become aware of tension in our bodies and say to ourselves 'breathe in for relaxation'. We then pause with the breath inside us, and then exhale, letting go of any tension, saying to ourselves 'breathe out tension'. Beware of funny looks if you say this out loud in a public place.

Some people go a stage further when going through this exercise by adding a visualisation to their breathing. As they exhale they imagine their stress and tension being released from them, often as red mist. This red tension mist then slowly wafts away and eventually disappears from view.

Better breathing 2: breath-less

'It was a nightmare,' said Emma Jane about her presentation. 'I'd done my preparation and thought I was ready for it. But then, as I knew my turn to speak was coming up, I started to feel a tightening in my chest and wondered whether I had enough breath so I breathed in deeply – but that still didn't feel like enough so I breathed in again and again. When I stood up I sounded really breathy and nervous.'

Emma Jane is describing a common complaint: When people feel panic or are put under stress they have a tendency to gasp: take in a breath and hold on to it. The resulting sensation of fullness and inability to get enough air produces quick, shallow breathing. This can trigger a stress response and the whole thing gets even worse.

Once again, diaphragmatic breathing is the key. But this time, rather than using a suggestion such as 'breathe out tension', try what is known as the ten-second cycle: first, inhale through your nose counting 'one . . . two . . . three'. Pause for 'four', and exhale through your mouth counting 'five . . . six . . . seven . . . eight'. Pause for 'nine' and 'ten' and then inhale again. What we are trying to do is exhale for longer than we inhale. By taking deeper breaths than we need to, we are attempting to reduce the number of breaths we need to take. The closer we can get to our optimum number of breaths per minute (see box above), and the longer the pauses between breaths, the more relaxed we will feel.

Every breath you take

The real pay-off of better breathing comes when we don't use it just as a last resort for dealing with stress but when we use it regularly, putting our bodies close to a state of relaxation for most of the time.

How can we create reminders for ourselves to regulate our breathing? In one of The Mind Gym's workouts, a participant described using Post-it notes stuck on their computer to remind them about diaphragmatic breathing and posture. Think about where and when such reminders might be useful, and give it a go. And remember this: if you can improve your breathing, the most basic of human functions, then you are infinitely better equipped to deal with stress, whenever it occurs.

(P) Tranquillity

It's Friday night. We're on our way home for the weekend, or rather we aren't because the train isn't moving. The conductor apologises for the hold-up, mumbles something barely audible about signal failures and the delay stretches from ten minutes, to thirty, to over an hour. We check our watch as our connection slips from comfortable to tight to forget it. In such a situation, our stress is instant, and we want instant relief.

Visualisation, as with better breathing in the previous chapter, acts as a sort of psychological headache tablet. Wherever we are, whatever the situation, it offers immediate relief and a rapid reduction of our stress levels. Scientifically proven, this technique may take a little time to master but it's well worth it – that missed connection will never seem as distressing again.

The vision thing

It may be a summer's day in the park. It may be having a deep and luxurious bath. It may be sunbathing on a Caribbean beach. When we have a hectic and stressful day, we all have an image in our head about where we'd rather be.

Visualisation is, in essence, similar to creating this pleasant daydream. Here's how it works. Every time we see an image, our mind gives it a meaning (in terms of what it means to us), and this meaning triggers an emotional or physical response. Take the two images which follow, for example: what responses do they conjure up in you? Hunger? Nausea? Yum? Ugh?

Feeling hungry?

Imagined images can trigger exactly the same reactions as real ones. In the eighties film *Weird Science*, an older brother is teasing his younger hungover brother by repeating the phrase 'greasy pork ashtray'. The hungover brother turns the words into images that are attached to meaning (revolting taste, smell and texture) and are converted into an emotional and then physical response ('I need a bucket').

In the same way that the image of a 'greasy pork ashtray' can trigger disgust, so the right type of visualisation can trigger a state of relaxation. All we need to do is to create images that we associate with calm and tranquillity. And unlike the real world where, say, that soothing Caribbean break is out of our reach, visualisation can take us wherever we want to go, immediately.

Emile or imagined?

Emile Coué was the French pharmacist who came up with the idea of visualisation, along with a whole host of positive thinking techniques. Coué knew that our imagination is one of the strongest mental 'tools' at our disposal. His stroke of genius was to work out that our imagination is more powerful than our will: we can't will our way into a relaxed state of mind, however much we'd like to. But, given practice, we can imagine our way into one.

Eyes wide shut

Some people think they can't visualise. This is, of course, nonsense. It's just that they suppose that visualisation is more complicated than it actually is. At its simplest, visualisation is simply imagining something that isn't actually there in front of you. It does require some effort, more than, say, watching a film, which is an almost entirely passive experience, but it is not difficult.

Here is a very simple example of visualisation.

Close your eyes. Imagine you are standing in front of the door to your home.

What colour is the door? Where is the keyhole? Is there a handle or doorknob? If so, what does it look like?

Well done. You have just been visualising. Albeit a simple visualisation but nonetheless you have done it.

You could build on this, making your visualisation more sophisticated. For instance, you could add in movement and start 'visualising' with your other senses (so far the focus has been entirely on sight).

Read the following and then close your eyes again.

You take your key out and hold it in your hand. What temperature is it against your skin? How heavy? What do the edges feel like?
You put the key in the lock. What does this feel like? Does it slide in gently or is there some resistance?
You turn the key. What do you hear?
You push the door open. How does this feel? Where is the pressure? In your arms, or elsewhere? The door opens, you step in. What is the smell?

If you followed this through, you have now done a very good visualisation and, hopefully, it wasn't too difficult. Rather like chess, getting the rules clear is the first step but mastering it takes a little longer and a lot of practice. Here are some general tips that may help:

1 **No distractions**
   We tend to imagine and visualise better if we are not distracted by what we are looking at in real life. As well as closing our eyes, finding somewhere quiet also helps.

2 Use better breathing

This prepares us to move into a state of relaxation in which we are more likely to visualise effectively. This is discussed in detail in the Deep breath chapter (p. 225).

3 Involve all the senses

Although the technique is called visualisation, there should also be sound, touch, taste and smell. When thinking of an apple, for example, what is the sound when we bite into it? Is its texture smooth? Does it taste fresh? Is there a soft, sweet smell?

4 Add details, movement, depth and contrast

Vividness comes from these details, and our eyes are attracted to movement. By adding depth and contrast our visualisation becomes much fuller and 3-D. Imagine again taking a bite out of the apple. What do the teeth marks look like? What is the contrast between the outside and the inside of the apple? If we put the apple down, does it roll gently across the table before stopping?

5 Include emotion

And positive ones at that. Don't just see an apple, for example, but think how we might feel when we bite into it: satisfied, happy, content?

6 Use metaphors and different styles

When we visualise it doesn't always have to be real. Anger could be a dark cloud rolling away into the distance and disappearing or, if it relaxes you, why not have a visualisation in a Cubist or Impressionist style?

7 Be positive

In order to get the most from visualisation we should approach everything that occurs or what we see from a positive perspective. Rather than the sea being rough, make the sea strong.

8 Suspend judgement

Visualisations are not the time to critique, analyse, scrutinise and evaluate. If we judge our visualisation we are more likely to restrict our imagination rather than unleash it.

9 Practise

As with most things, our ability to visualise will get better with time and effort.

10 Be patient

In many ways you can't force visualisation to happen; it takes time and at first may feel a little awkward and clumsy – persevere.

Now wash your hands

Here is another, more in-depth visualisation, although, once again, focusing on a situation that we are all familiar with.

Doing it with your eyes closed

It is impossible to read the guidelines for these visualisations and keep your eyes closed at the same time.

One way round this is to visit The Mind Gym website (www.themindgym.com), where a spoken version is available. Alternatively, use a recordable mini-disc player, or something similar, to record the checklist and listen back.

Or you can simply read through and memorise as many of the instructions as possible. If it's too much to memorise the whole thing, that's fine: the first time, just do the first couple of steps, then add a few more as the process becomes familiar.

This example makes more use of all the senses and might take some practice to get right. But by learning to focus on the small details, we're going a long way to cracking visualisation.

STEP ONE   Close your eyes and imagine a familiar bathroom basin in front of you.

STEP TWO   Imagine the taps and some soap. Note the contours of the basin and how the colour changes shade at different points. Look at the taps: the design, the reflection they may give, the shadows they make. What colour is the soap? What shape? Does it look like it is stuck to the basin or loose or can't you tell?

STEP THREE   Now reach down and put the plug in. Then reach over and turn the taps on, hearing the splash of the water falling into the sink. How does the sound change as the basin starts to fill up? Look at where the edge of the water touches the side of the basin. Is it a straight line or a wave? How quickly is the water level rising? Notice how the light glints on the water's surface. Once the basin is fairly full, turn off the taps.

STEP FOUR   Put a hand into the water and check the temperature. If it is too hot or too cold, turn the taps on again until it is the right temperature for you to wash in. Put both hands into the basin so the water laps against your wrists. How does this feel? Leave them there for a moment.

STEP FIVE Now take your hands out of the basin and pick up the soap. Notice its colour, its shape and its texture. Bring the bar up to your nose. What does it smell like?

STEP SIX Fold the soap over in your hands and notice how it lathers and how your hands glide over one another. Put the soap down and notice the sound it makes as it rests on the basin. Continue washing your hands.

STEP SEVEN Put your hands back in the basin. Hear the noise as they break the surface of the water. Note how it feels as you leave them in the water and how it changes as you start to rub them together to remove the remaining lather from the soap. Notice how the water changes colour and the bubbles appear on the surface. What else can you see as you look into the basin?

STEP EIGHT Take your hands out of the basin. Pick up a towel, noting its colour and texture. Use it to dry your hands. Note how this feels and the patterns the towel makes as you use it.

STEP NINE Pull out the plug. Watch the water disappear. What do you hear? What does the basin look like now? How is it different from when you looked at it, empty, a few moments ago?

STEP TEN Open your eyes and come out of the visualisation.

This visualisation went into far more detail than the previous one about opening the front door. Once you get used to the process it becomes easier to delve deeper and conjure up the specific sensations that you feel. You can also do something that alters the circumstances and leads to a whole new string of experiences; for example, the soap bar could slide out of your hand and fall on the floor.

If you aren't yet comfortable with visualising, keep practising with these two examples, or try something else, say peeling an apple or making a cafetière of fresh coffee.

A place called peace
Some people find the visualisation about washing their hands is itself a relaxing experience. This is partly because it takes their mind off things that worry them and partly because they find the experience itself (putting their hands in warm water) and the pace (fairly slow and reflective) calming.

The next stage in using visualisation to help us relax is to create a place (real, imaginary or a bit of both) where we feel completely relaxed. This place is unique to us. And though we create it through a fairly detailed visualisation, once we have imagined it fully we can return quickly, whenever we want to feel calmer.

This example is a little longer than the ones we have tried so far so, again, logging on to The Mind Gym website, where there is an audio copy, or making your own recording, would be useful. Otherwise, as before, memorise each step and slowly build the visualisation up.

Ready to start? Relax using diaphragmatic breathing and close your eyes . . .

STEP ONE   Visualise yourself walking down a path. What can you see? What can you smell? What is the weather like? What's the temperature? What is the path made of? What are you wearing on your feet or are you barefoot? What sound do you make as you walk? What else can you hear? What else are you wearing? Is your mouth dry? Can you taste anything?

STEP TWO   You come to a bend in the path and as you walk round the corner, maybe speeding up, eager to find out what is there, you see a building. It is a building where you instantly know you will be relaxed, happy and calm. What kind of building is it? What does it look like? What are the walls made of? Are there windows, doors? What do they look like? What is the roof made of if it has one? Is there smoke coming out of the chimney or a flag blowing in the breeze or anything else moving?

STEP THREE   You walk up to the door and push it open, knowing it will be safe inside. What is the door made of? Is it heavy or does it swing open easily? Is there a squeak or other sound or is it silent? You step over the threshold/hearth and into the building and close the door behind you.

STEP FOUR   Look round the place and take in the doors, walls and windows. What do you see? What is on the walls, if anything? What kind of flooring? What is the ceiling like? (If things are unclear experiment with what is on the walls. Feel free to alter, change and amend what you see – if you don't like anything, just remove it and put something else in its place.)

STEP FIVE   Put in some furniture and other decorations, as you like. Turn around and look up and down so you have a good idea of the whole inside of the building. If you want to, go and look in some other rooms. Once you are as familiar with the inside of the building as you want to be, go to each window and look out – what do you see? If you want, each window can have a very different view. Are the windows open? If so, what can you see or feel or smell from the outside?

STEP SIX   Now add some sound: have something that creates music, whether it be wind chimes or the latest Bang & Olufsen super-stereo. Play some music – it could be trance, jazz or a Verdi aria.

STEP SEVEN   Tell yourself that when in this place you can do anything and no one will care. Here you can be relaxed, content and creative. Sit or lie down somewhere where you are completely comfortable. If you are hungry or thirsty, help yourself to something delicious. What is it? Savour the flavour.

STEP EIGHT   It is now time to create a symbol for stress. The blinds or curtains or shutters close and block the view through the windows. Now imagine, for example, a pile of metal knives, forks and spoons, each with a life of its own, wrapping themselves around each other, stretching and twisting, with the prongs of a fork trying to trap a spoon, or a knife trying to cut off one of the prongs of a fork. You can hear the screeching sound of metal scraping against metal and perhaps even the cries of anguish and determination as they do battle. They are tying themselves up in ever-increasing knots, sliding in and out of each other faster and faster like snakes, forming more and more distorted shapes, each trying to get the better of the other.

STEP NINE   There is then a release of tension – relate the image to how you feel. Imagine, for example, that the knives, forks and spoons are uncoiling from one another, sighing as they do so, gently flopping away and resuming their original shape. Perhaps they all lie down together, the spoons neatly fitting against the spoons, the forks against the forks. Or they form a neat table setting, a knife, a fork and a spoon happily together, maybe rolled up in a comfortable, thick napkin. Focus on the knives, forks and spoons finding their comfortable place and, as they do so, the blinds (or curtains or shutters) open to let in warm sunshine. And you feel totally calm, peaceful and at ease.

STEP TEN   Look around you again. Stand up and wander around your room, make improvements and changes wherever you like, perhaps looking out of the window at the view. Notice what you see. Enjoy the feeling of calm control.

STEP ELEVEN   And, when you are ready, open your real eyes.

This visualisation should create a sense of calm – if it didn't work for you, then it may well be worth giving it another go, perhaps in a place where you are less likely to be distracted or have more time to indulge your senses.

Some people find that trying to come up with their own imaginary place is too demanding. If you feel like this, then use a place you know. Maybe sitting in your garden with the smell of recently cut grass or lying in bed on Sunday morning with the aroma of toast and freshly ground coffee wafting in. As long as it is somewhere that you associate with being relaxed, it should work.

The perfect place

If you want to create a new place for peace then the following questions may help.

1 As you walk towards it, what does your place look like?

2 How do you enter your place?

3 What can you hear?

4 What can you see as you walk in and look around?

5 What are the details of, for example, the pictures, the furniture, the floor?

6 Does your place have a particular smell?

7 What can you see out of the windows?

8 What time of day is it?

9 What was the weather like outside?

10 How do you feel as you walk around or sit down in this place?

And remember you can always change any details you don't like. Try painting the walls a different colour and see how this changes your mood.

Some people also find it useful to write down what their place is like, to help jog their memory for the next time.

Visualisation: a final recap

Visualisation has many uses. Athletes, for example, often visualise the race they are about to run (or row or ride) and find that this mental preparation increases their chances of success. Indeed, the scientific research suggests that effective visualisation increases our chances of achieving our goals in all walks of life (poor visualisation, however, can decrease them, so beware).

But above all, visualisation is brilliant for helping relaxation. Once you have created your place of peace you'll have a highly effective way of coping with stress wherever you are. And when you've really got to know it, you will find that you won't need to go through the whole visualisation each time. Simply going back to your room will be enough to help you relax, and leave it to the other passengers to fret about the late running of the 18.43.

Creative juices

A recent television advert for cooking sauce featured a woman making spaghetti Bolognese for a group of friends. Chatting away, the woman accidentally knocked over the bottle of sauce, splashing it into the Bolognese. But rather than throw it away, she tasted it and guess what? It was delicious. By sticking to her usual recipe, she'd have made just another ordinary meal. By trying something different (albeit accidentally), she created something far more individual and appetising.

Most of us don't think creatively that much as we journey through our regular patterns of life. And in many situations this is a good thing: Bolognese with vanilla milkshake might not be such a winner. Indeed, if we thought afresh every time we found ourselves in a familiar situation, we'd never leave home. *What else could one use an alarm clock for? What if it could answer my emails? Why just an 'alarm' clock; what about a distress clock that warned us about getting over-anxious; a panic clock which told us when to do our day's panicking . . . ?*

This is because we have trained our brain to make practical short cuts. As we progress through life we learn more and more mental short cuts that help us do the regular things in our lives faster, leaving more time for everything else. Once we know how to make a cup of tea, we don't rethink the whole process each time we fill the kettle; we've got better things to do.

But as useful as these short cuts are, there are times when thinking creatively can be an enormous help. One thing that does look like a load of spaghetti is the London Underground: lines criss-cross each other, stations bunch together in the centre, and are hugely spread out in the outskirts. In 1931, Harry Beck had the creative brainwave of designing a topographical rather than a geographical map of the system: the key to usage was how the stations linked to each other, not the actual distance between them. The result was a user-friendly map that Londoners and tourists continue to use virtually unchanged over 70 years later (and sparked the idea for the structure of this book).

In our own lives, too, there are many situations where it pays to be creative. For example:

1   To solve a problem

2   To spot (or discover) an opportunity

3   To find a better, quicker or easier way of doing something

4   For the pleasure of being creative, be it writing a story or decorating a cake

5   To add a little sparkle, humour or romance

6   To make life more interesting

Unfortunately, most of us are so adept at creating mental short cuts that even when we want to, we have difficulty turning them off and thinking creatively instead. Which is where this section comes in: it is for those who want to be able to make the switch and so make more and better use of their creative potential.

The first chapter, Let the juices flow, is filled with ways to spot the mental short cuts (or filters) that have become second nature to us and to remove them, even if only temporarily. The subsequent three chapters are filled with techniques to help us come up with original ideas: Creativity for logical thinkers offers techniques that not only allow but actively encourage logical thinking and yet, in the process, generate lots of fresh ideas; Creativity for free thinkers suggests tools to get the mind going in all sorts of unusual and unexpected directions; and Creativity for wannabe daydreamers explores how we can tap into our unconscious mind to think the unthinkable (also perfect for when someone asks why you've spent the last half hour gazing out of the window).

(Q) Let the juices flow

Making a spectacle of ourselves

A man is driving a black car on a blackened road without street lights and without headlights on his car. A black cat crosses the road right in front of his car and still he is able to apply brakes to save the cat. How come? In this chapter we'll not only reveal the answer to this intriguing brainteaser but more importantly the way to solve it: how to think about things creatively.

When people look back at the past nostalgically they are often described as having rose-tinted spectacles. Similarly, the patterns in understanding and problem solving we have developed are so second nature that it is as if we are wearing 'problem-solving' spectacles: we have forgotten we are wearing them, but they provide a useful (if for our own eyes, distorted) view of reality. The trick to thinking creatively is to take off these problem-solving spectacles or 'filters' and perceive the world differently once more.

Would we want to take these filters off all the time? Definitely not. Just like a pair of glasses they help us see the world in a way which is useful, recognisable and clear. But when we want to be creative, we want to remove our glasses and see the fuzzy edges, the different shapes, the mass of interlocking colour that breaks down our assumptions and makes us think differently about the world around us and the challenges we face.

This chapter explores the different kinds of reality spectacles we all wear and how to go about taking them off. Let's start by shedding some light on why that black cat wasn't run over.

Five ways in which we see the world

1 I know the question

A donkey is tied to a rope 6 feet long and there is a bale of hay 8 feet away. How can the donkey get to the hay if he does not bite or undo the rope?

Can you work out the answer? It has nothing to do with using his hind legs or gusts of wind blowing the hay in his direction. If you can't work out the answer then try to work out what assumptions you have made. The question has been deliberately worded to encourage you to think in a certain way but this is the wrong way if you want to solve the problem.

What are the assumptions you have made about the donkey that aren't in the question? That a donkey has four legs, perhaps. And what about the rope? We know it is tied to the donkey but what is it tied to at the other end? Aha. It doesn't say and therein lies the answer to this question. The rope is not tied to anything and so the donkey has no problem getting to the bale of hay.

Frustrating though this brainteaser is, it highlights a common filter that hinders creativity: knowing the problem. We often make assumptions about the problem before we try to solve it. This will automatically reduce the range of possible answers. If our assumptions are correct, they may help us get to an answer faster. But if they are wrong, they prevent us ever getting one.

Sometimes there is a conscious effort to mislead. Let's go back to the black car and the black cat at the beginning of the chapter. Can you spot the assumption that most people make when defining this problem? Most of us imagine the scene and because the word 'black' occurs so often and because there is a mention of street lights and headlights, we assume that it is night-time. However, it doesn't say so. Once we realise that it could be daytime we can solve the puzzle immediately.

Except in brainteasers, the narrow definition of a problem isn't usually deliberate. It occurs because we haven't challenged the way it has been expressed or what lies behind the expression.

The idea of introducing ATMs (machines in the wall used primarily for withdrawing cash) came out of some rather tired market research. Bank customers had said for years that they wished that their branch was open longer and at weekends. But when the banks calculated the cost of this they decided it wasn't worth it. It was only when someone spotted that the customers didn't necessarily want the branch to be open, only to be able to withdraw cash outside normal banking hours, that the idea of the ATM took off.

Were you told at school to make sure that you read the question in the exam properly before answering? With our busy lives there is often a similar rush to answer, assuming we know what the question is without checking. The consequence is the same: the wrong answer.

Creative thinking in the real world: air travel

Stuart needed to be in the States on two separate occasions about six weeks apart from each other. So he bought two return tickets. He even thought he'd been quite clever by using the web to find some good deals.

The flights are about a third of the price if you stay a Saturday, something he couldn't have done on either of the trips. However, he could have bought two return tickets, the first from London to New York; the second from New York to London and back (with his US credit card). He could then have used the first legs of both tickets on his first trip and would have saved himself £500.

2 I know the answer (or, at least, how to work it out)
Look at the two lines below. Which do you think is the longer one, A or B?

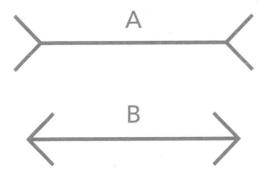

Now measure them. Go on, use the edge of your mobile phone, a pen, the spine of another book or any other straight edge and find out for sure which line is longer.

Were you surprised? Most people think the lines are the same length because they have seen a puzzle that looks like this before where the lines were the same length. But this is not the same puzzle. And these lines are not the same length.

The 'I know the answer' filter occurs when we assume that either we know how to solve the problem or that we already know what the solution is. Whilst this might happen at the same time as 'I know the question', they are often quite separate.

A man was unhappy with his job because, even though he was earning good money and liked the company, he hated his boss. Eventually, he decided to go and see a recruitment consultant who assured him that there would be no problem finding him a new job as there was a shortage of people with his skills and experience.

At home that night he re-examined the assumptions he was making about how to solve his problem. The next day he went back to the recruitment consultant and, as well as discussing the job opportunities that were available, gave the consultant his boss's name, praising his boss very highly. The boss was surprised when, a few days later, he was called about a new opportunity and, suspecting nothing, investigated further and took on the new role in another company.

This happy solution for all concerned was reached only by thinking completely differently about how to approach a familiar problem.

3 I live in the real world
When Einstein developed his theory of relativity, he did it in such a way that he left reality behind. He pictured himself sitting on a beam of light and imagined the journey he was going to take.

Our thinking is often influenced by the 'reality' we inhabit. In one of The Mind Gym workouts, there is an objective 'to generate ideas for a new tourist attraction'. One of the component parts of the problem is the opening times for this tourist attraction.

At first the group usually groans (or looks as if it would like to) – what could be more boring than coming up with times that a tourist attraction might open? And with their reality filter firmly on, they list all the possible variations they can think of. An abridged version of their brainstorm looks something like this:

1 9 to 5	7 Weekends
2 10 to 6	8 24/7/365
3 8 to 6	9 Lunchtime
4 Evenings	10 5pm to 9am (all night)
5 Mornings	11 10pm to 3am
6 Afternoons	12 Breakfast

Creative thinking in the ancient world: Archimedes

The phrase 'Eureka moment' comes from the apocryphal story that Archimedes screamed 'Eureka' from his bath tub when he had a sudden flash of inspiration. (This is a widely reported phenomenon that is explored further in Creativity for wannabe daydreamers.)

According to the tale, Archimedes was lying in his bath thinking about how to measure the volume of an irregular object (which is what very clever people do, unlike most of us who make ourselves a Mohican hairdo out of the bubbles. Or maybe that's just us). As Archimedes was thinking, no doubt considering all the traditional ways of measuring volume, he noticed how the water level rose as he sank further into the bath. He then realised that you could measure the volume of an irregular object (in this case himself) by measuring the volume of water that was displaced when it was submerged in a tank. Eureka indeed.

A (retrospectively) simple solution to a highly complex problem, found only by removing the 'I know how to solve this' filter and so changing the way of answering the question.

At the end of this they tend to feel that they have been rather creative – who would have thought about just breakfast as an opening time?

It's true that there's nothing wrong with this list but it doesn't exactly sparkle with originality. Why? Because all these ideas are based around what we are used to in real life. In the workout we then discuss what would happen if we dismissed all our knowledge about what opening times normally look like and thought about alternative ways of deciding when to open the attraction. The next list looks very different. Here is an example from one group:

- The first 15 minutes of every hour

- Only when there are 20 people in the queue

- Only if people are carrying water

- When people are wearing red clothes

- If half the group is under 10 years old

- For groups of 6

- Only with a bag of peanuts

- Only when no one is there

- When the moon is full

- Months with an 'R' in them

These opening times then sparked new ideas. If we take when the moon is full as an opening time, they mused excitedly, what about a surfing competition at night with a full moon (the group suggested calling this 'Night Surfari').

One Manchester United fan said that we could take people who are wearing red clothes as wearing the Manchester United football strip, and they could get into the football museum or into specific bars with it on. The idea about the first 15 minutes of every hour was also popular as the group thought that it would help with congestion inside, thereby allowing an effective flow of people through the attraction itself.

The point is, by letting go of the reality we're used to, the ideas we generate are likely to be more quirky, different and engaging.

4 I am an expert

Sometimes our knowledge or expertise can get in the way of seeing different solutions, or cause us to make assumptions about a particular problem.

Creative thinking in the inventing world: the roll of the outsider

Many inventions we take for granted today had the strangest of beginnings. Here are just a few.

- **The roll-on deodorant**
  The original deodorant was invented in 1888 in Philadelphia, but it wasn't until the 1950s that the roll-on appeared. The inspiration? The ballpoint pen: an inventive employee worked out that the same idea could be used to spread deodorant evenly as it could for ink.

- **The microwave oven**
  This invention came about as a by-product of World War Two radar research. While working on magnetrons (vacuum tubes that produce microwave radiation), engineer Percy LeBaron Spencer discovered that a chocolate bar in his pocket had melted. Working out that the microwaves were the cause, he experimented and discovered that not only could microwaves cook food, they could do so much faster than normal ovens.

- **The Alcopop**
  This came about because an Australian farmer was throwing away a good proportion of his lemon crop, simply because the lemons weren't the right size. Rather than letting them rot, his neighbour, a brewer, took them, used his knowledge of brewing and a family recipe for lemonade, and the 'Two Dogs' lemon brew was created.

A group of expert magicians was asked to watch one of their fellow conjurors do a trick where an ace appeared from the middle of a shuffled pack. A group of novices was also asked to observe the same trick.

When asked what technique the magician used to get the ace to appear, the experts gave long convoluted explanations that involved complex and skilful sleight of hand. The novices simply said that the pack contained only aces. In this instance the novices were right – the expertise of the magicians got in their way.

There is a tale of the older boys in a school teasing a younger one by offering him a nickel (worth 5 cents) and a dime (worth 10 cents) and telling him he could have whichever one he picked. The younger boy would always choose the nickel 'because it's bigger'. The older ones would give him the coin and laugh at him for being so stupid.

It was a game they would play again and again and each time he would choose the nickel, 'because it's bigger', and each time the older boys would give him the coin and laugh at him.

A kind teacher spotted this and, feeling sorry for the younger boy, said, 'Did you know that a dime is worth more than a nickel?'

'Of course.'

'So why do you keep picking the nickel?' asked the teacher.

'Because if I took the dime they'd stop offering me the money.'

The older boys and the teacher have their 'expert' filter on. They know that a dime is worth more than a nickel. But the younger boy has removed his expert filter so is able to think differently about the situation. As a result, he is quids, or at least cents, in.

The expert filter comes in when we assume that we have special knowledge that helps us see something better than people without that knowledge. While this can be true it can also have the opposite effect.

5 Is and could
Take a look at the picture below – what do you see?

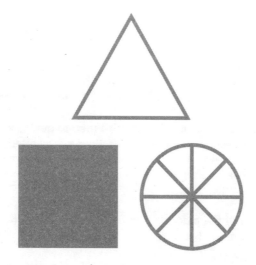

Some people say 'a triangle, a shaded square and a circle with lines in it' or 'three geometric images'. Others say, 'a tractor on a sunny morning', 'a set of children's building blocks', 'a clown's face', or 'the different windows from the children's TV programme, *Play School*'.

When it comes to thinking creatively, being too literal doesn't pay. Don't worry if you still can't see a clown's face in the picture, that isn't really the point. Creativity is not, in the main, about being right or wrong but about seeing things differently. Looking at a picture and imagining what it could be as opposed to what it actually is, can release a fresh train of thought.

What are the next three numbers in this sequence: 1, 8, 15, 22, 29, 5? This is a row of numbers. We could spend ages trying to find a formula that links them but we wouldn't get very far. What else could they be?

Instead of a row, they could be a column. Instead of numbers they could represent something that is usually represented by numbers.

If you haven't worked out what the next three numbers are, draw them as a column. Imagine there is a grid and fill in the rows with the missing digits.

What does this look like? A calendar? The next three numbers are 12, 19 and 26. The numbers represent the same day of the week in a month with 31 days.

Children often exhibit this kind of 'could be' creativity. They are uninhibited by assumptions about what is or the concern about getting things wrong (there is no 'wrong'). A twig becomes an aeroplane, the water from a hose a mountain stream, a hole in a wall is a dark and dangerous cave, the petals from a flower the hidden treasure.

We can gain from doing much the same. Richard James was a naval engineer who was working on tension springs to support equipment on battleships. When one of the springs accidentally fell to the ground and kept on moving, Richard had a thought: his iffy tension spring could be a children's toy. The result? The invention of the Slinky and one very rich naval engineer.

Pick up an object in front of you. What is it? What could it be?

(Using images, sounds, smells and words as stimuli to encourage fresh thinking is explored in more detail in the chapter Creativity for free thinkers.)

Guidelines for boosting creativity

There are no rules for creativity. But here are five guidelines that, when we follow them, will mean that we tend to come up with fresher, more innovative ideas.

1 Go for quantity. 'I find that the best way to have a good idea is to have lots of them,' remarked two-time Nobel Prize-winner Linus Pauling. When it comes to creativity, more is better, partly because we never know when we are going to hit on something great and partly because, by going for volume, we force ourselves to think more widely.

2 Don't judge or evaluate the ideas as you go along. This is the hardest rule to stick to. No sooner do we have some zany thought than we dismiss it as, well, absurd. All ideas are good ideas because at the moment we have them we don't know where they might lead.

3 Write down or capture in some other way all the ideas you have, otherwise you may concentrate on trying to remember what you've already thought of rather than putting these ideas, however brilliant, to one side and thinking afresh.

4 Have an objective. Aimless creativity is usually just that. Some sense of purpose greatly increases the odds of coming up with something that is not only original but also worthwhile.

5 Love half answers. The moment of genius may come from letting an earlier thought that you liked (but weren't quite sure why) gestate. Ambiguity is great. Don't dismiss partial solutions as they can often lead to the complete answer, though, frustratingly, usually not straight away.

Prepare for creative take-off: removing the spectacles

Once we know which spectacles are on and how they are affecting the way we are thinking, then it is relatively easy to take them off. The challenge is noticing them in the first place. The most common spectacles that inhibit our creative thinking are outlined above: simply by knowing what they are, we should find it easier to recognise when they are on.

Sometimes this is enough, but for the times when it isn't, here are four techniques that help us both spot what filters are on and turn them off.

- Rephrase the problem or issue. Imagine, for example, explaining the challenge out loud to someone who doesn't speak very good English. As you do so, look out for the assumptions you are making that may not be true (not about their English but about the problem).

- Look at answers that don't help and ask, why not? Once we can see why the ideas we are coming up with aren't appropriate we may start to think differently about what could be.

- Keep asking questions. While 'What assumptions am I making?' is a good place to start, it is usually not enough. Probe further, examining the definition of each word or alternative meanings of what has been said, or the reason behind it.

- Put on a different filter. For example, take on different people's perspectives. How would a doctor look at this challenge? How would someone who had never seen anything like it before think about it?

The following chapters are packed with more complex techniques that help us think differently by removing or changing the filters for different types of creative challenge and for different kinds of mind. At its essence, though, thinking more creatively doesn't need to be complicated.

If we look at the world through rose-coloured glasses then it is no surprise that everything is rosy. This can be very pleasant but if we want to think creatively then we need to realise we've got the glasses on and (mentally) take them off.

Now, where did I put them?

Give your mind a workout

I SPY Can you spot the filters that the following brainteasers are encouraging you to put on and so take them off and solve these problems?

1   Which three numbers are next in the sequence 1 0 1 1 1 2 1 2 ?

2   There are three light bulbs in a room and three separate switches the other side of a solid wooden door. You cannot see any of the light bulbs from the light switches. You are one side of the door and can go

into the room only once and cannot come back. How will you find out which switch is for which light bulb in one go?

3   A woman has five children and half of them are male. Is this possible? If so, how?

4   A woman with no driver's licence goes the wrong way down a one-way street and turns left at a corner with a no left turn sign. A policeman sees her but does nothing. Why?

5   What's the next letter in this sequence: W, T, N, L, I, T ?

6   There is a barrel with no lid and some wine in it. Without any measuring implements and without removing any wine from the barrel, how can you easily decide whether it is more or less than half full?

Answers at The Mind Gym Online

I TRY 1   Take a sheet of blank paper. Spend a couple of minutes writing down as many different types of transport as you can. When you feel you are running out (but not before) read on.

How creative did you get?

Different coloured bicycles – come on, have another go.

Kitesurfing; pogo sticks – OK, you're roughly where most people get to.

Magic carpet; Star Trek transporter; Tardis – OK, now we're going somewhere but your thinking is still limited by your interpretation of the objective.

Go back and read it again. What assumptions are you making about it? What do you assume the question is about but it might not be?

If you're still stuck go online.

2   Take another sheet of paper. Draw a dot in the middle of a large circle (see illustration) without removing the pen from the paper.

There are several ways of doing this. Once you spot the filters you have on (in this case the reality filter is likely to be strongest) you will find it much easier to come up with a solution.

If you are still stuck visit The Mind Gym website.

ⓇCreativity for logical thinkers

'I'd love to be creative,' said Martin, a participant at one of our workouts, 'but I'm not.' When pressed for an answer as to how you could spot a creative person, Martin was clear. 'Flamboyant,' he said, 'long messy hair.' 'Outrageous clothes,' suggested a fellow participant. 'Temperamental,' offered another.

Martin's perception of what a creative person looks and behaves like is a common one. It's also wrong. The description he and his colleagues came up with isn't of a creative person: it's of a caricature. The good news about creative people is that they are just as likely to look like Martin, with his short hair and shirt and tie, as anyone else.

This chapter explores what logical thinkers have to do to think creatively and offers two very well tested tools that require structured thinking to generate original ideas. And all without taking off our 'sensible' shoes.

The number one challenge for logical thinkers who want to think creatively

As logical thinkers, we have one natural advantage when it comes to thinking creatively, and one disadvantage. The key strength is the ability to follow a process. This is exactly what is needed and gives us an advantage over less structured thinkers. The key danger is our ability and appetite to continually assess and evaluate. In many situations this is a great asset; however, it gets in the way when we want to think creatively.

Our biggest challenge therefore is to ignore this instinct to assess. When we come up with an idea, we will want to evaluate it: we may like it or, more likely, we may find some fault with it. This is a temptation we need to resist if we want to be creative.

But how? Here are some tips and techniques that may help:

1   We can put a limit on how long we spend generating ideas and so relax, confident that assessment will happen in due course. The logical thinker is usually happier when deferring judgement rather than postponing it indefinitely.

2   Remember, there is no risk with having creative ideas. The risk comes with the evaluation and, even more, with implementation. Any ideas that we come up with in this idea development phase can be thrown away. There is no chance that something will go wrong as a result.

Spot the creative genius

3 Write everything down (or say it out loud if you are with other people). What may seem like a lousy idea now may be the springboard for an amazing idea for someone else, or to us later.

4 Put aside time just for coming up with ideas. Promise not to consider whether this is a good use of time until it is over. You cannot evaluate who has won a football match until the final whistle blows and, similarly, you cannot tell whether you have come up with a good idea until your time is up (and often not even then).

5   Spot when you are evaluating. Pay a penalty, say, having to come up with three more ideas in the next 30 seconds.

6   Time pressure. Too much makes us panic but some can be a good thing as it means there isn't enough time to evaluate on the go.

7   See quantity of ideas as a measure of successful creative thinking, not quality.

Thinking about an idea without evaluating or judging it can be particularly difficult at first. It may take practice to get used to it.

Tool 1: outrageous opposites

Opposites attract. Every action needs an equal and opposite reaction. Heroes have their villains. Yins have their yangs, McEnroes their Björn Borgs, Sherlock Holmes their Moriartys. Whether we're talking physics, folklore or cliché (there's two sides to every story), they all suggest that there is an opposite.

This is exactly how this creative technique works. It considers the normal and traditional way of solving a problem and then uses the opposites as a springboard to create new and different solutions. In footballing terms, it is like having a forward line of both a traditional centre forward (tall, strong, good in the air) and a more unorthodox partner (small, creative, capable of the unexpected).

A different meaning of opposite
The key part in using this creativity tool is generating opposites. At first glance this is easy enough, as we consider the literal opposite. Below are three examples and three for you to answer.

Traditional	Opposite
Black	White
Rich	Poor
Tall	Short
High	
Early	
Day	

The challenge is to come up with as many other opposites as possible. The trick is not to stick to the literal opposite, but to find other alternatives to the traditional ideas. The literal opposite to black may be white, for example, but other colours are also opposites: in money terms, for example, you're either in the black or in the red. It is here that we need to ignore our instincts to assess and put our evaluating skills to one side.

Remember, we are using this tool to help us think creatively, not to force us to think analytically. In the box overleaf, the examples are worked further, using our new definition of opposite (and some space for yours too).

Traditional	Opposite
Black	White, red, green, orange, pink, light
Rich	Poor, well-off, comfortable, respected, shrewd, generous, understated, barren, plain, happy, light, sincere
Tall	Short, long, strong, tiny, microscopic, giant, wide, narrow, true
High	
Early	
Day	

For some suggestions on more outrageous opposites, see later in this section.

This is fine for single items but not yet extremely useful. The power of this tool is if we have more than one component to play with. Imagine we are thinking about going on holiday and want to do something different from last year's cottage in Wales. Here we have two parts to the equation – the cottage and Wales – and can look for the opposite either in part or in entirety. For example:

Traditional	Opposite
Welsh cottage	Italian cottage, Italian villa, Welsh barge, Dutch windmill, French castle, Marine adventure (whales)

In this way, without stopping to assess, we can come up with many more different and interesting options. Again, it is vital to remember why we are doing this: to come up with innovative ideas rather than a comprehensive list of accurate opposites.

Think of the opposite – the process
Having understood how to generate creative opposites, here are the steps to get the most from this technique.

1   Ensure that the objective is clear and that everyone has the same understanding of it (eg, going somewhere on holiday).

2   Brainstorm ideas we would normally produce, in other words the traditional solutions (eg, Welsh cottage).

3   Find the opposites (eg, Italian villa, French castle, etc).

4   Don't forget to evaluate afterwards.

Earning a crust: the story of the stuffed pizza

Do you ever think about how people come up with ideas for the products you use every day?

Imagine your objective was to create a new type of pizza. Using the outrageous opposites tool, your initial chart might have looked like this:

Traditional	Opposite
New topping	
Different size of pizza	
Different price of pizza	

OK, so what are the opposites to these traditional ideas? The grid may well have looked like this:

Traditional	Opposite
New topping	Old topping, no topping, old topping in the crust, upside down, fruit topping
Different sizes of round pizza	Square, rectangle, by the metre, one size fits all, sell in slices to make a whole
Price based on topping	One price fits all, price based on time of day, number of pizzas purchased, price based on crust, price based on loyalty (ie, buy five and the price comes down, buy ten and the price comes down further)

From here a number of ideas would have been evaluated against criteria such as whether there was a market for the ideas, how the new products would fit into the delivery process and so on. And then you might have hit upon the concept of a stuffed crust pizza, currently selling in a supermarket freezer near you now.

Opening a restaurant: the outrageous opposites approach

In The Mind Gym's Creativity for logical thinkers workout, a group was asked to come up with ideas for opening a new restaurant. Some of the traditional ideas that were considered to start with were price, type of food, opening hours and so on.

The question of price might not be the most exciting place to begin, but it generated the most interesting ideas. To start with, the discussion centred on whether to have set meals or individual prices. Thinking a little more creatively, someone suggested rather than set prices why not have different prices for different days: cheaper meals on Mondays, for example, when the restaurant would be quiet?

Starting to think outrageously, someone suggested that rather than just having different prices on different days, why not have different prices on the same day? An idea that came out of this was a restaurant in a financial district where the prices are on an electronic board and go up and down based on how much each opinion is ordered. Each table has an electronic box so they can place orders when they want and will get the price showing at the time. Should I order my pudding now or wait to see if it gets cheaper? It also means that the restaurant can manage the inventory by lowering the prices of slow-selling dishes and pushing them up when they have only one left (it would also save money as you wouldn't need waiters to take orders or issue the bill). There could also be a price based on loyalty. If customers come back more than once a week they get cheaper food, thereby encouraging people to eat there more regularly.

Sounds far-fetched? In fact, great minds clearly think alike as there is a bar in Paris called Footsie based on a similar principle: bar prices are modelled on shares which rise and fall depending on how many people buy them. The Time Out Guide to Paris says of the system, 'This is such a plummy idea it should be floated on the stock market.' If such a great concept can come about from thinking creatively about something as everyday as price, who knows what might be thought up once we get on to the question of decor?

Your turn

Here's a grid for you to complete for your own subject. There is also an online version of this tool.

- What is your objective?

- What normal/traditional ideas might you come up with?

- What are the opposites/alternatives of these ideas?

Objective:

Traditional	Opposite

How did it go?

People often find they are very surprised at both the quantity of ideas they produce using this technique and the broad range of ideas they may not otherwise have thought of. There are, however, some common problems people find with this tool. Below are a few along with suggestions about what to do to overcome them.

Advantages and disadvantages

The main advantages of this tool are that it is simple, easy to use and generates a wide variety of ideas. The disadvantages are that the ideas which we tend to produce are based around our initial thoughts, and so do not always move us far enough away from our traditional solution.

Problem	Solution
I seemed to come up with the literal opposites but not the alternatives	This is a common problem. For example when people generate the traditional idea of 'topping' they believe the opposite is 'no topping'. Don't take the word 'opposite' too literally. Consider what broader category the traditional answer is in, and then consider all the different items within that category. So, for the example earlier, the opposite of 'Welsh cottage holiday' is 'no Welsh holiday'. But if I consider that cottage is a component, then I could say the opposite of cottage is anything from castle to windmill to a hole in the ground
All the ideas seem useless	Unfortunately, that's creativity. If you come up with a fantastic idea every time you try, it's probably not that fantastic an idea or not that different from a load of ideas that you've had before. Persevere. Try coming back to it later, using a different technique, or think about your goal from a different perspective

Problem	Solution
The ideas didn't seem very different	Think through the opposites. Are you considering every item within the traditional idea (eg, Welsh and cottage, and not just Welsh cottage?), or even articulating the idea in full (a new topping in the middle of a pizza)? If you do this the ideas should get different fast. The alternative is to use a more quirky creativity tool – read on
It was difficult coming up with traditional ideas	You're probably using the wrong tool. Try brainstorming first with your 'internal filters' off to generate ideas. Then pick out the more traditional ones and take them through the outrageous opposites process
There were too many alternatives for each of the traditional ideas	Lucky you – that's a great problem to have. Record the ideas in as much of an order as possible. Consider what criteria you should use to evaluate. For example, one of my 'must have' criteria for the holiday might be a high level of comfort. I could run through my list of ideas and remove many using that criterion alone

And from earlier

Here are some opposites (or alternatives) to the earlier example on p. 258. These are by no means right or wrong, simply suggestions.

Traditional	Opposite
High	Low, short, distant, close, ground, basement, sober, straight, fresh
Early	Late, premature, never-ending, long, first, last, average, evening, behind
Day	Night, week, month, year, century, nocturnal, hour, minute, suspended animation

Tool 2: the morphological matrix

The morphological matrix is an ugly name for a very elegant creativity tool. It has been used by everyone from philosophers to car designers to scriptwriters. Its method is simple: break down a goal into its component parts, consider these parts separately and then recombine them to find new solutions.

What's more, on an ideas per second basis, no other technique can beat the morphological matrix.

The key to the matrix
Without coming over all Keanu Reeves, here is the key to the matrix: attributes. An attribute is a component part of a problem. So if the question is coming up with ideas for a surprise party, an attribute might be the theme, the location or the music. An attribute is different from an 'item' which is a possible answer to each attribute question. So for the attribute location, two items that might fit in are boat and rooftop.

Making the matrix work is all about understanding the difference between attributes and items, and not confusing the two.

Let's suppose, then, that our objective is to hold a surprise party. We can then select three or four of the best attributes. In this instance we might choose dress, location and music. Once the best attributes have been selected we can come up with a list of items under each attribute.

Dress	Location	Music
Wild West	Boat	String quartet
London Underground	Rooftop terrace	Jazz band
Film star	In the country	DJ
School	Underground club	Acoustic
Something beginning with 'P'	Warehouse	Pianist
Someone else	Posh hotel	Gospel choir
1960s	At home	Abba tribute band
Medieval banquet	By the seaside	Blues guitarist
Toga	Favourite bar	Karaoke
Black tie	Shop window	Sounds of nature

We then take one item from each column to generate a new idea. For example:

- A Wild West party on a rooftop terrace with a blues guitarist in the corner

- A toga party in a shop window with a gospel choir singing in the background

- Everyone dressed as something beginning with P, in a posh hotel with a pianist playing on a grand piano

There are ten items in each of these three categories and so we have 1000 possible combinations or solutions to our objective. Add one more column and we have 10,000 possible ideas. And by using the matrix in this way we are sure to generate ideas that we would not normally have considered. Professional party planners can eat their party hats.

Your turn
Consider a goal or problem that you are facing at the moment. The objective is best described as either a how question or a statement. For example, 'How can we decorate our living room?', or 'To generate ideas for decorating our living room'. Objectives become unhelpful when they are either put too specifically or in a yes/no manner, for example 'Should we decorate the living room?'

What are the attributes of your objective? If we were considering what the attributes were for the objective of decorating the living room, 'deckchairs' would not be an attribute, but an item within an attribute (furniture).

Select the best attributes. Best could mean anything from the most interesting to the one that seems to make most sense given your objective. You could have as many attributes as you like (remember that you're going to create a list of items for each) and no less than two. For the first go, three or four attributes is probably best.

Brainstorm items within each attribute. Work through one attribute at a time, coming up with as many ideas as possible.

Objective:

Attribute 1	Attribute 2	Attribute 3

Make the combinations you particularly like and evaluate them.

Logical or creative? When it comes to thinking logically or creatively, we can have our cake and eat it. One type of thinking doesn't preclude the other; in fact it can help it. And best of all is when both are combined. Elementary, my dear Watson.

(S) Creativity for free thinkers

In his Oscar-winning film *Bowling for Columbine*, Michael Moore visits an American bank where, by opening an account, you get a free gun. The scene is typical of his satire: topical, contemporary and razor-sharp. At the other end of the humour spectrum is the classic Monty Python film, *Monty Python and the Holy Grail*. In one scene, the hero is stopped by the Knights who say 'Ni!' He is only allowed to pass if he brings them a sprig of shrubbery. Two brilliant films: both extremely funny, but with completely different senses of humour.

The previous chapter, Creativity for logical thinkers, deals with creativity in a more structured and rational sort of way. This is good but it is not the full story. To harness fully the power of creativity and to come up with even more exciting and original ideas, we need to tap into our intuition as well. In terms of our film examples, it is a question of thinking a little less like Michael Moore and a little more like Monty Python.

Free-range Bacon

Six Degrees of Kevin Bacon is a popular film trivia game from the 1990s. Building on the idea of Six Degrees of Separation (the theory that anyone can contact anyone else in the world in six steps), the game challenged players to link any film star to the film star Kevin Bacon. So, for example, if the actress in question is Carrie Fisher, then you could link her to Kevin Bacon as follows: Carrie Fisher was in *Star Wars* with Harrison Ford; Harrison Ford was in *The Fugitive* with Tommy Lee Jones; Tommy Lee Jones was in *Batman Forever* with Val Kilmer; Val Kilmer was in *Heat* with Robert De Niro; De Niro was in *Sleepers*, as was . . . Kevin Bacon.

In the same way as the Kevin Bacon game uses our film knowledge to link together two seemingly unconnected actors, we can use our minds to pull seemingly disparate objects together.

Let's pluck a trio of nouns drawn at random from a dictionary, and see if we can find a way of connecting them; say, electricity, herring and one-armed bandit.

Can we link the three together? It's tricky, yes, but not impossible. One way of linking them could be that a one-armed bandit needs electricity to function, and that the machine has a fish theme, the jackpot is when you get three herrings in a row. Or maybe there was a Mexican bandit who only had one arm, who liked nothing more than frying herrings on his electric cooker. The words in question are so far apart that thinking logically we could never have connected them. By thinking more freely, we can.

Grundies

In a creativity workout participants were asked to create a product or service for the elderly. One suggestion was for people with osteoporosis or prone to brittle bones to wear something over their underpants that contained the equivalent of a miniature spirit level controlling something like an air bag in a car. If the person wearing this device started to fall, the air bag would inflate, leaving them with a soft landing rather than broken bones.

The idea was sparked by a slightly abstract picture of some life vests.

Have a go yourself with these sets of words.

- Spanner, dove, artichoke

- Monkey, door, world atlas

This is like mental free-wheeling, generating random and disparate 'could be' connections and ideas. It is the same sort of mindset that jazz musicians use when they solo or many stand-up comedians get into when they perform. Eddie Izzard, for example, is a master at talking about one subject, and then linking it to another: in one popular routine he describes how cats purring behind the sofa are doing no such thing – they are surreptitiously drilling for oil. To use free association thinking effectively we need to let our mind go on an adventure where we have an objective and a starting point but the destination remains unknown.

Free association thinking is a bit like connecting apparently unrelated words (or films) except we have only one word to start with and no final destination in mind. We start with that one word (or some other stimulant – see later in this chapter) and use it to generate ideas related to whatever we want to think about creatively (our objective). Because there isn't a pre-determined end point, we can let our mind explore in all sorts of different directions and, if we get stuck or bored, we can go back to the original word or stimulant and start again.

Putting it into practice

All this sounds great and creative, but how does it actually relate to our normal lives? Here is an example of using free association to help with a real challenge. The 'spark' we are going to use in this instance is the 'random word'.

One of our best friends runs a small local theatre. The plays put on are fantastic but no one goes to see them and the company is facing closure. In desperation, our friend asks us if we would put some time aside and help come up with some original ideas to promote the theatre. The good friends that we are, we agree (in return for two free tickets and a backstage pass).

Traditional ideas could be to appear on television and radio, get some press coverage and reviews, tell all our friends about it. But we decide to look at things in a different way: let's see if we can use something from a play itself to kick-start some thoughts. Plucking three numbers which stand for a page number, a line number and a word number, we come up with 127, 16 and 6, turn to the script the cast is currently rehearsing and discover the word is 'out'.

Free-wheel association: Picasso

Put together a bicycle seat and pair of handlebars, and what have you got? Not much, might be the initial response. Two wheels, a frame, a chain, and a set of brakes short of a bicycle, might be another. Certainly, the answer 'a work of art' would not be high up the list of the most common replies. But in 1943 Pablo Picasso put the two together to create a legendary sculpture using the bicycle seat as the head and the handlebars as the horns: he created 'The Bull's Head'.

Oh dear, you might think – this might be difficult. But let's try connecting the word to our objective. What does the word 'out' remind us of, and how could that have anything to do with marketing the theatre?

One thought is that 'out' makes us think of exits, so we could hand out leaflets at tube stations, or stand by the exits of stadiums or other theatres distributing flyers.

Another is it reminds us of 'coming out', or disclosing sexual orientation, so we could consider doing tours of gay venues, or having a gay night.

What about outside or out in the open, so why not have an open-air performance in order to generate interest? This gets us thinking of the Open golf championship and maybe a competition at the end of the play with a prize of tickets to the event.

Then out-patients – maybe a five-minute sketch in a local hospital waiting room where people are bored and want to be entertained, with flyers to hand out afterwards.

The master of free association: B A Baracus

One group of people who knew all about the secrets of free association were four TV action heroes, *The A-Team*. Almost without fail, each episode would feature a key scene where their attempts to rescue a hostage looked all but over. Whereupon B A Baracus would look at the random objects about him – say a golf cart, a lawn mower and a watering can – and five minutes with a soldering iron later one improvised armoured tank was ready to roll.

Another thought would be going on an outing – we could connect the play with some sort of related tour; maybe you could receive money off a tour or a visit to a museum with every ticket purchased (or vice versa).

Very quickly, we have moved away from our traditional way of thinking to coming up with a range of different ideas by free associating from our original word. We have also managed to remove our 'internal noise filter': any thoughts or concerns or preconceptions that may hinder our creative thinking. At no point have we evaluated any of these thoughts (as you can see), or worried about whether they would work or the practicalities; that can all come later. For now, we have let our creative juices flow and come up with a fresh selection of new solutions.

Your turn

- **Choose an objective that you want to consider creatively**

  It is best if the objective is either stated as a problem, opportunity or a 'how' question. Closed questions like 'Should we go to the moon?' don't leave much room for creativity, so make sure you're asking the right question. Furthermore, when you start practising this technique it is best used for fairly straightforward objectives like 'ideas to throw a great party' or 'easy ways to move house'. Very complex, controversial or overly simple objectives like 'finding ways to create world peace' or 'how should I eat this carrot?' should probably be left, at least for now.

- **Write down some of your traditional ideas**

  It's always a good idea to write down some of your traditional ideas first. Primarily because it gets them out of the way (and there may also be an excellent idea in there), but also because it gives you something to compare with later.

- **Now look at the problem again using some random words**

  Try to generate ideas which link the word to your objective (remember to free wheel and make connections)

  Apricot
  Tape recorder
  Catapult

Whoosh

In a pharmaceuticals company, the objective was to create an oral healthcare product for people too young to care about looking after their teeth and gums. The idea was sparked by a picture of lightning (which, in turn, made people think of the sound of a storm). The concept was to create a canister (similar to those that contain whipped cream) but filled with a tooth cleaner. The substance would come in many flavours and be literally squirted into the mouth. There it would solidify and the chewing action clean the teeth and gums.

My catalogue

In a creativity workout participants were asked to develop a new innovation for a clothes retailer. They used objects to spark ideas, and the object that helped most on this occasion was a glove. From the phrase 'fits like a glove' came the thought of customers sending a photograph and their measurements to the clothes retailer. The retailer could then send back a catalogue featuring the customer wearing the clothes from their range that would most suit them.

Words are not enough

There are a number of different stimulants besides words that we can use to get our mind free associating. Because our minds all work in different ways we will find some more helpful than others. The only way to discover which work best for you is to give them all a go.

- **Sound**
  Sounds can be a great stimulus for new ideas though best to avoid music, and ideally choose something that isn't immediately recognisable. For each sound, listen to it, spend a minute writing down every idea that comes to mind, thinking about how the sound relates to your objective.

  For example, supposing your objective is to come up with a surprise present for your partner's birthday, and the sound stimulus makes you think of a train speeding along the tracks. Putting aside obvious thoughts you might have about tickets for a train journey, one idea you might have written down is Thomas the Tank Engine. From here you remember that the TV series was voiced over by Ringo Starr, from which one idea is to 'buy' your partner a star in a galaxy far, far away.

- **Vision**
  Using visual images can also help with breaking down our traditional patterns of thinking. If the image is slightly abstract, so much the better. This is because the less specific and the more abstract the stimulus, the more likely we are to think conceptually as well as practically, and so come up with something original. Again, look at the image and, for one minute, write down as many ideas as you can, and then sift through for the most appropriate. You might also like to try playing music while looking: combining stimuli has been shown to help creative problem solving.

PhonePets

Another objective was to come up with a product for teenagers for which advertising space could be sold. The idea was sparked by sound. The thought was to build a Tamagochi (a cyberpet who needs love and attention to survive) into mobile phones. The user would then look after the pet, making sure it was healthy and happy. Users could download new moods, reactions and presents for their pet from a website with advertisements.

- **Scramble**
  Here we use letters to kick-start our ideas. Using a handful of Scrabble pieces, or a selection of letters written on scraps paper, spread them out on the table in front of you. Then, rather than trying to form complete words, use them to make sounds or sections of words (ie, the first few and last few letters of a word). Build on these to develop some ideas.

- **Objects**
  Like sound and vision, objects can be used to help pattern break. They also have the advantage of adding a kinaesthetic (touch) dimension to creativity. Hold and feel the chosen object in your hands. What thoughts come up?

- **Smell**
  Another sense we can draw on is our sense of smell. Having chosen our particular scent, be it eucalyptus, orange or whatever, think of not only ideas but also memories the smell evokes: this may lead you on to a train of thought you hadn't previously considered.

Dead ends and cognitive cul-de-sacs

If you get stuck or come to a standstill at any point, don't worry. Try the same problem using a different word. Alternatively, use sounds, objects or pictures. If you do use sounds, slightly abstract ones work best as different people respond to them in very different ways.

Remember: patience is also a virtue in creativity. If you think you are going to generate award-winning ideas every time you think creatively you are going to be disappointed. And if you do, you're probably not thinking creatively often enough.

City scentres

The objective in this creativity workout was to make a city look, feel and smell cleaner. The idea was sparked by the smell of sandalwood incense. The concept was to build a small amount of perfume into street lamps (in much the same way as you can put a couple of drops of incense in an incense burner). The lamp would then give off a fragrance and make the area smell nice. This was thought particularly good for urban areas where plants or trees would struggle to grow. A development on this idea was to introduce different smells for weekends and evenings.

(T) Creativity for wannabe daydreamers

The Economist has for many years run a series of iconic poster adverts that illustrate the sharp thinking behind its writing. 'Great Minds Like a Think' was one slogan; 'B#' was another. But then there was another series: carefully positioned near train lines, the poster read 'No one ever got successful staring out of the window'.

Daydreaming and watching the world go by are not normally seen as the best way of getting ahead in life. Far better to buy a copy of *The Economist* and get up to date on world affairs. But one person often found staring into space was Albert Einstein: indeed, this was when he got his best ideas. Many other great thinkers are also at their most creative when in fact they aren't really 'working' at all.

How come? It's all about putting our conscious train of thought to one side and tapping into our unconscious mind. This chapter shows how (without reaching for mind-bending drugs). It isn't for everyone. It's risky, it may well feel uncomfortable, the outcome is uncertain and for most of us it's definitely very different from how we normally go about thinking creatively. But it's a fantastic way of generating new ideas and coming up with the sort of creative leaps we would be unlikely to make if we stuck with conscious thinking.

Three ways in which we think

In Guy Claxton's book *Hare Brain, Tortoise Mind* he describes three different modes of thinking.

The first is wits. Have you ever noticed how you are able to navigate a busy shopping precinct or railway station without having to think about it? We adjust our stride, pace and direction according to the movement of hundreds of people around us without thinking. Indeed, the moment we start thinking about what we are doing, we can't seem to stop bumping into people. Wits are also responsible for jamming on the brakes if someone pulls out in front of us in a car – there's no time to think then react: we react first, then think about what has happened afterwards.

The second way we think is the intelligent conscious. This is where we actively go about solving problems – how can I get to work in the least amount of time? Where shall we go on holiday? The intelligent conscious is interested in solving the problem, is literal and is explicit. Explaining and coming up with solutions to the situation are more important than simply observing it.

The intelligent conscious is where we spend most of our thinking time: it is what we have been trained to use in our education and jobs and so forth. Reading *The Economist* will help here. In Guy Claxton's book, he describes this type of thinking as 'the Hare Brain mode': quick, decisive and focused.

The third form of thinking is our intelligent unconscious. The intelligent unconscious is more interested in the problem than necessarily finding a solution. It tends to be imaginative and playful, meandering around a particular topic or issue, 'messing about' to get to an answer. This mode of thinking is more useful when dealing with complicated or thorny issues, where attempting to solve the problem directly yields frustration and little else.

This third mode of thinking Claxton calls our 'Tortoise Mind': rather than hurrying to try to solve the issue, we mull over and ruminate on things instead. It is here, according to Claxton, that our most creative ideas occur.

But is it allowed?
'If you can't solve a problem in five minutes, you either aren't clever enough, or the problem isn't solvable,' said a participant in a workout.

Our schooling, education and work train us to do the intelligent conscious approach very well, while the quirkier, unconscious methods of problem-solving are often ignored. We learn to solve problems logically, whether it is a maths question or completing a comprehension test. Speed and showing how we worked out a problem are appreciated. However, the more playful and meandering approach (and in particular daydreaming) is discouraged.

Imagine you told your colleagues at work that you were going to spend the day sitting under a tree in the park thinking; and that you were going to take the whole team with you to do the same; and then, when you come back, you freely admit that you didn't come up with any useful ideas the whole day.

This would not be popular.

But if you came back with an earth-shatteringly brilliant and original idea you would be heralded as a genius.

While the process of reaching into our unconscious may not be to everyone's taste, being able to use this very different way of thinking can be remarkably useful – especially when our normal, quick, solution-orientated approach doesn't seem to be generating any answers.

Our boss or partner (or *The Economist* advertising agency) may not think much of it but tapping into our unconscious as a way of thinking creatively has a pretty impressive pedigree.

Tool 1: into the incubator

Shakespeare called it 'The spell in which imagination bodies forth the forms of things unknown'. Einstein said that as well as staring into space, some of his best ideas occurred when he was taking a shower; Nobel Prize winner Leo Szilliard revealed that the concept of a nuclear chain reaction came to him while he was waiting at some London traffic lights. William Blake saw visions which he later drew or used for his poetry. Mozart and Tchaikovsky both said that their most creative sequences emerged as spontaneous passages that they could hear.

And you don't have to be one of the world's geniuses for ideas to come to mind at unexpected moments. In the middle of the night, walking the dog or driving on the motorway – many of us have had brainwaves in places and at times when we weren't aware that we were even thinking about the problem.

The process is called incubation. Incubation is allowing our minds to mull over the problem whilst doing something else. Building in incubation time to a problem-solving exercise can be a very worthwhile investment.

One person who employs a sort of incubation process in his work is the novelist Martin Amis. He describes a crucial stage in his writing as 'marinating': having an idea and then leaving it in the unconscious mind for all the flavours to infuse. Only once this has happened does he then put pen to paper.

There is a story (perhaps apocryphal) in the advertising industry about the creative who was given the brief for Carlsberg. The creative involved worked away on the brief trying to come up with the idea for the ad and a suitable strapline for the brand. The deadline was drawing nearer and he still had nothing decent. Exasperated, the creative decided to take a holiday to clear his head in the hope that, on his return, feeling fresh, he'd be better placed to come up with the idea and present it to Carlsberg. While he was relaxing, sitting by the swimming pool, the strapline and the advert struck him. Awards, accolades and a campaign that has lasted 25 years followed.

This is a fine example of the power of incubation. By framing the problem up front, and then going about our daily business, it is possible that the activation in other areas of our brain will create a connection to help solve our problem.

The most important principles to follow in order to get the benefits of incubation are:

1   Build in time to allow for incubation. Start thinking about the problem or challenge before you need the answer.

2   Don't allow yourself to get frustrated or feel under pressure to get an answer. If you do it is likely to be the wrong one, or at least a paler, weaker version of what you could come up with.

3   Have faith in your unconscious mind. Let it whirr away undisturbed and unhurried.

The most important thing about allowing our intelligent unconscious to shine is not so much tools or techniques (unlike the types of creative think-ing explored in the other chapters), but getting ourselves into the right frame of mind which means giving our intelligent unconscious the chance to work at a problem.

We put the meat in the oven and expect it to be cooked in half an hour, or plant a tree and assume that if we keep watering it every now and then it will grow. In a similar way, we need to leave the idea in our mind and trust that a creative idea will emerge without trying to force it (any more than we can force the meat to cook faster or the tree to grow more quickly). Sure, we can go back to it every once in a while, but if we keep looking at it, it won't help (like watching the kettle boil).

Tool 2: daydream believer

Another way of dipping into our unconscious mind is sometimes called reverie or even daydreaming: this is the kind that Shakespeare talked about. Each of us can generate great creative leaps, where we make sense of concepts, link different thoughts together and produce some truly original ideas.

'Whenever I get a brief from a client, I go and visit churches,' said the creative director from an ad agency who came to a workout. He found that wandering around these old holy places was how his best ideas came to him. So what can we do to hook into this mode of thought?

Daydreaming is a state we can all recognise: that moment between wakefulness and slumber when we half dream; or when we peer out of a window and our imagination takes us on a bizarre and quite unexpected journey.

This isn't about the daydreams where we reminisce about the past. This is the daydreaming where we construct a new reality for ourselves. We might be pirates, astronauts, people with very long fingers – we distort or amend reality in such a way that a new situation occurs, however freaky or strange that might be.

So how do we go about getting ourselves into this state?

Dream catcher

The answer is in visualisation (or unconscious imagining as it's sometimes called). For those who have read the Deep breath and Tranquillity chapters, this process is similar in many ways, but is designed for creativity rather than specifically for relaxation (though it should be relaxing and enjoyable too) and so is slightly different in important ways. There are three elements that will help us get into a reverie which will generate ideas:

Hard at work

1 **Relax**

The first step in this creative visualisation process is to quieten our mind (ie, stop consciously thinking). One way of achieving this is by concentrating our focus on our breathing. We often don't breathe as effectively as we might. When concentrating on our breathing we can begin to let all other thoughts leave us.

2   Visualise a special location

The special location is a visualised setting where we can relax and think clearly, feeling safe and comfortable. It can be real or imagined, like a beach, park, stream, cave, forest, a place we have read about in a book, seen in a film or simply generated ourselves.

3   Introduce a creative guide

The creative guide is a visualised guide whom we trust, value and respect. It is someone who is wise and original. Again the creative guide can be real or imagined. They can be a person, character, animal or another type of being. Our guide may respond to us verbally or may give us an object or show us an image.

The process requires us to use all our senses to bring ideas to life as much as possible. By using sight, sound, touch, smell and taste we make the experience much richer and more engaging. Let's look at the process in detail.

The visualisation process

Breathe in deeply through your nose, filling both the top and bottom of your lungs. Breathe out easily through your mouth. Concentrate on the rhythm of your breathing and really focus on inhaling and exhaling and nothing else.

Do not actively push your thoughts away as this can be distracting. Let your thoughts drift away. If a thought comes into your mind imagine it as a cloud that will get blown away with your next breath. Don't fight your thoughts; just let them drift in and then drift away again.

Imagine arriving at your special location. Use all your senses to visualise this place in as much detail as possible so you feel like you are really there. You should imagine how it smells, what sounds you can hear and how calm and relaxed you feel. Spend a few moments enjoying the tranquillity of your special location and drifting into a deeper state of relaxation.

Now imagine you can see a figure moving towards you from the distance. As the figure gets closer you see that it is your creative guide who has come to help you with your objective. Imagine your guide arriving next to you wherever you are and greeting them. You feel relaxed and inspired in the presence of your guide and are very happy to be in their company.

Imagine you are explaining your objective to your guide. You may want to explain this verbally or write it down or even use telepathy to inform your guide, whatever you prefer.

You wait for a response, confident that your guide will help you come up with an original and innovative solution. Your guide may talk to you, give you an object or even show you a scene.

The symbol, object or idea may be abstract or cryptic and so you may need to spend a few minutes deciphering the various symbols.

Having thought about what the symbol or gesture may represent you can then relate it back to your objective and see what it may mean. You mustn't worry about your ideas being too strange or difficult to put into action – part of the creative process is simply generating ideas themselves.

Dream on

People find that they come up with ideas they never would have reached using the more logical approaches to problem solving; or at least an initial thought that, with incubation, leads to a great idea. Part of this may well be that we find it difficult to self-censor in the generation of our ideas when using this mode of thinking, hence the interesting and more quirky products generated from using this technique.

This process doesn't work for everyone right away – it improves with practice so if you enjoyed it use it regularly. It seems that the more practised we become at visualisation the more likely we are to generate useful and interesting ideas from it.

Tool 3: automatic writing

Automatic writing is rather like recording a stream of consciousness. By capturing all our thoughts as they occur, it is difficult to evaluate as we go along and so we are more likely to drift into new and unexpected places somewhere at the back of our unconscious mind. First, find a space you are comfortable in, making sure you have a pen and paper, and then get into a relaxed state of mind (the previous exercise should have done this).

Surreally good

André Breton was a French Surrealist who was interested in expressing 'the actual functioning of thought'. He felt that with automatism we were able to get a pure form of expression. Automatic writing dates back much further, to Horace Walpole who wrote *The Castle of Otranto* in 1764 in a purely automatic manner.

Start writing as quickly as you can and without thinking. If the flow of writing is broken then you take a new line and start writing again. If you want to, use a trigger word to get your sentences going. Be prepared for your ideas to come from a deeper, more intuitive place and don't be alarmed if they are odd – when we explore in this more extreme form of free association, we are more likely to produce ideas that are unusual and out of context; after all, that's the point.

A few tips

1   Let go. No one is watching and no one will see what you've written. Let it rip.

2   Write as fast as you can.

3   Have a trigger word. If you dry up don't worry, but use your trigger word to get you going again.

4   There should be some grammatical sense (rather than just a string of words) but it doesn't need to be perfect or a work of literature.

5   Use it as a starting point. It won't give you 'the answer' but it may take you to it. Review, amend or adjust afterwards, not as you're going along.

Sean Connery's character in *Finding Forrester* is teaching someone to write. He explains, 'First you have to write with your heart, then you have to write with your head.' Automatic writing is like writing with your heart.

Automatic writing: Bob Dylan's vomit

In 1966, Bob Dylan found himself writing the words to a song and 'a long piece of vomit about twenty pages long' is how he described his outpourings. To begin with, there was no structure, no rhyme, no direction, just 'an ill-formed mass of words' in the opinion of one critic. But as Bob went back to what he'd written, sifted through it and started to edit and shape it, he knew he'd come up with something special. His 'vomit' became the words to 'Like A Rolling Stone'.

More than half a brain

People often find that this is a great place to start the creative process, but their ideas then need to be significantly refined, improved, discarded or amended before they can be used. In other words, once our 'Tortoise Mind' has come up with the ideas, it is time to switch back to 'Hare Brain' mode to analyse them. For the first time in a long while, we are using all of our brain rather than just half of it: by doing so, the possibilities of what we can achieve are endless. Sweet dreams.

The beginning

The difference between the accomplished apprentice and his master is that while the former may be skilled at each element of the task, the latter knows how and when to bring all the elements together.

This final chapter suggests how to combine all the various tools and techniques in this book and elsewhere to multiply their effect: how to turn some neat ideas into a new, more satisfying and more effective way of living.

This 'helicopter' view on how we can use our mind better does make two assumptions:

1   That we can tell the difference between doing things right and doing them wrong (which is what the rest of this book and everything else in The Mind Gym is all about).

2   That there is something we want to achieve or improve upon.

If you are happy with these assumptions then you are ready to discover a fresh way of using your mind that will help you get more out of your life and give more to others. Maybe even a new beginning.

Focus pocus

If we could tune into other people's thoughts, what might we hear? For some people, like Freda, it would be the equivalent of talk radio, a non-stop conversation with herself about everything and anything:

'What if interest rates go up? Where would that leave me? Perhaps I should pay off my loans, there again it would be great to go trekking in the Himalayas.' And without pausing for breath, she's off on to the next subject. 'Oh look, the broccoli is on discount, I wonder if something is wrong with it; shall I get the low fat? Better not, it might be disgusting. There again, Kate has put on weight recently. Mind you, she'll probably get offended if I get only healthy food.'

To put it mildly, there's a lot of chat going on in Freda's head. If you asked her, 'Freda, what are you thinking about at the moment?' she would be able to tell you confidently and fairly accurately. And at length.

But not everyone's like Freda. Tuning in to Cath would be more like turning the dial to Silent FM. If you asked her what she was thinking, she would look at you slightly startled and reply, 'Er, I was looking at that picture.' Or 'I was just listening to that song – she has an amazing voice, doesn't she?' Or even 'I wasn't really thinking, I was just writing an email.'

Sometimes Cath is simply going through the motions of a familiar routine: shopping, travelling home or washing the car. At other times she is totally caught up in what she is doing, so absorbed that it would be difficult to get her attention.

The difference between Freda and Cath is all to do with their focus, and where it is pointing. Freda is an example of someone with an exclusively internal focus: she is always aware of what she is doing and what she is thinking, like an observer of her mind. Cath, by contrast, has an entirely external focus: she is oblivious to how she is thinking or what she is doing; she is just doing it.

Internal focus: a touch of Freda
When our focus is internal we are usually having some kind of conversation with ourselves. It may be the voice that you can hear now as you read these words, asking yourself whether it's worth continuing to read this chapter, or if now is the time to have a cup of tea (or something stronger). It could also be the thoughts about whether you left the oven on, wondering where to go on holiday next or how to deal with a tricky colleague.

When our focus is internal we are conscious of the fact that we are thinking; we can hear and pay attention to the running commentary in our heads.

External focus: calling Cath
Take in where you are at the moment – what is happening around you? What are the noises that you can hear? Who is nearby? What are all the colours that you can see? What can you notice that is new or different?

External awareness occurs when we focus on things outside our own head. And when we do so, we aren't aware of what we are thinking. Our attention is on what is going on and not what we think about it, how we interpret it or whether it could have an impact on our future.

When we are really caught up in something, whether the thrill of a football game or the latest twist in our favourite soap, we are externally focused. When we think, 'I must be mad doing this', 'How can the government justify taking so much?' or 'Darren is behaving like a complete ****', then we have returned to an internal focus, although possibly for only a few moments.

Of course, as soon as we ask ourselves where our focus is it automatically becomes an internal focus, which is one of the reasons why it is easier to move to an internal focus than to an external one.

Where's your head at?
Our mind is always occupied in one of two places: what is going on in our head or what is going on outside it. It is, however, as impossible to do both at the same time as it is to do neither.

What is possible, though, is to switch between them, which, with a little mental discipline, we can do pretty much whenever we want (though it normally happens involuntarily).

For better and for worse
So which is best? Do I want to be more like Freda or more like Cath? The answer is neither, or both. Different personality types tend to spend more of their time in one world than the other but all of us spend time in both and we need to – it is both natural and sensible to switch between an internal and an external focus.

The qualitative difference comes within each focus rather than between them. The internal focus and the external focus have both a helpful side and a harmful one.

The helpful side is when the *way* we are focusing, either internally or externally, increases the likelihood of success, effectiveness, efficiency or elegance.

The harmful side is when the *way* we are focusing, either internally or externally, hinders us from achieving our aims or delivering to our potential, whether we are trying to relax, giving a presentation or arguing with our partner.

Inside and out

Take a blank sheet of paper and a pen and draw a picture of a house in the countryside on a sunny day.

There will be times during this when you think to yourself, 'Am I doing this right?' or 'I really can't draw' or 'This is a really good picture'. There will be other moments when you are so absorbed in, for example, making the smoke that is coming out of the chimney look realistic, that you won't be aware of what you are doing.

You will find it impossible to be aware of the conversation in your head and absorbed in what you are doing at the same time. But you can quickly move between the two, going internal by asking yourself a question (say, how well am I doing this?), and going external by focusing on the picture or some element of it.

Put it all together . . .

When we combine the different *types* of focus (internal and external) with the different *ways* of focusing (helpful and harmful), we generate four different states of mind.

When things aren't going so well we are usually spending lots of time in the 'critical' and 'autopilot' boxes. Ideally, and when things are going swimmingly, our time is spent in 'thinking' or 'engaged'.

Our challenge, then, is to spend as much time as possible in the helpful states swapping neatly between 'thinking' and 'engaged' to support our desires and suit the situation. To do this we need, first, to be good at spotting which mode we are in.

	Thinking	Engaged
Helpful	Thinking	Engaged
Harmful	Critical	Autopilot
	Internal (Freda)	External (Cath)

1 Autopilot

Habits of mind

Good morning. My name is Mark and I will be your autopilot for the day. We will be setting off for work this morning five minutes late as usual and then will be travelling along the same route we have taken every day for the last three years. Later on, someone will ask how we are, and we will reply 'Fine, thank you' without a moment's thought. There is a possibility of turbulence at the meeting when someone makes a political statement we disagree with. But don't worry: we have a stock response of tired and familiar arguments to bat straight back at them . . .

We all have mental short cuts we use every day. Without them, very little would ever get done, but because of them we tend to miss out on opportunities and fail to perform at our best. We've all been shown some short cut or other on the computer, some keyboard whiz holding down a couple of buttons to do what would otherwise take us half a dozen steps: rather than being grateful our response is more likely to be an annoyed 'Why didn't anyone *tell* me I could do that?'

Who's running the show?

In effect, the lights are on but no one is at home.

Why does it happen?

Autopilot kicks in when we allow what was once exciting and challenging to become boring or mundane. We stop thinking about the situation and respond in pre-programmed ways. There are several factors that can turn on the autopilot (and turn off our thinking mind).

- **The familiarity trap**
  We give something a category that helps us to understand how it fits with the world around us, eg, we see someone crying and we think 'this person is upset'. This stops us from considering alternative explanations. The person crying could be acting, have dust in their eyes, have been chopping onions, crying with laughter and so on, but because we are caught in the familiarity trap we are unlikely to consider these alternatives.

Some pianists learn their pieces away from the keyboard so that they don't become too familiar and so won't fall into autopilot when they perform.

The familiarity trap also explains why security officials at the airport rotate roles. If you look at a screen for long enough, a nuclear bomb could go through and you wouldn't notice it.

- **The single view**
  When we start trying to solve a problem we tend to assume that the way we see it is the right way to see it. This isn't always the case. Thinking creatively demands that we look at a familiar problem with fresh eyes (see Let the juices flow). However, to do this we need to spot that we are in autopilot, temporarily fixed by our own world view, in the first place.

Priests under pressure

One of the many things that can send us into autopilot is pressure.

This was demonstrated by the psychologists John Darley and Daniel Batson who asked a group of trainee priests to prepare a talk on the good samaritan parable that they were to deliver at a nearby location. With the idea of stopping and helping those in need at the forefront of their minds, the trainees were then asked to walk over to where they were delivering their talk.

Straightforward enough you might think, but this is where the cunning psychologists made life difficult – they decided that on the way to their talk the trainees should happen upon someone lying in the road, coughing, spluttering and calling for help. To make things more difficult still, they told half the trainees that they were late for their talk and the other half they had plenty of time.

How many would stop? And which ones?

61% of those who were told they had plenty of time stopped to help the injured person but only 10% of those who were told they were late stopped, with some trainees literally stepping over the 'injured' person.

This slight change of situation moved the 'hurried' trainees into autopilot, forgetting what had been on their mind just moments before.

When to avoid autopilot

There is nothing wrong with autopilot for mundane activities that we have to do and have no desire to change. Autopilot is, however, unhelpful when:

- We want to achieve something we haven't done before or where the circumstances are different from last time

- We want to do something better than we did it last time

- There might be a better way of doing something that we're used to doing in the same way.

2 Critical

Your own worst enemy

Sports commentators are not always complimentary about the sports stars they are reporting on: 'Oh, that was a dreadful tackle!', 'Scotland have only got themselves to blame . . .', 'That's a schoolboy error.' Similarly, when we are in 'critical' mode, we hear an inner voice giving us a running commentary on what we are doing and what we should be doing differently: 'You're making a fool of yourself', 'What are you going to do next? Do something', 'Smile, go on, smile, not like that, a friendly smile not a grimace, you don't want to frighten him, that's better.'

This is accurately described by the expression 'you are your own worst enemy'. In sports terms, it is the equivalent of that old commentary cliché: 'They're playing against two teams tonight, Ron: the opposition and themselves.'

The critical noise often arrives when we are doing something that matters to us. It could be playing tennis, making a point in an important meeting, negotiating with the plumber or in the midst of a passionate embrace.

A voice pops up and starts to talk to us about what we are doing, how we are doing it, whether we are doing the right thing and so on. We may be fooled into thinking that this voice is being helpful, but in fact it is a distraction. It's a bit like when we try to get to sleep but can't. We say to ourselves 'must get to sleep, must get to sleep', become anxious about getting to sleep, and so end up becoming more awake.

It is the same when dealing with people. Our internal voice suggests, 'Say this', or 'I'm being boring', or 'Come on, you should have generated some ideas by now.' These instructions distract us, knock our confidence and get in the way of what we are doing.

Timothy Gallwey, the professional tennis coach turned management guru, calls this 'Self 1'. He considers it as the most common and most pernicious influence on tennis players and the primary obstacle that people face to improving their game and, by extension, their performance in any arena where they want to succeed.

Impostor syndrome

If you have ever thought, 'I'm not able to do this; it's only a question of time before they find out' then you have suffered from impostor syndrome.

This is a common example of being in a 'critical' state of mind.

The good news is that almost all white-collar workers suffer from impostor syndrome at some stage in their careers, and some of the more successful people experience it the whole way through their working lives. This means that all those people you are worried might expose you are probably busy worrying that you might be about to show them up. What a relief.

3 Thinking

I think therefore I am doing something worthwhile
We are in this state of mind when we are assessing options, deciding on a course of action, working through a problem, estimating the likely consequences or chain of events or simply organising our thoughts to make more sense of them. At its best, thinking feels clear, precise and positive.

This mode is particularly useful when:

* **Solving problems**
  We weigh up the pros and cons of taking a new job. We decide whether we prefer grapefruit or orange juice for breakfast. We consider where to go on holiday and how to spend our weekend. We plan how to have the difficult conversation with our lover/friend/boss.

  It is in this state that we 'think through a problem' and then decide what we ought to do and how we ought to do it. We then, ideally, move to an external focus to carry out our plan of action.

- **Oops, it's going wrong**
  When things don't seem to be going as we want, we need to rethink and respond. At this moment we move into 'thinking' as we consider what is happening and the options available to us (as opposed to being 'critical', where we castigate ourselves for being in the situation in the first place).

- **Reflection**
  One of the most effective ways of developing ourselves is to learn from our past experience is to consider what we did well and what we could do better if we were in a similar situation again. It is through this kind of reflection that we become more self-aware, more knowledge-able and, in due course, more capable.

- **Making sense**
  Am I redecorating my home to increase its value or to make it a nicer place for me to live in? What is it about my personal relationships that means they start so passionately and end so abruptly? Why do I want to change jobs?

  Asking, and trying to answer, some of the 'big' questions can be a very helpful mental tool, so long as we ask the right questions and do something with our answers (otherwise it can turn into self-indulgent navel-gazing).

Most of the suggestions in this book and elsewhere in The Mind Gym are designed to trigger 'thinking' by suggesting approaches, tools and techniques to help us think differently. All of this is essential if we want to use our minds better. Equally, when it comes to using some of these techniques (as opposed to deciding which techniques to use), they tend to have more impact when our focus is external, ie, when we are 'engaged'.

4 Engaged

Engaged, locked in, in the moment, absorbed, in the zone, in flow. There are many phrases that we use to describe this state of mind.

It exists when our focus is external, on something in our immediate environment, and we are performing at our best or, at the very least, are on form. If you can drive, you may recall the moment when you first drove somewhere on your own without thinking 'check mirror, change gear, indicate right', but, instead, your attention was completely on the road ahead and the other motorists while you sang along to the radio. Or the first time you skied to the bottom of the slope and you were not quite sure how you got there, but it felt great.

Equally, it could be writing an email, contributing in a meeting, talking with people at a party or reading a book. The key is that we didn't have any distractions, either internal voices telling us what we should or should-n't be doing, or external ones, looking up at the clock or around for other people to talk with. When we are totally absorbed by what we are doing, the people we are talking to, the characters in the story. At this moment, we are engaged.

Timothy Gallwey calls this focus 'Self 2' (in contrast to the 'critical' mode, which is similar to his 'Self 1'). He says that we can improve our tennis game by focusing on things such as where the ball bounces or by not forc-ing but noticing where our racket is when we play a game.

The idea is that rather than judging how we are playing and distracting ourselves from a great game, we are, instead, totally present. Also, by not judging ourselves as we act, we interfere less with the task at hand, and allow our potential to take over. Mihaly Csikszentmihalyi describes this state as finding flow. It is where we are likely to feel peak performance and immersion in what we do.

(If you have read The joy of stress, you will recognise some similarities with zone 2 – the thrill zone. When we are 'engaged' then we are likely to be in zone 2. However, just because we are in zone 2 does not mean that we are necessarily 'engaged'; we could be in any of the four states of mind.)

Moving to the helpful modes

Thinking – turning off the autopilot
Need to turn the autopilot off? Here are best ways to switch back to manual:

- **Looking for something new**
  Here we scan our environment, consciously looking for what is new, different and unusual. We might ask ourselves questions like, was that

flower out last time I passed? What shoes are the people opposite me wearing? By doing so, our focus is on the present and we become more aware of our surroundings. Rather than being on autopilot, we are constantly searching for what's different.

We may then start to look for patterns or meaning in what we see. Has spring arrived? Is there a new fashion emerging? By now, we are clearly in 'thinking' mode.

Engaging racing

Leading the 1950 Monaco Grand Prix, Juan Manuel Fangio approached a blind corner and, instead of continuing at his normal 100mph, for some reason braked hard and took the bend at a crawl.

As he rounded the turn he saw a nine-car pile up. If he had been travelling at his usual speed he would almost certainly have been caught in the crash and might well have died. Instead, he drove safely past.

So, what was it that caused Fangio to brake suddenly and for no obvious reason? It wasn't until some time later that even Fangio could explain why. Without being aware of it at the time, a part of his mind had noticed that the faces of the spectators in the stand ahead, which were usually fixed on him as the race leader, were turned away, as it happened looking towards the crash.

If he had been in 'thinking' mode it would have taken too long to process this piece of information to react in time, and in autopilot he wouldn't have spotted that anything was different. But Fangio was completely engaged, as any Grand Prix champion would be, and so he picked up on this unusual feature, realised that it could mean danger and took an intuitive, split-second decision that saved his life (and won him the race).

- **Always to often**
  One of the reasons why we can get caught in autopilot is that we tend to see the world as a set of absolutes. We like to believe that such-and-such will always happen as this is a mental short cut which saves us having to think about it again. As a result, our thinking can fall into patterns of our own making and we are, in effect, switching on the autopilot.

To see the world as less absolute and more conditional (where things happen often or regularly rather than always) is to keep ourselves mentally on our toes. When thinking creatively, offering counsel, managing conflict or any of the other topics we have looked at in this book, it is better to think of the techniques conditionally rather than absolutely the right thing to do in all situations. Without this conditional approach we use a wrecking ball when a hammer would have been just fine.

- **Other people's perspectives**
  Have you ever had a boss or colleague who you thought was overbearing, dogmatic, aggressive or rude? Do you think they saw themselves in that way? Surprisingly enough, they might not. If they were asked to describe themselves they would probably say they were assertive, direct, honest and candid (you might want to add 'lacking in self-awareness').

  One of the reasons why conflicts can go so badly wrong is that we behave on autopilot, and respond without thinking, or without considering the other person's perspective. By staying alert to other people's perspectives we move out of autopilot and into a more constructive state of awareness.

Thinking – removing the critical noise

Sometimes it can be easier to move directly from 'critic' to 'engaged' as, by focusing externally, we automatically banish the critic (see Getting engaged p. 295).

When we want to move from 'critic' to 'thinker', we can do so by:

- Bringing objectivity and analysis into our thinking: for example, asking ourselves what are the facts and what are the assumptions?

- Thinking like an attentive optimist (see Lucky you p. 24).

Building reflection time into our routine

Having completed a task we should reflect back on what we have achieved, what we did well and what we would like to have done differently. Golf players could do this between shots but not while taking them. All of us can do it at the end of each day.

Getting engaged

When we want to get engaged in a task but hear the critical noise make its entrance ('You don't want to do THAT'), or find ourselves busy thinking in our head rather than absorbed in the moment, there are several things we can do.

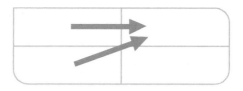

- **Vital components**

  Vital components are things that are part of what we are doing, and may well be essential, but aren't tied directly to the outcome. For example, if we were dealing with people on the telephone, a vital component would be the other person's tone of voice. If we were playing tennis, a vital component would be the speed of the ball. If we were being interviewed, a vital component would be the posture of the interviewer.

  The trick with these vital components is not allowing the critical noise to start: 'He's folded his arms; I'm clearly boring him.' Instead, we need to observe or report on what is happening without commenting on it, and trust ourselves to do what is right as a result.

  Focusing on the vital components makes us more present and aware of our surroundings. Most importantly, as it moves us towards an external focus (Cath) it helps silence the critical noise.

- **Process not outcome**

  When we focus on the eventual outcome it is all too easy for the critical mode to take centre stage. 'I'm never going to make it to the top of the mountain'; 'the sales targets are impossible'; 'it'll be years before we finish redecorating the house'.

  To quieten this critical voice and get engaged we need to focus on the process, ie, the steps we are taking. The mountaineer will focus on getting to the next ridge or, when really exhausted, simply on taking the next step, one at a time. The salesperson will concentrate on the call to a specific potential client. The DIY unenthusiast will devote themselves to each stroke of the brush.

  By concentrating on the steps to get there, rather than the eventual outcome, we can switch from critical to engaged. However, if we don't keep our focus on the process, it's just as easy to glide back again.

- **Balancing challenge and skill**

  The balance between challenge and skill is a sensitive one. If there is too much challenge (cooking for 25) and not enough skill (can't even boil an egg) we feel anxious about completing a task. If there is too much skill (Michelin Star chef) and not enough challenge (an order for beans on toast), we feel apathetic towards it. If neither skill nor challenge is needed we are bored.

  However, if we are skilled in something and there is a challenge to meet we can become immersed and enjoy what we are doing. We are also most likely to achieve our potential by managing this mix between skill and challenge. We can make even the most mundane things more challenging – when mowing the lawn, we can focus on how well we have mowed, try mowing in strips as on a football pitch and challenge ourselves to mow in the quickest time, but still have the neatest lines.

Thinking and engaged – how to dance

The ideal is to move between 'thinking' and 'engaged' as the situation demands. There isn't a formula that dictates when to be in one mode and when to be in the other but, rather like dancing, we need to find a rhythm and delicately move as the situation (or music) requires.

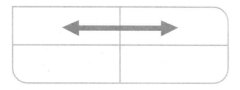

Claire thinks 'What shall I wear? I've got the marketing meeting so I'd better look smart'. She chooses her favourite suit and then thinks no more about it as she returns to her automatic routine for getting ready for work. On the drive in, however, she is fully engaged in her environment, noticing that road works are planned for next month ('I'll need to find another route', she briefly thinks to herself) and the preponderance of purple that women are wearing (she isn't aware that she has noticed this yet but it will influence her views in the meeting later on).

On the way up to her office she bumps into Peter, her old boss who has recently been made a Director. 'Congratulations', she enthuses and chats away totally engaged in the conversation. It is only when Peter starts explaining his new role that she thinks, 'He could be a useful sponsor for my project; I wonder how can I persuade him'. Claire quickly develops an influencing strategy (using a selection of the tactics covered in the

Influence chapter) and when there is a suitable moment in the conversation broaches the subject, 'Peter, when you say . . .'

It seems to Claire only seconds later, though it is in fact several minutes, that Peter is suggesting a meeting with his whole management team – result. As Claire gets herself a coffee she reflects on what she did well that helped gain Peter's support and whether she can apply any of these lessons when it comes to the marketing meeting.

Claire glides between the different modes as the situation requires. Most of the time she is either engaged or thinking, moving to an internal focus (thinking) when she needs to assess the situation or decide what to do and then to an external focus (engaged) when she does what she planned, getting completely involved in what she is doing.

Our challenge is to do much the same.

The end of the beginning

Congratulations (and thanks) for reading this far. Hopefully you feel that you have gained a good knowledge about how to wake your mind up in order to use it better and so get more of what you want out of life.

The next challenge, however, is much harder. It is putting the theory into practice. There is no book, workout or virtual exercise that can do this for you (a shame, we know). Whether what you have discovered in these pages will be helpful or not is now largely up to you.

But you are not alone. At The Mind Gym Online you can find like minds – people with similar challenges to yours who can offer their advice and experience, or simply act as a helpful buddy or coach (and you can do the same for them). There is also a range of exercises, games and additional hints and tips to help guide and support. Some techniques will work first time, others will require practice and some won't suit you at all. Pick out what helps and feel free to dismiss what, after you have tried it, doesn't work for you. But don't give up trying.

Our world is what we make of it and the tips, techniques and ideas that you have uncovered will help you make of your world what you want. There may be slip-ups on the way but, as Albert Hubbard remarked, 'The greatest mistake you can make in life is to be continually fearing you will make one.'

Bibliography

Alloy, L. B. & Abramson, L. Y. (1979). Judgement of contingency in depressed and nondepressed students: Sadder but Wiser. *Journal of Experimental Psychology: General, 108,* 441–485.

Bandura, A. & Locke, E. A. (2003). Negative self-efficacy and goal effects revisited. *Journal of Applied Psychology, 88* (1). 87–99.

Bee, F. & Bee, R. (1998). *Constructive Feedback.* CIPD.

Bernardi, L., Spadacini, G., Bellwon, J., Hajric, R., Roskamm, H., Frey, A. (1998). Effect of breathing rate on oxygen saturation and exercise performance in chronic heart failure. *The Lancet, 351,* 9112, 1308–1311

Bernardi, L., Slieght, P., Bandinelli, G., Cencetti, S., Fattorini, L., Wdowczyz-Szulc, J. & Lagi, A. (2001). Effect of rosary prayer and yoga mantras on autonomic cardiovascular rhythms: comparative study. *BMJ, 323,* 1446–1449

Bernieri, F. J. (1988). Coordinated movement and rapport in teacher-student interactions. *Journal of Nonverbal behaviour, 12B.* 120–138.

Bernstein, D. A., Borkovec, T. D., Hazlett-Stevens, H. (2000). *New directions in Progressive Muscle Relaxation Training: a guidebook for helping professionals.* Praeger Publishers.

Bowins, B. (2004). Psychological defence mechanisms: A new perspective. *American Journal of Psychoanalysis, 64* (1), 1–26.

Brotchie, A. (1991). *Surrealist Games.* London: Redstone Press.

Burka, J. B. (1990). *Procrastination.* Cambridge: Perseus Books.

Burley-Allen, M. (1995). *Listening: The Forgotten Skill.* New York: John Wiley & Sons Inc.

Cialdini, R. (2001). *Influence: Science and Practice.* Allyn & Bacon.

Clance, P. (1985). *The Impostor Phenomenon: Overcoming the Fear that Haunts your Success.* Peachtree Pub Ltd.

Claxton, G. (1998). *Hare Brain Tortoise Mind*. London: Fourth Estate Ltd.

Claxton, G. (1999). *Wise Up*. London: Bloomsbury.

Csikszentmihalyi, M. (2002). *Flow: The Classic Work on How to Achieve Happiness*. Rider.

Danner, D., Snowdon, D. & Friesen, W. (2001). Positive Emotions in Early Life and Longevity: Findings from the nun study. *Journal of Personality and Social Psychology, 80*. 804–813.

Darley, J. & Batson, D. (1973). From Jerusalem to Jericho: A study of situational and dispositional variables in helping behaviour. *Journal of Personality and Social Psychology, 27*, 100–119.

Darley, J. M. & Latane, B. (1968). Bystander intervention in emergencies: Diffusion of responsibility. *Journal of Social Psychology, 8*, 377–383.

Davison Ankney, C. (1992). Sex differences in relative brain size: The mismeasure of women, too? *Intelligence, 16*, 329–336.

Dilts, R. B. (1994). *Strategies of Genius*. California: Meta Publications.

Duruy, V. (1883). *History of Rome*, Vol. V (1883); Suetonius, 'Life of Julius Caesar' in Davis, William Stearns, *Readings in Ancient History* (1912).

Farhi, D. (1996). *The Breathing Book*. New York: Henry Holt.

Fenno, R. (1959). *The President's Cabinet*, Cambridge, Mass: Harvard University Press.

Ferrari, J. R., Johnson, J. L. & McCown, W. G. (1995). *Procrastination and Task Avoidance*. New York: Plenum Press.

Fiore, N. (1989). *The Now Habit*. New York: Penguin Putnam Inc.

Fisher, R. & Ury, W. (1992). *Getting to Yes*. London: Random House Business Books.

Furedi, F. (2004). *Therapy Culture: cultivating vulnerability in an uncertain age*. London: Routledge.

Gallwey, W. T. (2003). *The Inner Game of Work*. Australia: Thomson Texere.

Gardner, H. (1993). *Creating Minds*. New York: Basic Books.

Goldberg, A. (1991). *Improv Comedy*. Hollywood: Samuel French Trade.

Gottman, J. & Silver, N. (2000). *The Seven Principles for Making Marriage Work*. London: Orion.

Gregory, S.W. & Webster, S. (1996). A nonverbal signal in voices of interview partners effectively predicts communication accommodation and social status perceptions. *Journal of Personality and Social Psychology, 70*, 1231–1240.

Guffrey, M. E. (1995). *Essentials of Business Communication* (3rd edn) Cincinnati, OH: South Western.

Hatfield, E., Cacioppo, J. T. & Rapson, R. L. (1994). *Emotional Contagion*. Cambridge University Press.

Hofling, C. K., Brotzman, E., Dalrymple, S., Graves, N. & Pierce, C. M. (1966). An experimental study of nurse-physician relationships. *Journal of Nervous and Mental Disease, 143*. 171–180.

John F. Kennedy 'Man on the moon' Speech. September 12, 1962, speaking at Rice University.

Knaus, W. J. (1998). *Do it Now: Break the Procrastination Habit.* John Wiley & Sons Inc.

Kolb, D. A. (1984). *Experiential Learning.* New Jersey: Prentice-Hall.

Langer, E. J. (1989). *Mindfulness.* Cambridge, Perseus Books.

Lazarus, R. S. & Folkman, S. (1984). *Stress, Appraisal and Coping.* New York: Springer Publishing Company.

Maguire, E. A., Gadian, D. G., Johnsrude, I. S., Good, C. D. Ashburner, J., Frackowiak, R. S. J. & Frith, C. D. (2000). Navigation-related structural change in the hippocampi of taxi drivers. *Proc Natl Acad Sci U S A, 10,* 4398–4403.

Mason, D. (2004). *The Piano Tuner.* London: Picador.

Matura, T., Colligan, R., Malinchoc, M. & Offord, K. (2000). Optimists vs pessimists: Survival rate among patients over a 30-year period. *Mayo Clinic Proceedings, 75,* 140–143.

Maynard, D. (1996). On 'realization' in everyday life: The forecasting of bad news as a social relation. *American Sociological Review, 61, (1)* 109–131.

McCrone, J. (2001). Mental gymnastics. *New Scientist, 172.* 30–31.

O'Shea, M. V. & Ragsdale, C. E. (1932). *Modern Psychologies and Education.* The Macmillan Company.

Pietsch, W. V. (1992). *The Serenity Prayer Book.* San Francisco: HarperSanFrancisco.

Provine, R. R. (1986). Yawning as a stereotyped action pattern and releasing stimulus. *Ethology, 72.* 109–122.

Provine, R. R. (1992). Contagious laughter: Laughter is a sufficient stimulus for laughs and smiles. *Bulletin of the Psychodynamic Society, 30.* 1–4.

Regan, D. T. (1971). Effects of a favour and liking on compliance. *Journal of Experimental Social Psychology, 7.* 627–639.

Reivich, K. & Shatte, A. (2002). *The Resilience Factor.* New York: Broadway Books.

Richardson, R. S. (1995). *The Charisma Factor.* Random House.

Salerno, D. (1998). An interpersonal approach to writing negative messages. *The Journal of Business Communication, 25,* 41–51.

Schulman, P., Seligman, M. & Oran, D. *Explanatory Style Predicts Productivity Among Life Insurance Agents: The Special Force Study* (unpublished manuscript available from Foresight, Inc. 3516 Duff Drive, Falls Church, Va 22041).

Seligman, M. E. P. (1988). Pessimistic explanatory style in the historical record: Caving LBJ, presidential candidates and East versus West Berlin. *American Psychologist, 43.* 673–682.

Seligman, M. & Schulman, P. (1986). Explanatory style as a predictor of performance as a life insurance agent. *Journal of Personality and Social Psychology, 50,* 832–838.

Selye, H. (1978). *The Stress of Life.* New York: McGraw-Hill.

Silverman, S. B. (1991). *Individual development through performance appraisal.* In K. N. Wexley (ed.), *Developing Human Resources,* pp. 120–151.

Smith, G. N., Nolan, R. F. & Dai, Y. (1996). Job-refusal letters: readers' affective responses to direct and indirect organizational plans. *Business Communication Quarterly*, 59.

Stanislavski, C. (1963). *An Actor's Handbook*. New York: Theatre Arts Books.

Sternberg, R. J. (2003). *Wisdom, Intelligence and Creativity Synthesized*. Cambridge: Cambridge University Press.

Stone, B. (1997). *Confronting Company Politics*. London: Macmillan Press Ltd.

Stone, D., Patton, B. & Heen, S. (1999). *Difficult Conversations*. London: Penguin Books.

Underhill, R. (2002). *Khrushchev's shoe*. Perseus Publishing.

West, M. A. (1997). *Developing Creativity in Organisations*. Leicester: British Psychological Society.

Wiseman, R. (2004). *The Luck Factor*. London: Arrow Books Ltd.

Yerkes. R. M. & Dodson, J. D. (1908). The relation of strength of stimulus to rapidity of habit formation. *Journal of Comparative Neurology and Psychology*, *18*, 459–482.

Yukl, G. & Falbe, C. M. (1990). Influence tactics in upward, downward, and lateral influence attempts. *Journal of Applied Psychology*, *76*, 132–140.

Without whom

The Mind Gym: wake your mind up has been written by Octavius Black and Sebastian Bailey, co-founders of The Mind Gym.

It would never have happened, however, without the insight, support and energy of many others.

The academic board chaired by the illustrious Professor Guy Claxton† and including Professor Michael West††, Professor Ingrid Lunt*† and Emeritus Professor Peter Robinson.†

The Mind Gym core team past and present, led by the invincible Sam Aspinall (especially when Octavius and Seb were away writing) and including the mighty Sam Scott (who has been a powerful force for good from the outset), Pui-Wai Yuen, Jonna Sercombe, Ben Oxnam, Joe McLewin, Caroline Smith, Debbie Taylor, Rachel Newton, Pui-Kei Chan, Jo Yates, Nicole Evans, Daz Aldridge, Georgie Selleck, Azim Khan, Samy De Siena, Camilla Jewson, Sarah Pearce, Cezzaine Haigh, Megan Korsman, Tania Stewart, Alice Jackson, Elizabeth Vivian-Wright.

The Mind Gym's overseas pioneers, especially Sean Clemmit (Australia) and Jonathan Law (Ireland).

Those clients who were brave enough to risk an untested concept and without whom The Mind Gym would not have survived its turbulent first year: Antonia Cowdry (Deutsche Bank); David Lavarack (Barclays); Tony Shaw (then TDG); Nick Viner and Richard Stark (BCG); Bryan Low (then Scottish Provident International); Sue Ryan (GCI); Susan Coulson (T-Mobile); Shaun Orpen (then Microsoft); Bruce Robertson (then Prêt A Manger); David Kean (Omnicom); Charles Sutton (who made the introduction to Guinness), as well as all those who have since taken The Mind Gym concept seriously by becoming corporate members, not just once but again and again, including Simon Linares, Claire Semple and Jenny Morris (Diageo); Lisa Day and Catherine St John-Smith (United Biscuits); Noel Hadden and Mike Molinaro (Deutsche Bank); Peter Wilkinson and Sarah Halling (Royal Mail); Chris Peck and Sarah Leonard (GSK); Hugh Spalding and Pam Rawlings (Hewlett-Packard); Antonella Milana (BBC); Neil Clarke and Cat Allen (3); Sheila Weatherburn (Norwich Union); Maggie Hurt (National Grid Transco).

The Mind Gym Coaches who have delivered the workouts in 20 different countries in 270 organisations. In particular, John Nicholson, Catherine Hoar, Giles Ford, Fiona Houslip, Andrew Pearson, Steph Oerton, Natasha Owen, Andrew Mallett, Jane Palmer, Patrick Medd, Annie Ingram, Helen Vandenberghe, Michelle Mackintosh, Simon Rollings, Linda Stokes, Tony Plant, Gregg Harris, Laurie Carrick, Jacqueline Farrington, Fiona Tordoff, David Ruef, Ben Avery, Pete English, Danny Easton, Mary Gregory, Paul Burton, Annette Kurer, Jessica Chivers, Scott Keyser, Neil Park, Paul McGee, Reuben Milne, Danny da Cruz.

The extensive range of advisers, many of whom gave their advice for free or at very reasonable rates.

IT: Phil Lea; Louise Collins; Will Loden; Oly Grimwood; Dave Watkinson; Nick Taylor; Nigel Colvert; George Sanders

Design: Julie Durber; Attik; Now Wash Your Hands; Danny, Mark and the team at mj impressions; Two by Two

Learning: Bill Lucas; Ben Cannon; Mike Leibling; Susie Parsons; Jonathan Brown; Penny Egan; Paul Crake

Business: Cathy Walton; Murray Poole-Connor; Michael Anderson; Brinsley Black; Martin Foreman; Martin Taylor; Rita Clifton; John Smythe; John Nicholson; Michael Bilewycz; Michael Birkin; Selina Hastings; Richard Wingfield; Caroline Taylor; Polly Hayward, Dave Coban

Editors and journalists who commissioned or wrote about The Mind Gym: Rufus Olins; John-Paul Flintoff; Susan Elderkin; Tiffanie Darke; Cath Ostler; Michael Gove; Claire Macdonald; John McCrone; Kate Reardon; Matthew Gwyther; Steve Crabb, Anabel Cutler

Juliet Bailey, for her exceptional patience when the book deadline coincided with the wedding day.

And, most poignantly, the irrepressible Tif Loehnis of Janklow & Nesbit, who as our agent kept at us to write a proposal for over two years, and the bold team at Time Warner Books who believed in the concept from the outset, led by the magnificent Jo Coen and aided by the sharp-witted Tom Bromley.

The greatest thanks of all are due to the tens of thousands of people who take part in workouts and share, every day, what they do and don't like. These honest (sometimes very honest) views are the basis on which The Mind Gym is constantly revised, refreshed and renewed. We hope that, as a reader of this book, you too will share your opinions and so make sure that The Mind Gym constantly improves and consistently gives you what you want. Well, as near as.

(† = Fellow of the British Psychological Society; * = former President of the British Psychological Society)

Index